The Cambridge Companion to Marga[illegible]

Margaret Atwood's international celebrity has given a [illegible] visibility to Canadian literature in English. This *Companion* provides a comprehensive critical account of Atwood's writing across the wide range of genres within which she has worked for the past forty years, while paying attention to her Canadian cultural context and the multiple dimensions of her celebrity. The main concern is with Atwood the writer, but there is also Atwood the media star and public performer, cultural critic, environmentalist and human rights spokeswoman, social and political satirist, and mythmaker. This immensely varied profile is addressed in a series of chapters which cover biographical, textual, and contextual issues. The contributors consider recurrent topics, for what emerges through the multiplicity of Atwood's voices, personas, and formal experiments are the continuities in her work across decades and across genres. The Introduction contains an analysis of dominant trends in Atwood criticism since the 1970s, while the essays by twelve leading international Atwood critics represent the wide range of different perspectives in current Atwood scholarship.

CORAL ANN HOWELLS is Professor of English and Canadian Literature at the University of Reading. Her books include *Private and Fictional Words, Margaret Atwood* (winner of the Margaret Atwood Society Best Book Award in 1997), *Alice Munro*, and *Contemporary Canadian Women's Fiction: Refiguring Identities*. She is co-editor of *Margaret Atwood: The Shape-Shifter* and editor of *Where are the Voices Coming From? Canadian Culture and the Legacies of History*. She is former President of the British Association of Canadian Studies and has been associate editor of the *International Journal of Canadian Studies*. She has lectured extensively on Margaret Atwood and Canadian women's fiction in the UK, Europe, Australia, Canada, USA, and India.

THE CAMBRIDGE
COMPANION TO

MARGARET ATWOOD

EDITED BY

CORAL ANN HOWELLS

CAMBRIDGE UNIVERSITY PRESS
Cambridge, New York, Melbourne, Madrid, Cape Town, Singapore, São Paulo

Cambridge University Press
The Edinburgh Building, Cambridge CB2 2RU, UK

Published in the United States of America by Cambridge University Press, New York

www.cambridge.org
Information on this title: www.cambridge.org/9780521548519

First published 2006

Printed in the United Kingdom at the University Press, Cambridge

A catalogue record for this publication is available from the British Library

Library of Congress Cataloguing in Publication data
The Cambridge companion to Margaret Atwood / edited by Coral Ann Howells.
p. cm. – (Cambridge companions to literature)
Includes bibliographical references and index.
ISBN-13: 978-0-521-83966-2 (hardback)
ISBN-10: 0-521-83966-1 (hardback)
ISBN-13: 978-0-521-54851-9 (pbk.)
ISBN-10: 0-521-54851-9 (pbk.)
1. Atwood, Margaret Eleanor, 1939 – Criticism and interpretation – Handbooks, manuals, etc. 2. Women and literature – Canada – History – 20th century – Handbooks, manuals, etc. I. Howells, Coral Ann. II. Series.
PR9199.3.A8Z565 2006
818′.5409 – dc22 2005024381

ISBN-13 978-0-521-83966-2 hardback
ISBN-10 0-521-83966-1 hardback
ISBN-13 978-0-521-54851-9 paperback
ISBN-10 0-521-54851-9 paperback

CONTENTS

Notes on contributors *page* vii
Acknowledgments x
Note on editions used xi
List of abbreviations xii
Margaret Atwood chronology xiii

Introduction 1
CORAL ANN HOWELLS

1 Margaret Atwood in her Canadian context 12
DAVID STAINES

2 Biography/autobiography 28
LORRAINE YORK

3 Power politics: power and identity 43
PILAR SOMACARRERA

4 Margaret Atwood's female bodies 58
MADELEINE DAVIES

5 Margaret Atwood and environmentalism 72
SHANNON HENGEN

6 Margaret Atwood and history 86
COOMI S. VEVAINA

7 Home and nation in Margaret Atwood's later fiction 100
ELEONORA RAO

8 Margaret Atwood's humor 114
MARTA DVORAK

9 Margaret Atwood's poetry and poetics 130
BRANKO GORJUP

10 Margaret Atwood's short stories and shorter fictions 145
REINGARD M. NISCHIK

11 Margaret Atwood's dystopian visions: *The Handmaid's Tale* and *Oryx and Crake* 161
CORAL ANN HOWELLS

12 Blindness and survival in Margaret Atwood's major novels 176
SHARON R. WILSON

Further reading 191
Index 196

NOTES ON CONTRIBUTORS

MADELEINE DAVIES is Lecturer in English at the University of Reading. Her major research interests include Margaret Atwood, Virginia Woolf, and female-authored narratives of war. She has also published widely in the areas of post-war British drama, where she is the author of *Peter Shaffer: Theatre and Drama* (1998) and editor of *British Television Drama Past, Present and Future* (2000). She is currently working on *Margaret Atwood: Writing Women, Women Writing*.

MARTA DVORAK is Professor of Canadian and Postcolonial Literatures and co-director of the Centre for Canadian Studies at the Sorbonne Nouvelle, Paris. She is the author of *Ernest Buckler: Rediscovery and Reassessment* (2001) and *Vision/Division: l'oeuvre de Nancy Huston* (2004), and editor of several books including *Lire Margaret Atwood: "The Handmaid's Tale"* (1999) and *Thanks for Listening: Stories and Short Fictions by Ernest Buckler* (2004). A book on Carol Shields is forthcoming. She is currently editor of *Commonwealth Essays and Studies*.

BRANKO GORJUP is the chief editor of the Peter Paul Bilingual series of Contemporary Canadian Poetry (English/Italian), which includes a volume on Margaret Atwood (2000). He has also edited several anthologies of short fiction by Canadian authors and a book of essays by Northrop Frye, *Mythologizing Canada* (1997), as well as a special issue of *Nuovi Argomenti* (2003) featuring Canadian contemporary writing in English. His most recent edited collection is *White Gloves of the Doorman: The Works of Leon Rooke* (2004). He has taught Canadian literature at universities in Canada and Italy, and currently lives in Los Angeles and Toronto.

SHANNON HENGEN is Professor of English at Laurentian University, Canada. In addition to numerous articles on Atwood, comedy, Canadian theatre, and *Beowulf*, she is the author of *Margaret Atwood's Power* (1993), editor of *Performing Gender and Comedy: Theories, Texts, Contexts* (1998), and co-editor of *Approaches to Teaching Margaret Atwood's "The Handmaid's Tale" and Other Works* (1996). From 1999 to 2001 she was President of the Margaret Atwood Society.

REINGARD M. NISCHIK is Professor of American Literature at the University of Constance, Germany. She has published numerous essays and is the author and editor of twenty books on Canadian, American, and comparative literature. Since 1992 she has been Managing Editor of the interdisciplinary journal *Zeitschrift fuer Kanada-Studien*, and since 1996 editor of the book series European Studies in American Literature and Culture for Camden House, New York. Her edited collection *Margaret Atwood: Works and Impact* (2000) received the Best Book Award of the Margaret Atwood Society.

ELEONORA RAO is Associate Professor of English at the University of Salerno. She is the author of *Strategies for Identity: The Fiction of Margaret Atwood* (1994) and *Heart of a Stranger: Contemporary Women Writers and the Metaphor of Exile* (2002). She has published numerous essays on contemporary women writers and has co-edited *Letteratura e femminismi*, an anthology of Anglo-American feminist theories in translation (2000).

PILAR SOMACARRERA teaches English and Canadian literature in the Department of English at the Universidad Autónoma de Madrid. She has translated Margaret Atwood's *Power Politics* into Spanish (2000) and is the author of a book in Spanish on the topic of power, *Margaret Atwood: Poder y Feminismo* (2000), as well as numerous articles on other Canadian women writers.

DAVID STAINES is Professor of English at the University of Ottawa. He is the editor of the *Journal of Canadian Poetry* and of the New Canadian Library. His books include *The Forty-Ninth and Other Parallels: Contemporary Canadian Perpectives* (1986), *Beyond the Provinces: Literary Canada at Century's End* (1995), *Northrop Frye on Canada* (with Jean O'Grady, 2003), and *Marshall McLuhan: Understanding Me* (with Stephanie McLuhan, 2003). In 1998, he received the Lorne Pierce Medal for distinguished service to Canadian literature from the Royal Society of Canada.

COOMI S. VEVAINA is Professor of English at the University of Mumbai, India. She is the author of *Re/Membering Selves: Alienation and Survival in the Novels of Margaret Atwood and in the Manawaka Novels of Margaret Laurence* (1996). She has written numerous articles on Canadian writing and is co-editor of several essay collections, including *Intersexions: Issues of Race and Gender in Canadian Women's Writing* (1996), and *Margaret*

Atwood: The Shape-Shifter (1998). In 2004, she received the Award of Merit from the Indian Association of Canadian Studies.

LORRAINE YORK teaches Canadian literature at McMaster University in Hamilton, Canada. She is the author of a book about photography and Canadian fiction, *The Other Side of Dailiness* (1988) and of *Front Lines: The Fiction of Timothy Findley* (2002). She has also edited *Various Atwoods: Essays on the Later Poems, Short Fiction and Novels* (1995) and *Rethinking Women's Collaborative Writing* (2002). She is currently writing a book on Canadian literary celebrity.

SHARON R. WILSON is Professor of English and Women's Studies at the University of Northern Colorado and founding co-President of the Margaret Atwood Society. In addition to articles on Atwood, Doris Lessing, Jean Rhys, Samuel Beckett, and other writers, she is the author of *Margaret Atwood's Fairy-Tale Sexual Politics* (1993), co-editor of *Approaches to Teaching Margaret Atwood's "The Handmaid's Tale" and Other Works* (1996), and editor of *Margaret Atwood's Textual Assassinations: Recent Poetry and Fiction* (2003).

ACKNOWLEDGMENTS

I am grateful to Margaret Atwood for permission to quote extracts from her private correspondence with several contributors.

Extracts from unpublished Atwood manuscript materials in the Thomas Fisher Rare Book Library at the University of Toronto and from the following poems: "The Circle Game" (*The Circle Game*), "The Double Voice" (*The Journals of Susanna Moodie*), "You Fit into Me," "They are Hostile Nations," "Small Tactics" (*Power Politics*), and "Half-Hanged Mary" (*Morning in the Burned House*), are reproduced with permission of Margaret Atwood and of Curtis Brown Group Ltd. London, Copyright Margaret Atwood 1966–71, Copyright O. W. Toad Ltd. 2001–03.

NOTE ON EDITIONS USED

In quoting from Margaret Atwood's novels, poems, and short stories, contributors to this volume have used a variety of British, Canadian, and American editions, usually paperbacks when available. Details of editions used are included in the endnotes to every chapter.

ABBREVIATIONS

AG	*Alias Grace*
BA	*The Blind Assassin*
BE	*Bluebeard's Egg*
BH	*Bodily Harm*
CE	*Cat's Eye*
DG	*Dancing Girls*
EW	*The Edible Woman*
GB	*Good Bones*
HT	*The Handmaid's Tale*
JSM	*The Journals of Susanna Moodie*
LBM	*Life Before Man*
LO	*Lady Oracle*
MBH	*Morning in the Burned House*
MD	*Murder in the Dark*
NWD	*Negotiating with the Dead*
O&C	*Oryx and Crake*
PP	*Power Politics*
PU	*Procedures for Underground*
RB	*The Robber Bride*
S	*Surfacing*
SP	*Selected Poems*
*SP*II	*Selected Poems* II
ST	*Strange Things*
SW	*Second Words*
THP	*Two-Headed Poems*
WT	*Wilderness Tips*
YAH	*You Are Happy*

MARGARET ATWOOD CHRONOLOGY

1939	Margaret Eleanor Atwood born 18 November, in Ottawa, Canada.
1940–45	Family based in Ottawa, but spends long periods every year in the bush of northern Ontario and Quebec, as her father an entomologist; they live in Sault Ste. Marie (1945).
1946	Family moves to Toronto, though summers spent up north, and Atwood only begins attending school regularly in 1951.
1952–57	Attends Leaside High School, where she writes a column for school newspaper; at 16 she "becomes a poet"; works as summer camp counsellor.
1957–61	Attends Victoria College, University of Toronto; publishes stories and poems in college literary journal and designs posters and programmes for college drama society; first poem accepted by *The Canadian Forum* ; begins reading her poems at the Bohemian Embassy Coffeehouse; graduates (1961) with honors degree in English, and wins Woodrow Wilson Fellowship to Radcliffe College (later part of Harvard University).
1961	*Double Persephone* (privately published chapbook) wins University of Toronto E. J. Pratt Medal.
1961–63	Attends Radcliffe College, where she gains MA and begins doctoral studies at Harvard University.
1963–64	Returns to Toronto, where she works at market research company; begins her first novel (unpublished); first trip to England and France in summer, 1964.
1964–65	Moves to Vancouver, to lecture in English at the University of British Columbia; drafts *The Edible Woman* and writes fourteen short stories and over fifty poems.
1965	Returns to Harvard to continue PhD research (thesis not completed).

1966 *The Circle Game* published, which wins Governor-General's Award for Poetry (1967).

1967 Marries James Polk, an American postgraduate student at Harvard; they move to Montreal for a year, where Atwood lectures in English at Sir George Williams University (now Concordia).

1968 *The Animals in That Country*; moves to Edmonton, Alberta.

1969 *The Edible Woman*; teaches creative writing at University of Alberta.

1970 *The Journals of Susanna Moodie* and *Procedures for Underground*; Atwood and Polk spend the year in England and France.

1971 *Power Politics*; return to Toronto, where Atwood is Assistant Professor at York University; joins board of directors of House of Anansi Press (1971–73).

1972 *Surfacing* and *Survival: A Thematic Guide to Canadian Literature*; Atwood is writer-in-residence at Massey College, Toronto (1972–73).

1973 Atwood and Polk are divorced; Atwood moves with Graeme Gibson to a farm in Alliston, Ontario; receives her first honorary doctoral degree from Trent University, Ontario.

1974 *You Are Happy;* TV script "The Servant Girl" for Canadian Broadcasting Commission; cartoon artist for *This Magazine*.

1976 *Selected Poems* (Oxford) and *Lady Oracle*; daughter Eleanor Jess is born.

1977 *Dancing Girls* and *Days of the Rebels: 1815–1840*; special Atwood issue of *The Malahat Review*, the first critical survey of her work.

1978 *Two-Headed Poems* and *Up in the Tree*; Atwood's first of many world book promotion tours (Paris, Afghanistan, India, Australia); family moves to Scotland, where Gibson is writer-in-residence at University of Edinburgh for three months.

1979 *Life Before Man*.

1980 *Anna's Pet*; family returns to Toronto; Atwood elected Vice-President of the Writers' Union of Canada.

1981 *Bodily Harm* and *True Stories*; wins Molson Prize and Guggenheim Fellowship; becomes a Companion of the Order of Canada; President of the Writers' Union.

1982 *Second Words: Collected Critical Prose*; *The New Oxford Book of Canadian Verse in English* (co-ed., with William Toye).

1983	*Murder in the Dark: Short Fictions and Prose Poems* and *Bluebeard's Egg*; receives honorary doctorate from University of Toronto; family moves to Norfolk (November 83–March 84), then to West Berlin (March-May 84).
1984	*Interlunar*; return to Toronto (summer 84); elected President of PEN International, Canadian Centre (English-speaking) (1984–86).
1985	*The Handmaid's Tale*, which wins Governor-General's Award for Fiction (1986), Arthur C. Clarke Award for Best Science Fiction, Toronto Arts Award, *Los Angeles Times* Fiction Award; Atwood is Visiting Chair of Creative Writing at Tuscaloosa, Alabama.
1986	*Selected Poems II: Poems Selected and New, 1976–1986* (Oxford) and *The Oxford Book of Canadian Short Stories in English* (co-ed., with Robert Weaver); Atwood holds Berg (Visiting) Chair at New York University.
1987	Edits *The CanLit Foodbook*, in aid of PEN International; elected Fellow of the Royal Society of Canada; writer-in-residence at Macquarie University, Sydney.
1988	*Cat's Eye*.
1989	*Selected Poems: 1966–1984* (Oxford) and *For the Birds*; wins Canadian Booksellers' Association Award; writer-in-residence at Trinity University, San Antonio, Texas.
1990	Attends Berlin Film Festival for premiere of Volker Schlondorff's film of *The Handmaid's Tale*.
1991	*Wilderness Tips*; Clarendon Lectures at University of Oxford; family spends winter in France (1991–92).
1992	*Good Bones*.
1993	*The Robber Bride*; Atwood is named Chevalier dans l'Ordre des Arts and des Lettres by Government of France.
1995	*Strange Things: The Malevolent North in Canadian Literature*, *Morning in the Burned House*, and *Princess Prunella and the Purple Peanut*; *The New Oxford Book of Canadian Short Stories in English* (co-ed., with Robert Weaver); series of radio interviews in French with Quebec writer Victor-Lévy Beaulieu.
1996	*Alias Grace*, which wins Giller Prize.
1997	*In Search of Alias Grace*.
1998	*Eating Fire: Selected Poetry 1965–1995* (Virago); receives honorary doctorate from University of Oxford.

2000	*The Blind Assassin*, which wins Booker Prize; Empson Lectures at University of Cambridge; attends premiere in Copenhagen of Poul Ruders's opera *The Handmaid's Tale*.
2001	Receives honorary doctorate from University of Cambridge.
2002	*Negotiating with the Dead: A Writer on Writing*.
2003	*Oryx and Crake* and *Rude Ramsay and the Roaring Radishes*; attends London premiere of *The Handmaid's Tale* opera.
2004	*Bottle* (Hay Festival Press) and *Moving Targets: Writing with Intent, 1982–2004*; "Margaret Atwood: The Open Eye" international symposium, University of Ottawa; Toronto premiere of *The Handmaid's Tale* opera; receives honorary doctorate from Harvard University.
2005	*Curious Pursuits: Occasional Writing, 1970–2005*; receives honorary doctorate from Université de la Sorbonne Nouvelle, Paris; *The Penelopiad*.
2006	*The Tent*.

This chronology shows only a selection of Atwood's numerous national and international literary awards and of her many honorary doctoral degrees.

INTRODUCTION

CORAL ANN HOWELLS

Introducing Margaret Atwood

In November 2004 Margaret Atwood and Dame Gillian Beer engaged in a public conversation about her writing at the British Academy in London, a very "Establishment" literary event, where they discussed the image of the labyrinth as an appropriate description of the processes of writing novels and reading them. Two months later, Atwood appeared on a popular Canadian television show, rigged out in full ice hockey gear, showing the host, Richard Mercer, how to deflect a puck in Canada's favorite national sport. These two images of Atwood, as internationally famous writer talking seriously with a Cambridge professor about the mysteries of her craft, and the other as Canadian celebrity advertising her national identity in a playful masquerade, illustrates the combination of high seriousness and witty ironic vision which is the hallmark of Atwood's literary production. In this book, our primary concern is with Margaret Atwood the writer, but there is also Atwood the literary celebrity, media star, and public performer, Atwood the cultural critic, social historian, environmentalist, and human rights spokeswoman, and Atwood the political satirist and cartoonist. The chapters in this volume address all these features in the Atwood profile, as they consider her career from a variety of perspectives and with very different emphases, though it is her Canadianness and her international appeal as an imaginative writer which are the two *leitmotifs*.

Atwood is a popular writer; as she has often said, "I write for people who like to read books,"[1] and her novels are bestsellers all over the world. They are also taught in schools and colleges all over the world on a wide range of courses: English literature, Canadian and postcolonial literature, American literature (in the United States, where Atwood is a "North American" or sometimes an "American" writer), as well as women's studies, gender studies, and science fiction courses. Our aim in this book is to encourage students to see more – not only in individual Atwood novels, short stories or poems which they happen to be studying, but also to place any single Atwood text or selection of texts in context, in relation to her other work and in a broader framework of contemporary issues and critical approaches. Appropriately for Atwood, we have assembled an international array of contributors here – there are critics from Canada, Britain, Australia, the United States, France, Germany, Italy, South Asia, and Spain – all of us Atwoodians who are engaged in this collaborative project which illustrates the variety of emphases in current Atwood scholarship.

This book does not follow a chronological design, but is arranged round a set of recurrent themes, for what emerges overwhelmingly through the multiplicity of Atwood's voices and personas and her formal experiments with language and literary conventions are the continuities across four decades of her writing. Most of the topics here have been visited before. After all, there is a huge international Atwood academic critical industry, and the Margaret Atwood Society Newsletter publishes annual updates of scholarly works on Atwood – articles and books – which average over fifty per year. However, revisiting these same topics from different critical and theoretical angles (e.g. recent emphases on postmodernism, postcolonialism, and environmentalism) and in the light of Atwood's own continuous production, may help to re-evaluate the major dynamics in her work.

The *Companion* and its chapters

To give a brief overview of this book: the first two chapters are biographical and literary, setting Atwood in her Canadian context and analyzing her role as international literary celebrity. The next five chapters are concerned with important topics with which Atwood engaged at the beginning of her career and to which she has returned again and again, exploring, expanding, and explaining these in her fiction, poetry, and essays. Chapter 8 is devoted to Atwood's language as it analyzes her distinctively Canadian brand of ironic humor; this is followed by three chapters which take an explicitly generic approach, looking at her poetry, short stories, and dystopian narratives, and highlighting her experiments across genre boundaries. The final chapter is the other "bookend" which balances the first chapter by offering a retrospective view of Atwood's whole career as a novelist. It extrapolates her Canadian themes of wilderness and survival and resituates them in relation to that other key motif in her "I" witness/eyewitness narratives, that of blindness and vision. The chapter ends with a provocative question which turns readers back with renewed attention to Atwood as writer, trickster, entertainer, moralist, and satirist.

In chapter 1 David Staines presents a profile of Atwood as the famous writer who is, "above all else, Canadian." Rich in biographical detail, his account traces Atwood's career in tandem with her responses to the Canadian cultural context from the 1950s onwards, emphasizing her innovative role as interpreter of her country's culture, first to Canadians themselves in the 1970s and since the 1980s as an increasingly popular spokesperson for Canada around the world. He sets out the major themes of her writing which are grounded in her Canadian context, like her fascination with Canadian history and landscape, but which over forty years have broadened into topics of international relevance with her scrutiny of cultural myths about women, her concern with human rights and threats to the environment, and her strong sense of moral responsibility in an increasingly globalized context of reference. Chapter 2 is also biographical in its basis, but with a difference. It is about biography and fiction, or perhaps about biography as fiction, for Lorraine York reads Atwood's biography through the discourse of literary celebrity. Her focus is not so much on the details of Atwood's life story (which are sketched in the Chronology) but on Atwood herself as a "star text." York analyzes the ongoing interrelation between media constructions of Atwood and her own active intervention in those constructions through her website, her deprecating self-irony and humor in interviews, and through the negotiations with fame of many of her fictional protagonists like Joan Foster, Elaine Risley, or Grace Marks. Not surprisingly, this chapter shows up the more sinister aspects of celebrity, so helping us to interpret Atwood's own ironic comments on the star status of the writer in her lectures and essays in *Negotiating with the Dead* and her latest invention, a remote book-signing device which would allow her to autograph copies of her novels from her desk in Toronto "without . . . having to traipse to bookshops across the globe."[2]

Chapters 3 and 4 discuss the theme of power politics. Pilar Somacarrera analyzes the treatment of national and sexual power politics and their curious intersections, as Atwood continues to investigate the question of "who gets to do what to whom."[3] Reading through a Foucaldian lens, Somacarrera analyzes the sexual power games in the early poems and novels, tracing the topic as it expands into national and international dimensions in her later work. Madeleine Davies also focuses on sexual power politics with a specifically feminist emphasis on Atwood's representation of female bodies, where social power structures are "written on to female flesh" and into women's psyches. Adapting the French feminist theorist Hélène Cixous's famous essay, "The Laugh of the Medusa," Davies shows Atwood's ongoing engagement with the concept of *écriture féminine* as her women's fictive autobiographies trace the emergence of female subjects from a position of powerlessness and silence to become duplicitous narrators as they struggle to reconnect "body" with "text."

The four middle chapters address various facets of how Canada and Canadianness are figured within the textual spaces of Atwood's writing, from her concern with landscape and environment to her responses to Canadian social attitudes and changing ideologies of nationhood and identity, all of which are marked by the distinctive manner of her storytelling. In her survey of Atwood's novels, poetry and non-fictional prose in chapter 5, Shannon Hengen explores Atwood's environmental ethics and the evolution of her ideas about what "being human" means. Her broadly ranging analysis argues for Atwood's insistence on the symbiotic relation between human and non-human nature, as she spells out the vital connection between science and art in defining the position of human beings as the nexus of nature and culture. In chapter 6 Coomi Vevaina discusses Atwood's postmodern versions of Canadian history, with her double focus on history as collective public memory and the private psychohistories of female immigrants, witches, criminals, and various trickster figures. These marginalized "her/stories" destabilize the truth claims of historical writing in a postmodern context. A similar skepticism about national and social myths is revealed in Eleonora Rao's analysis in chapter 7 of Atwood's discourses of home and nation in her later novels. Focusing on their postcolonial implications, Rao argues that any discourse about "home" is an extension of discourses of nation and national identity and related to concepts of belonging and homelessness, dislocation, and alienation. Rao traces patterns of exile and self-division from *Cat's Eye* through to *Oryx and Crake*, where Snowman is the ultimate outsider. Here Atwood the Canadian nationalist moves beyond national boundaries in a post-catastrophe world where "home" exists nowhere but in imagination and memory. It would be an oversight, however, to neglect the wit and humor of Atwood's storytelling, no matter how serious the subject matter, and in chapter 8 Marta Dvorak offers a fascinating rhetorical analysis of her skillful use of irony and satire. Harking back to the deadpan humor of rural Nova Scotia, the home of both Atwood's parents, Dvorak argues that the manner of Atwood's storytelling derives from the tall tales and yarns of that oral tradition, though she goes on to situate Atwood's writing in a broader framework of humorous literary production that includes the burlesque, the grotesque, and the Bakhtinian carnivalesque.

The first of the three "genre" chapters, Branko Gorjup's overview in chapter 9 of Atwood's poetry from the 1960s through to the 1990s, also focuses on language, this time on the distinctively "Atwoodian" idiom and the evolution of her poetic voice. Whereas the early poetry was characterized by irony, emotional detachment, and a lethally precise vocabulary, there are shifts in her later poetry towards a multiplicity of voices and corresponding changes in tone towards compassion and elegy. Reading though imagery, Gorjup highlights Atwood's "poetics of metamorphosis" in her poetic world of mutations and mirrors and the palimpsestic quality of experience and landscape, filled with unseen presences and memories. "Nothing goes away" in the fluid reality of this created world, where Atwood is presented not as a cultural historian but as a mythographer of the Canadian imagination. In chapter 10, Reingard Nischik surveys Atwood's three short story collections and her three collections of (short) short stories written since the 1980s. Or should they be called prose poems? Dramatic monologues? Flash fictions? As Nischik comments, the critical terminology is as yet unfixed for in these new short text formats Atwood has exploded the boundaries of the short story genre. This scholarly analysis pays attention to the high degree of intertextuality and generic hybridity in these short prose pieces, while at the same time it takes up Atwood's feminist focus on the theme of gender relations, playing variations on the same themes explored in her novels and poetry. Like Dvorak, Nischik draws attention to techniques of irony and humor as she traces Atwood's development as a social and political critic. Coral Ann Howells's chapter on the two dystopian novels also stresses her role as satirist and moralist, with her urgent warning to an international readership to pay attention to the world we live in before it is too late. Howells argues that the two novels represent a synthesis of Atwood's political, social, and environmental concerns, transformed into speculative fiction, where Atwood continues to ask awkward questions. What difference does it make when a dystopian narrative is told from a marginalized feminine perspective, and perhaps more radically, what difference does it make when the tale is told by the Last Man alive? Not only do these questions challenge the limits of the dystopian genre, but they also probe the possible functions and purposes of storytelling.

The final frame is provided by Sharon Wilson in chapter 12, who begins with Atwood's endgame in *Oryx and Crake* where human beings and civilization are on the brink of extinction. Returning to Atwood's fictions as early as the 1970s, Wilson discerns signs of that end-of-the-world theme and perceives a consistent emphasis on the failure of Atwood's protagonists to see clearly – from defective sight to distorted vision and moral blindness. While symbolic blindness may be a necessary beginning for narrative quests, regaining some vision is arguably necessary for survival. But how useful would it be to emerge from moral blindness in a post-apocalyptic world? Wilson is prompted to ask, given the ferocity of Atwood's satiric vision of the future in *Oryx and Crake*, whether her vision is growing more pessimistic. This novel asks the same question as *Survival* over thirty years earlier, but with very different inflections in a postmodern globalized context: "Have we survived? / If so, what happens *after* Survival?"[4] For Snowman, the implications at zero hour look dire, and his last words in the novel are, "Time to go."[5]

Overview of Atwood criticism since the 1970s

This *Companion* is the latest in a long line of critical anthologies on Margaret Atwood's work, and the remainder of this Introduction offers an overview of the most significant of these anthologies published since the 1970s, as a method of surveying the dominant trends and shifts of emphasis in Atwood criticism over thirty years. In 1977 the first collection of critical essays appeared in *The Malahat Review: Margaret Atwood: A Symposium*, edited by Linda Sandler. It was designed as a tenth anniversary tribute celebrating Atwood's 1967 Governor-General's Award for *The Circle Game*. Already Atwood was being hailed as "the presiding genius of Canadian letters," with six collections of poetry, three novels, and one controversial book of literary criticism to her credit,[6] and the contributors included eminent Canadian poets, novelists, and literary critics. In many ways this is a remarkably prescient volume, for it laid out the key issues in Atwood's writing and mapped major directions for Atwood criticism throughout the 1980s; it is also a very domestic production, featuring Sandler's interviews with Atwood at her Ontario farmhouse shortly before her daughter, Eleanor Jess, was born, together with a photograph of the young mother with her baby, and a photostat page of a worksheet for one of her "Circe/Mud" poems covered with chaotically crossed-out scribbled lines. Not surprisingly, the main emphasis was on Atwood's relation to Canadian literary traditions, her fascination with the wilderness and her ecological concerns, and her role as a mythographer, with much of the evidence drawn from her poetry. Many essays also identified her concerns with the new North American feminist movement, and several essays on her novels paid attention to her narrative techniques of revisioning myths and fairy tales, and her use of a "derailed observer" as the central narrating voice. Interestingly, her "Swifitian" satire was flagged as a sign of her Canadianness, with her books being seen as "mirrors where almost every reader finds his own reflection,"[7] and even her Gothic imagery was read through a Canadian lens where forests substituted for haunted castles.[8] There were also foreshadowings of later criticism on Atwood's postmodernism, with commentaries on the generic hybridity of *Lady Oracle* and a description of the artist as "that prime trickster"[9] (though it is not clear whether the essay refers to Atwood or to her fictional protagonist). Here too appeared the first Atwood checklist and the first essay on archival research into the newly acquired Atwood papers in the Thomas Fisher Rare Book Library, University of Toronto.[10] Jerome Rosenberg records his excitement at looking into the professional correspondence relating the beginnings of Atwood's career and the evidence there of her "wit and energy" and her refusals to compromise with publishers' demands. At this early stage, it is perhaps surprising to find an analysis of Atwood as cult figure, and even more surprising to register the ambivalent tone of its ending: "For the media, Atwood is endlessly re-usable because she is endlessly Protean. There are many more Atwoods to come."[11]

As Atwood's reputation in North America and Britain continued to grow through the 1980s,[12] four important anthologies were published. In 1981 Arnold and Cathy Davidson's *The Art of Margaret Atwood: Essays in Criticism* appeared, edited in Japan by these two Canadians on a sabbatical year away from teaching in the United States. This collection took up the same topics as *The Malahat Review*: Atwood's Canadianness, her feminism, her woman-centered revisions of myths and fairy tales, though developing these topics in different directions. Many of these essays emphasize Atwood's literariness and her intertextuality, some in relation to Northrop Frye's myth criticism and his theory of romance, others in relation to female literary traditions with her Circe and Penelope figures and her stories of transformation and female empowerment, while Atwoodian Gothic was doubly located in relation to European traditions and to the "wilderness Gothic" of Native mythology. That fascination with doubleness as a fundamental Atwoodian concern informed several studies of her "poetics of duplicity" and there are also signs of a new critical interest in the artifice of Atwood's fiction, where "truth" in her novels is seen as "a shifting construct, or a series of tricks with mirrors,"[13] a phrase taken from one of her poems and used again as the title of Branko Gorjup's Italian/English selection of Atwood's poetry in 2000.

The 1983 anthology edited by Sherrill Grace and Lorraine Weir showed the influence of the new critical theories of structuralism and poststructuralism, as its title suggests: *Margaret Atwood: Language, Text, and System*. So, in the first essay, Grace argues for the coherence of Atwood's "system" (the codes that structure a writer's work), identifying patterns of binary opposition, but also demonstrating how Atwood deconstructs such dualities as culture/nature and male/female, as she searches for "a third way of being outside of the either/or alternatives which her system resists."[14] These essays were preoccupied with the central importance of language and writing, best illustrated perhaps by the extreme example of Robert Cluett's detailed examination of the syntactic profile of *Surfacing* by computer analysis. More fascinating, however, is the essay on "Atwood's Poetic Politics," the most deconstructive in the book, which intimates that Atwood's creative writing exceeds the limits of any system, and that moreover "Atwood" may be a figure created by the reader's imagination, "to satisfy our cultural needs as these have arisen. Feminist, nationalist, literary witch, mythological poet, satirist, formulator of critical theories."[15]

With the publication of *The Handmaid's Tale*, the Atwood critical industry shifted into a higher gear, and this made Judith McCombs's anthology, *Critical Essays on Margaret Atwood* (1988) doubly welcome, for this was a retrospective of Atwood criticism up to 1987, drawn mainly from Canadian and American journals and newspapers. Arranged chronologically, these essays and reviews covered every Atwood text up to and including *The Handmaid's Tale*, sometimes singly but often several texts grouped thematically or generically. McCombs provided an extremely useful analysis of critical trends and a summary of debates around Atwood's major texts to date. A reminder of the historical context of the collection are her perceptive comments on what was yet to come in critical studies on Atwood: "The linguistic, formal, structuralist, postmodern, and manuscript approaches have been fewer [than thematic and genre-based criticism], but will no doubt increase."[16]

The next collection, *Margaret Atwood: Vision and Forms*, edited by Kathryn Van Spanckeren and Jan Garden Castro, appeared at the end of 1988. Both these American editors were longstanding Atwood enthusiasts: Castro was founder of the Margaret Atwood Society and Van Spanckeren the first editor of the Atwood Society Newsletter, and this book was designed to introduce the writer to a wider American readership. The collection begins and ends with Atwood's personal views on the United States in an autobiographical foreword and an interview, and a preoccupation with Canada–US relations characterizes the book. There are two essays on *The Handmaid's Tale*, together with an essay based on archival research in the Atwood Papers entitled "Politics, Structure, and Poetic Development in Atwood's Canadian–American Sequences," which looks at two unpublished poems suggestively entitled "The Idea of Canada" and "America as the aging demon lover" and traces the evolution of Atwood's ideas on national power games into her poetry of the late 1970s. For the first time, more attention is paid to her novels and criticism than to her poetry, and one further innovation is the inclusion of an essay by Sharon R. Wilson on Atwood's visual art, illustrated with eight color plates of her watercolor paintings in the Fisher Library archives.

In 1994 the first anthology on Atwood was published in Britain and featured British and European critics as well as North Americans. Edited by Colin Nicholson, *Margaret Atwood: Writing and Subjectivity: New Critical*

Essays departed from the usual agenda by considering Atwood's Canadianness not in the contexts of nationalism and Canada–US relations but from a postcolonial perspective. Twenty years after *Surfacing* and *Survival*, these texts could now be seen as writing against a colonial mindset: "*Survival* establishes parameters . . . for much of the recent theorising of postcolonial representations of literary subjectivity, whether Indian, African, Caribbean or Australian."[17] There was also a strong awareness of Atwood's "continually historicising consciousness" (Nicholson, "Introduction," p. 15), an important feature of her work which was signaled by a few Canadian critics back in the 1970s but then neglected because of critical interest in more topical social and literary concerns like her feminism and her postmodern narrative experiments. Though these issues are represented in the essays on individual novels (now including *Cat's Eye*) and in three on her short stories up to *Wilderness Tips*, the consideration of colonial history and prehistory was privileged here. This perspective cast a new light not only on the archaeological imagery in her poetry but also on Atwood's revisionary narratives, now seen as central to her ongoing project of cultural retrieval and postcolonial differentiation.

Lorraine York's 1995 Canadian anthology, *Various Atwoods: Essays on the Later Poems, Short Fiction, and Novels*, laid out its agenda in the title, with its reference back to Robert Fulford's comments on Atwood's multiplicity and inventiveness, and its subtitle declaring its selective focus. As York explained, this was a project inherited from Arnold Davidson, joint editor of the 1981 anthology with the same publisher, and a "supplement" to it, where several of the original contributors revisited and revised their earlier critical positions, while it also introduced a new generation of Atwood critics and new theoretical approaches. Many of these essays are retrospective in impulse, tracing continuities between later and earlier works in relation to thematics (wilderness, sexual power politics, Canadian nationalism) or to narrative techniques, though the influence of postcolonial theory, deconstruction, and new ideologies of multiculturalism had altered the lenses through which more traditional topics were being considered. This collection also contained what was perhaps the first essay on the emergence of a new Atwoodian genre, the prose poems of the 1980s and 1990s in *Murder in the Dark* and *Good Bones*.

In contrast to the selectivity of York's anthology, *Margaret Atwood: Works and Impact* (2000), edited by Reingard Nischik, follows a grand design which aims at a comprehensive survey and evaluative assessment of her work up to her 60th birthday in 1999; it is also the international scholarly community's tribute to her on that occasion. As well as essays by academic critics, Nischik assembled contributions from several of Atwood's editors, publishers, translators, and her literary agent, as well as appreciations from fellow Canadian writers, together with twelve pages of photographs, six pages of cartoons, and an interview with Atwood in Frankfurt. To accommodate such a variety of materials and contributors, the volume is designed as a series of short chapters arranged in sections: on biography, surveys of the different genres within which Atwood has worked, insights into Atwood's working practices as a creative writer, and a series of "overview" chapters which treat her work from a variety of critical and theoretical angles. These range from feminist, constructionist, generic, and mythic perspectives to environmentalism and cultural theory. As we might expect in a birthday tribute, the tone of the volume is very positive though, if anything, that enhances its value as a full dress parade of Atwoodian scholars and enthusiasts (indeed, the two cannot easily be separated), all of whom direct attention towards Atwood's versatility and the challenges that her writing presents.

It is a measure of Atwood's canonical status that the editor of a critical anthology can now assume an interested readership both for a comprehensive survey (like Nischik's or this *Companion*) and also for a more eclectic selection of essays which push out the boundaries of Atwood scholarship. *Margaret Atwood's Textual Assassinations: Recent Poetry and Fiction*, edited by Sharon Rose Wilson (2003) belongs to the latter class. This book draws attention to the allusions to violence and crime coded into the titles of many of Atwood's works since 1980 – *Murder in the Dark, The Robber Bride, Alias Grace, The Blind Assassin, Moving Targets* – and the emphasis in this collection as the editor explains, is on Atwood's "'assassinations' of traditional genres, plots, narrative voices, structure, techniques, and reader expectations."[18] In this context, academic criticism becomes a kind of sleuthing, not only in the Atwood archives and in those of her works which have as yet received little scholarly attention, like the short stories, prose poems and later poetry, but in the novels themselves, as these essays explore the metafictional dimensions and postmodern strategies of Atwood's storytelling, with their trickster narrators and their generic hybridity. Atwood's fictional and poetic worlds are strange indeed, though that strangeness is masked by her wit and humor, challenging readers to find a critical language adequate to describe her ironic mixture of realism and fantasy, verbal artifice and moral engagement.

An introduction is not a conclusion, but at this point I would like express my thanks to all the contributors to this volume, who have worked so enthusiastically within fairly rigid constraints of time and format; also to Sarah Stanton at Cambridge University Press for her warm encouragement of this project, and to Eva-Marie Kröller for her friendly editorial advice. Special thanks to my daughter Miranda for her expert help in preparation of the typescript, and to Jan Cox at the University of Reading for her thoughtful assistance throughout.

NOTES

1. Earl G. Ingersoll, ed., *Margaret Atwood: Conversations* (London: Virago, 1992), p. 144.
2. *Guardian*, 8 January 2005, p. 1.
3. Interview with Jo Brans (1982), Ingersoll, *Conversations*, p. 149.
4. Margaret Atwood, *Survival: A Thematic Guide to Canadian Literature* (Toronto: Anansi, 1972), p. 246.
5. Margaret Atwood, *Oryx and Crake* (London: Virago, 2004), p. 433.
6. For an outline of the fierce nationalist debates over Atwood's "Canadian Victim" thesis in *Survival* during the early 1970s, see Judith McCombs, ed., *Critical Essays on Margaret Atwood* (Boston: G. K. Hall, 1988), p. 7.
7. Linda Sandler, Preface, *Margaret Atwood: A Symposium*, ed. Linda Sandler, *The Malahat Review* 41 (January 1997): p. 5.
8. Eli Mandel, "Atwood Gothic," *A Symposium*, ed. Sandler, p. 71.
9. Jane Rule, "Life, Liberty and the Pursuit of Normalcy – The Novels of Margaret Atwood," *A Symposium*, ed. Sandler, p. 49.
10. Atwood made her first donation of manuscripts and correspondence to the Fisher Library in 1970, followed by major donations since; the latest accession (2003) contains materials related to *Oryx and Crake*. There are now three massive Atwood manuscript collections, though back in 1976 there were only eleven boxes.
11. Robert Fulford, "The Images of Atwood," *A Symposium*, ed. Sandler, pp. 95–98.
12. The Modern Language Association held its first special session on Atwood in 1977, and has held regular sessions since 1984; the Margaret Atwood Society was founded in 1983.
13. Robert Lecker, "Janus through the Looking Glass: Margaret Atwood's First Three Novels," *The Art of Margaret Atwood: Essays in Criticism*, eds. Arnold E. and Cathy N. Davidson (Toronto: Anansi, 1981), pp. 172–203.
14. Sherrill E. Grace, "Articulating the 'Space Between': Atwood's Untold Stories and Fresh Beginnings," *Margaret Atwood: Language, Text, and System*, eds. Sherrill E. Grace and Lorraine Weir (Vancouver: University of British Columbia Press, 1983), pp. 1–16.
15. Eli Mandel, "Atwood's Poetic Politics," *Margaret Atwood*, ed. Grace and Weir, pp. 53–56, quoting Robert Fulford's essay in *Malahat*, p. 95.
16. McCombs, "Introduction," *Critical Essays*, ed. McCombs, pp. 1–28.
17. Colin Nicholson, "Introduction," *Margaret Atwood: Writing and Subjectivity: New Critical Essays*, ed. Nicholson (Basingstoke and New York: Macmillan and St. Martin's Press, 1994), pp. 1–10.
18. Sharon Rose Wilson, "Introduction," *Margaret Atwood's Textual Assassinations: Recent Poetry and Fiction*, ed. Wilson (Columbus: Ohio State University Press, 2003), pp. xi–xv.

1

DAVID STAINES

Margaret Atwood in her Canadian context

For more than forty years, Margaret Atwood has been a published author, well known for the intricacies of her poetry, the power of her fiction, and the illumination of her literary criticism. As her reputation has grown steadily in international circles, she has produced more than forty books that have been translated into more than forty languages. But she has rooted most of her writing in her own country of Canada. She is, above all else, Canadian.

The early years

Born in the city of Ottawa, Canada's capital, on 18 November 1939, Atwood spent her early years in wintry Ottawa and in northern Quebec, where her father, a biologist, pursued his entomological studies. Moving to Toronto in 1946, her parents continued to take young Atwood and her older brother to the northern wilderness in the summers. "I didn't spend a full year in school until I was 11," Atwood recalls. "Americans usually find this account of my childhood – woodsy, isolated, nomadic – less surprising than do Canadians: after all, it's what the glossy magazine ads say Canada is supposed to be like."[1]

Atwood's parents are from Nova Scotia, and her extended family lives there: "The orientation of my entire family was scientific rather than literary . . . So while the society around me, in the fifties, was very bent on having girls collect china, become cheerleaders, and get married, my parents were from a different culture. They just believed that it was incumbent on me to become as educated as possible."[2] Her parents were great readers, and though they did not encourage her to become a writer, "they gave me a more important kind of support; that is, they expected me to make use of my intelligence and abilities, and they did not pressure me into getting married."[3]

Although Atwood began to write at the age of five, "there was a dark period between the age of eight and sixteen when I didn't write. I started again at sixteen and have no idea why, but it was suddenly the only thing I wanted to do" (Oates, "Poems and Poet," p. 15). It was at Toronto's Leaside High School that the sixteen-year-old Atwood realized that writing was her goal:

> Up to 1956, I'd thought I was going to be a botanist, or, at the very least, a Home Economist . . . There was nothing at Leaside High School to indicate to me that writing was even a possibility for a young person in Canada in the twentieth century. We did study authors, it's true, but they were neither Canadian nor alive . . . I contemplated journalism school; but women, I was told, were not allowed to write anything but obituaries and the ladies' page; and although some of my critics seem to be under the impression that this is what I ended up writing, I felt that something broader was in order. University, in short, where I might at least learn to spell.[4]

But Canada was not a home for writers in the fifties. Atwood remembers her high school days:

> we had no Canadian poetry in high school and not much of anything else Canadian. In the first four years we studied the Greeks and Romans and Ancient Egyptians and the Kings of England, and in the fifth we got Canada in a dull blue book that was mostly about wheat. Once a year a frail old man [Wilson MacDonald] would turn up and read a poem about a crow; afterward he would sell his own books . . . autographing them in his thin spidery handwriting. That was Canadian poetry. ("Travels Back," p. 31)

In the fifties Canada was a country not conversant with its own cultural identity. For many of the writers of the period, publication had to take place elsewhere, their band of readers distinctly negligible in Canada. In the twenties Morley Callaghan began his literary career from Toronto, yet he never identified the Toronto settings of his novels or short stories, only daring to name Toronto with the 1948 publication of his young adult novel, *The Varsity Story*. For such writers as Hugh MacLennan and Sinclair Ross, their first novels of the forties appeared in the United States. Mordecai Richler's first novel, *The Acrobats*, appeared in 1954 in American and English publications, but it was never published in Canada, a country still with little or no respect for literary endeavors.

Armed with a determination to write, Atwood enrolled in the honors English Language and Literature program at Victoria College in the University of Toronto in 1957. Her colleagues "read Evergreen editions of Sartre and Ionesco, wore black turtleneck sweaters, if men, and black turtleneck sweaters, if women. They too drank coffee in the student union . . . I didn't have a black turtleneck sweater, but I did have an old blue one of my father's which had shrunk. Besides, I wanted to be a writer."[5] At Victoria College she made her first foray into Canadian literature:

> When I did discover Canadian writing it was a tremendously exciting thing because it meant that people in the country were writing and not only that, they were publishing books. And if they could be publishing books, then so could I. So then I read a lot of stuff, and I was lucky enough to know somebody who had a fairly extensive library of Canadian poetry which I read from beginning to end, so that by the time I was about 21 I had certainly found my tradition."[6]

Among her Victoria College teachers were Jay Macpherson and Northrop Frye. Macpherson, a good friend and mentor to the young Atwood, was a distinguished poet and scholar who had the "fairly extensive library of Canadian poetry," where she discovered for the first time the writings of such poets as Margaret Avison, P. K. Page, and James Reaney. Frye was another non-intimidating mentor:

> I was never intimidated by Dr. Frye. The deadpan delivery, the irony, the monotone, the concealed jokes, the lack of interest in social rituals, may have seemed odd to those from Ontario, but to me they were more than familiar. In the Maritimes they're the norm. Puritanism takes odd shapes there, some brilliant, most eccentric, and no Maritimer could ever mistake a lack of flamboyance for a lack of commitment, courage or passion. Light dawned when I found out Frye had been brought up in New Brunswick. Not quite the same as Nova Scotia, where the relatives all lived, but close enough. ("Fifties Vic," p. 21)

Frye was the major figure of Canadian criticism, penning, for example, the yearly review of poetry in the fifties in the *University of Toronto Quarterly*. And he advised Atwood to go to graduate school, where she would have "more time to write."

Before Atwood graduated in the spring of 1961, she won the E. J. Pratt Medal for her small collection of poems, *Double Persephone*, which was privately printed by John Robert Colombo's Hawkshead Press. Then, with her Woodrow Wilson Fellowship, she began her master's program in English Literature at Radcliffe College in Harvard University, where she would study with Jerome Hamilton Buckley, the renowned Victorian scholar.

Harvard University is the home of Widener Library, and its extensive and endowed holdings in Canadian literature supplemented Macpherson's library. It was at Harvard, too, that Atwood took a seminar with Perry Miller on the American Puritans that offered her a way of thinking about her country of Canada:

> it [Harvard University] was the place where I started thinking seriously about Canada as having a shape and a culture of its own. Partly because I was studying the literature of the American Puritans, which was not notable for its purely literary values – if one can study this in a university, I thought, why not Canadian literature? (you must understand that at the time Canadian literature was simply not taught in high schools and universities in Canada) – and partly because Boston was, in certain ways, so similar, in climate and landscape, to part of Canada. One began to look for differences.[7]

As with many Canadians of her generation, Atwood's time outside of Canada gave her a necessary distance from, and a perspective on, her own land.

Mapping her Canada

After two years at Harvard, Atwood returned to Toronto and found employment in a market research company. The following year she accepted a lectureship in English at the University of British Columbia. Then she returned to Harvard for two more years: she completed her doctoral examinations and began to work on her thesis on "The English Metaphysical Romance," including the novels of Rider Haggard. The dissertation remains incomplete because Atwood's creative writing assumed dominant interest in her life, even during her time at Harvard. She continued to write poetry while she was attending graduate school, wrote even more in her two years away from Cambridge, and had her first full-length volume of poetry, *The Circle Game*, published in 1966. No longer an academic poet as she was in the poems of *Double Persephone*, she was now a mature poet, delving into the interconnectedness of human relationships and the games people play in the way of these connections. The voice, alive with wit and humor, is distinctive. In the opening poem, "This is a Photograph of Me," Atwood depicts the danger of misperceiving the role people play, yet this poem is not about Atwood herself: "The photograph was taken / the day after I drowned." From her earliest writing, she was determined to be a lens focusing outwards on the world around her. When she looked back in 1980, she would comment: "One of the things I would like to squash underfoot like a cockroach is the idea of art as self-expression. You must say something about the world at large."[8]

The Circle Game won Canada's highest award for poetry, the Governor-General's Award, which led to two important connections. First, early in 1967, William Toye, editorial director of Oxford University Press Canada,[9] telephoned Atwood and informed her that Oxford would like to publish her further collections of poetry. Thus began a collaboration between a gifted poet and an equally gifted editor, which ended upon his retirement in the early nineties. *The Animals in That Country* appeared the following year, and *The Journals of Susanna Moodie*, which Toye accepted the morning after he read it, appeared in 1970.

From "The Settlers," the closing poem of *The Circle Game* and the winner of the President's Medal from the University of Western Ontario, to such poems as "Progressive Insanities of a Pioneer" from *The Animals in That Country* and the entire volume of *The Journals of Susanna Moodie*, Atwood is fascinated by the history of Canada, still relatively unknown, and by the presence of the past in the fabric of contemporary human life. And she is the first writer in Canadian literature to evoke an artistic figure from the past, Susanna Moodie in her case, and make her a major presence in a new work of art. Four years later, Margaret Laurence would do the same with Susanna Moodie's sister, Catherine Parr Traill, in her novel *The Diviners*.

In *The Journals of Susanna Moodie*, Atwood pens a series of meditations on pioneer life, on nature's relationship with its animal and human inhabitants, and on human dislocation, all of them in the voice of Susanna Moodie, a nineteenth-century immigrant to Canada. She first came upon Moodie's *Roughing It in the Bush* (1853) in her family bookcase when she was a young girl.

> I did not read this book at the time. For one thing, it was not a novel, and I was not interested in books that were not novels. For another, my father told me that it was a "classic" and that I would "find it interesting to read some day." I tended to shy away from books that were so described.[10]

A small excerpt from the book appeared in her school reader: "every author in the Grade Six reader came to us clothed in the dull grey mantle of required reading, and I forgot about Susanna Moodie and went on to other matters, such as Jane Austen" (*Roughing It*, p. viii).

It was during Atwood's doctoral studies at Harvard that Moodie reappeared.

> I had a particularly vivid dream. I had written an opera about Susanna Moodie, and there she was, all by herself on a completely white stage, singing like Lucia di Lammermoor. I could barely read music, but I was not one to ignore portents: I rushed off to the library, where the Canadiana was kept in the bowels of the stacks beneath Witchcraft and Demonology, got out both *Roughing It in the Bush* and Mrs. Moodie's later work, *Life in the Clearings*, and read them at full speed. (*Roughing It*, p. viii)

Atwood's Moodie is the schizoid personality. Her personal dislocation – from the old country of England, which provides her perspective for seeing the new country, from the trappings of civilization, from neighbors and even family – dominates her character. She attempts to distance herself from her neighbors, even from her husband, only to discover her need for human beings as a garrison against the wilderness. She tries to explain her fascination with the Canadian landscape, yet she ends fearing her own destruction by that same landscape. She embodies what Atwood regards as the distinctly Canadian condition of living with a violent duality. She makes her final appearance on a bus along Toronto's St. Clair Avenue, a bus route Atwood knows very well. "I have my ways of getting through," Atwood's Mrs. Moodie affirms, and one of these ways is the art of Margaret Atwood. Complete with collages and artwork created by the author, *The Journals of Susanna Moodie* has never been out of print, having gone through a total of twenty-four reprintings until now.

The second telephone call arising from the Governor-General's Award came from Jack McClelland, president of the publishing firm of McClelland and Stewart, "The Canadian Publishers" as their imprint states. Interested in securing the publication of the first novel by this Governor-General's award winner, he invited her to consider his publishing firm, only to discover that she had already submitted it in October 1965 and that the novel was still sitting with no decision taken. He promised prompt action, suggested some revisions, and *The Edible Woman* was published in the fall of 1969. In a manner that was new to most Canadian authors, the book was also published that same fall in England and in 1970 in the United States.

Although *The Edible Woman*'s publication coincided with the rise of feminism in North America, Atwood sees the novel as protofeminist rather than feminist:

> there was no women's movement in sight when I was composing the book in 1965, and I'm not gifted with clairvoyance, though like many at the time I'd read Betty Friedan and Simone de Beauvoir behind locked doors. It's noteworthy that my heroine's choices remain much the same at the end of the book as they are at the beginning: a career going nowhere, or marriage as an exit from it. But these were the options for a young woman, even a young educated woman, in Canada in the early sixties. It would be a mistake to assume that everything has changed . . . The goals of the feminist movement have not been achieved, and those who claim we're living in a post-feminist era are either sadly mistaken or tired of thinking about the whole subject.[11]

Atwood's dissection of her society is rooted firmly in the society around her, and as a lens focused on the present, she gazes steadily on her own world.

For Marshall McLuhan, another Toronto-based author, the artist is the only person living in the present of a situation. Others are driving the car, looking out the rearview mirror at what is in the past and assuming that they are staring directly at the present; they remain wholly unaware that they are securely lodged fifty years behind. The artist is the passenger in the car, staring resolutely at what is taking place around him. For this reason, McLuhan concluded, the artist is often regarded as avant-garde when there is no such term; all there is are those who are staring at the past and those few who view life as it is happening now. The continuing importance of *The Edible Woman* is proof of McLuhan's vision of the artist and Atwood's position as an artist.

Surfacing offers a more optimistic view of its protagonist than *The Edible Woman*. While *The Edible Woman* is lighthearted, it is also pessimistic; the couple is not united, and the wrong couple gets married. At the end of *Surfacing*, the woman returns to the surface, having shaken off past encumbrances and willing now to begin anew. "*The Edible Woman* is a circle and *Surfacing* is a spiral," Atwood observes.[12] And although the terrain of *Surfacing* is bleak, the portrait of the nameless protagonist is sensitive and sympathetic.

Although a feminist novel, *Surfacing* is simultaneously a study of victimization. The nameless heroine "wishes to be not human, because being human inevitably involves being guilty, and if you define yourself as innocent, you can't accept that." Atwood confesses:

> what I'm really into in that book is the great Canadian victim complex. If you define yourself as innocent then nothing is ever your fault – it is always somebody else doing it to you, and until you stop defining yourself as a victim that will always be true. It will always be somebody else's fault, and you will always be the object of that rather than somebody who has any choice or takes responsibility for their life. And that is not only the Canadian stance towards the world, but the usual female one. Look what a mess I am and it's all their fault. And Canadians do that too. Look at poor innocent us, we are morally better than they. We do not burn people in Vietnam, and those bastards are coming in and taking away our country. Well the real truth of the matter is that Canadians are selling it.
>
> (Gibson, *Eleven Canadian Novelists*, pp. 22–23)

This theme of victimization stands behind Atwood's 1972 volume of literary criticism, *Survival*, a bold attempt to isolate "patterns, not of authors or individual works; the point is not to divide up citations on an equal-space basis but to see as clearly as possible those patterns of theme, image and attitude which hold our literature together."[13] Proclaiming at the beginning that her book was "not an exhaustive, extensive or all-inclusive treatise on Canadian literature" (*Survival*, p. 11), Atwood nevertheless incurred the wrath of many Canadian critics who failed to admit that she had done for her own literature what had not been done before.[14]

Addressed to the average Canadian reader, *Survival* is "something that would make Canadian literature, as *Canadian* literature – not just literature that happened to be written in Canada – accessible to people other than scholars and specialists, and that would do it with simplicity and practicality" (p. 13). The tone of the book suggests a guided tour through the pages of Atwood's own reading: like "the field markings in bird-books: they will help you distinguish this species from all others, Canadian literature from the other literatures with which it is often compared and confused" (p. 13). The book is "an attempt to say, quite simply, that Canadian literature is not the same as American or British literature."[15]

Dealing with Canada was not an easy choice, though it was a natural one. The book invoked the ire of many who could not tolerate the belief that there was a literature in Canada: "I drew certain conclusions relating to Canada in the world today, and I prefaced the whole thing with a few reasons why people should read their own literature and not just everybody else's. Worst of all, I said that Canada was a cultural colony and an economic one as well."[16] Still available in print today, *Survival* has sold more than 100,000 copies; it has never been published outside Canada.

Before *Survival* there was no volume of criticism on Canadian literature designed for the general reader. With its publication Atwood's reputation was secure throughout Canada. In this early period, which culminates with the 1972 publication of *Survival*, she had accomplished what she set out to do: forge an identity as a Canadian writer, something almost unique on the Canadian scene.

For Frye in 1965, there was no great Canadian author:

> Canada has produced no author who is a classic in the sense of possessing a vision greater in kind than that of his best readers . . . There is no Canadian writer of whom we can say what we can say of the world's major writers, that their readers can grow up inside their work without ever being aware of a circumference.[17]

As Atwood discovered her voice as a Canadian writer of poetry, fiction, and literary criticism, she helped the country discover its own life as a literary landscape. "Everything was interesting," she reflects, "but the important thing was discovering the fact of our own existence as Canadians" (Sullivan, *The Red Shoes*, p. 9).

"None of us thought it was really possible to be a genuine writer and remain in Canada" (Sullivan, *The Red Shoes*, p. 9), Atwood comments, but remain she did, and became the major exponent of Canadian literature, a wholly viable and emerging voice of power and urgency.

Interpreting Canada abroad

In the second phase of her career, which ran from the early seventies until 1985, Atwood began to review more widely. In the first phase, "I was reviewing Canadian books exclusively" (*SW*, *p.* 19); now her reviewing practices changed. In the mid-seventies she began "to get requests for reviews from publications other than the Canadian ones. They too often wanted me to review women, but not always Canadian women. So a certain amount of cross-fertilization took place, and I found myself reviewing Canadians for Americans and Americans for Canadians and sometimes Canadians for English and English for Canadians" (*SW*, p. 106). Atwood now found herself interpreting Canada for a world outside her country. Her success as a poet, novelist, and critic propelled her into larger frames of reference, though her Canadian roots still dominated in her writing.

In her fiction Atwood showed a masterful eye and ear for comedy. In *Lady Oracle*, her third novel, she fashioned her own *Bildungsroman* of a young Toronto girl who blossomed to 245 pounds by the age of nineteen. Red-haired and excessively overweight, her heroine is a romance writer who imagines alternative lives. But the Canadian media still tended to read fiction as autobiography. On her first public interview for the new novel, Atwood was asked when she dyed her hair and how she managed to lose so much weight! Less comic is her fourth novel, *Life Before Man*, where Toronto's Royal Ontario Museum is the background for a series of personal imprisonments. And her fifth novel, *Bodily Harm*, removes her heroine from Canada. In choosing a Caribbean setting, the first time she has moved her major fictional setting outside Canada, Atwood delivers a scathing commentary on her own country and its smug preference for the security of non-involvement. More than any of her contemporary Canadian writers, she devotes much of her creative energy to her country's aspirations and fears. Her own passionate commitment to Canada is audible in the admission of Dr. Minnow, the leader of the Justice Party and later the victim of an assassin's bullet: "The love of your own country is a terrible curse, my friend. Especially a country like this one. It is much easier to live in someone else's country. Then you are not tempted to change things."[18]

Bodily Harm is much more than Atwood's indictment of Canada's insensitivity to social issues that plague so much of the world. It is an impassioned and pained plea to everyone who stands back passively, preferring the role of voyeur to that of participant in the drama of life. The vacuum that is her heroine's life is finally her own creation, the consequence of her fear of commitment and her unwillingness to assume personal responsibility for her actions and her world. In the closing pages of the book, the heroine flies back to Canada, yet this closing is only her fantasized ending: we leave her still facing death in her Caribbean prison.

Her final novel in this second phase, *The Handmaid's Tale*, is set in Cambridge, Massachusetts. Society has returned to a constricted re-creation of Puritan New England. The brilliance of this international bestseller rests in the creation of a future that is a too logical extension of many dimensions of the present, the horrors her heroine witnesses not far removed from the contemporary atrocities depicted in J. M. Coetzee's South African fiction or from the narrow rules of the religious right in the United States.

Perhaps only a Canadian, a neighbor as well as an outsider to the United States, could create such an unsettling vision of the American future. In implied contrast to Gilead is its northern neighbor, once again the final stop of a new underground railroad, this time one that smuggles handmaids to the freedom of Canada. Readers may wish to shy away from Atwood's warning about the present, which leads to Gilead, preferring to regard the book only as science fiction. But the heroine realizes that mankind, unable to bear very much reality, escapes into the hope that reality is only fiction. "I would like to believe this is a story I'm telling," she laments. "I need to believe it. I must believe it. Those who can believe that such stories are only stories have a better chance."[19]

It was Marshall McLuhan who defined one of the features of the Canadian imagination: "Canada has no goals or directions, yet shares so much of the American character and experience that the role of dialogue and liaison has become entirely natural to Canadians wherever they are. Sharing the American way, without commitment to American goals and responsibilities, makes the Canadian intellectually detached and observant as an interpreter of American destiny."[20] With her readings in American Puritan literature and her eyes focused relentlessly on the present, Atwood offers a too convincing analysis of the future directions of the American destiny. She dedicated this novel to Perry Miller, her Harvard teacher.

From a writer who was trying to explain her experiences as a Canadian to Canadian audiences, Atwood now became a writer on the international level, explaining her country to international audiences. And as her audiences grew, so, too, did her stature inside and outside of Canada.

In her poetry of this period, Atwood published two collections of *Selected Poems* as well as four new volumes. In *Two-Headed Poems* and *True Stories*, she is experiencing her position as a Canadian agent for change in her society. In the former volume, neither voice of bilingual Canada's two founding peoples can hear what the other side is saying; the consequence is what one does hear, a "duet / with two deaf singers." In the latter volume the more public voice of the artist is now clearly heard as she confronts the tortures that confront people elsewhere. Now there is only one truth: "The facts of this world seen clearly / are seen through tears."[21] As she says in *Second Words*, the compilation of fifty reviews and essays,

> I have always seen Canadian nationalism and the concern for women's rights as part of a larger, non-exclusive picture. We sometimes forget, in our obsession with colonialism and imperialism, that Canada itself has been guilty of these stances towards others, both inside the country and outside it; and our concern about sexism, men's mistreatment of women, can blind us to the fact that men can be just as disgusting, and statistically more so, towards other men, and that women as members of certain national groups, although relatively powerless members, are not exempt from the temptation to profit at the expense of others. Looking back over the period, I see that I was writing and talking a little less about the Canadian scene and a little more about the global one.
>
> (*SW*, p. 282)

The world becomes her center, while her focus is distinctly Canadian.

It is during this second phase of Atwood's career that she undertook a variety of new tasks: she became a cartoonist under the name of Bart Gerrard, creator of Kanadian Kultcher Komics in *This Magazine*; an historian of Canada in *Days of the Rebels: 1815–1840*; a short story writer in *Dancing Girls and Other Stories, Bluebeard's Egg*, and *Murder in the Dark*; a children's writer in *Up in the Tree* and *Anna's Pet*; a screenwriter in *Snowbird*; and an editor of *The New Oxford Book of Canadian Verse in English* and *The Oxford Book of Canadian Short Stories in English*. And she received the first of several honorary degrees from Canadian universities with a D. Litt. from Trent University (1973), and from American universities with a degree from Smith College (1982).

Throughout this second phase in her career Atwood developed and defined her position as a writer. Faced with a barrage of criticism from Canadians angered that someone should consider literature, indeed Canadian literature, as part of their landscape, she defined the writer's position in society:

> Far from thinking of writers as totally isolated individuals, I see them as inescapably connected with their society. The nature of the connection will vary – the writer may unconsciously reflect the society, he may unconsciously examine it and project ways of changing it; and the connection between writer and society will increase in intensity as the society (rather than, for instance, the writer's love-life or his meditations on roses) becomes the "subject" of the writer.
>
> (*SW*, p. 148)

The writer becomes, not Shelley's isolated bird who may be overheard by society, but rather a Victorian singer, consciously confronting his society. This outlook is less romantic than Victorian, more the position of the later Tennyson or Browning, who wanted his critics to confront the work of art and to know nothing about the personal identity of the creator. Long criticized for being too autobiographical, Atwood as a poet and fiction writer defies any tendency to read her writings as autobiographical.

Furthermore, Atwood has a deep understanding of the nature of art:

> Poetry is the heart of the language, the activity through which language is renewed and kept alive. I believe that fiction writing is the guardian of the moral and ethical sense of the community. Especially now that organized religion is scattered and in disarray, and politicians have, Lord knows, lost their credibility, fiction is one of the few forms left through which we may examine our society not in its particular but in its typical aspects; through which we can see ourselves and the ways in which we behave towards each other, through which we can see others and judge ourselves.[22]

Fiction allows us to "see others," to move outside the paralyzing entrapment of self and to focus our gaze outside ourselves: "If writing novels – and reading them – have any redeeming social value, it's probably that they force you to imagine what it's like to be somebody else. Which, increasingly, is something we all need to know."[23] And writing, the act of making contact with something outside the self, she would ultimately call

> an uttering, or outering, of the human imagination. It puts the shadowy forms of thought and feeling – heaven, hell, monsters, angels, and all – out into the light, where we can take a good look at them and perhaps come to a better understanding of who we are and what we want, and what our limits may be. Understanding the imagination is no longer a pastime or even a duty but a necessity, because increasingly, if we can imagine something, we'll be able to do it.[24]

Canada in the world

In the third phase of her career, which goes from the mid-eighties until the present, Atwood again focuses on contemporary Toronto in her fiction. *Cat's Eye* and *The Robber Bride* focus on Toronto, the former portraying a painter who returns from Vancouver to confront the many submerged layers of her past, the latter looking at one evil woman who shapes and constantly reshapes the lives of her contemporaries. Then in 1996 she returned to the Canadian past in *Alias Grace*, her favourite period of mid-nineteenth-century Canada, to tell the tale of Grace Marks and her trial for murder;

the novel even includes a brief appearance by Susanna Moodie, that remarkable nineteenth-century immigrant who had already cast her lot in Atwood's imagination. From *Alias Grace* to *The Blind Assassin* is not a long journey, for the latter's realm is less remote in history, but Atwood is still using her knowledge of early twentieth-century Canada as she charts her heroine's journey through her life. Then in *Oryx and Crake* she again ventures into the realm of science fiction or speculative fiction with an account of the last supposed human being on the face of the earth. Whereas *The Handmaid's Tale* is a classic dystopia, *Oryx and Crake* is an adventure romance that depicts intellectual obsession leading to personal destruction. Alongside these five novels are two more collections of short stories, one remarkable volume of poetry, *Morning in the Burned House*, and another compilation of criticism, *Moving Targets: Writing with Intent 1982–2004*.

It is during this third period that Atwood started to pen criticism of Canadian literature that spoke about Canada and the world. In 1991 she was invited to give four lectures at Oxford University as part of the Clarendon Lecture Series in English Literature. Although she was "a non-scholar – and a Canadian non-scholar at that – presuming to address an audience that might contain not only some real scholars, but some real scholars from England," her lectures, published as *Strange Things: The Malevolent North in Canadian Literature*, opens with her non-apologetic statement:

> Canadian literature as a whole tends to be, to the English literary mind, what Canadian geography itself used to be: an unexplored and uninteresting wasteland, punctuated by a few rocks, bogs, and stumps. Note that I do not speak of the Scots, Welsh, or Irish, nor of the ordinary reader; however, for a certain kind of Englishperson, Canada – lacking the exoticism of Africa, the strange fauna of Australia, or the romance of India – still tends to occupy the bottom rung on the status ladder of ex-British colonies. (*ST*, p. 2)

Although she is speaking to "a certain kind of Englishperson," she is using her Oxford position to address a larger world on matters that still go back to *Survival*, when she addressed only Canadians.

Nine years later, Atwood was invited to the University of Cambridge to give the Empson Lectures on the broad subject of "Writing, or Being a Writer." Now she mingles Canadian writers with great writers from around the world, the published series, *Negotiating with the Dead: A Writer on Writing* (2002), having Carol Shields discussed on the same page as Jorge Luis Borges, Alice Munro on the same page as Plato; many Canadian writers take their place alongside some of the world's greatest writers and thinkers. Atwood's position is that of a distinguished writer who has laboured effectively for many years to bring her country's literature to the eyes of the world.

In this period, too, Atwood continued to receive honorary degrees, Oxford University (1998), Cambridge University (2001), Harvard University (2004), and the Sorbonne Nouvelle (2005), among many top institutions.

For Margaret Atwood the journey of the writer parallels the journey of the Canadian, the writer a young girl in her teenage years, determined to embark on what would be a distinguished writing career, and the Canadian, slowly realizing that her country has a literary life still unexplored and unknown. From her first forays into the world of Canadian literature, Atwood was intrigued and entranced with the treasures that lay at her feet, treasures that lay still undiscovered.

In the first phase of her career Canada was, for Atwood, a country to be explored, examined, and explained, and she set about doing this. In the second phase she moved beyond the discovery of "our existence as Canadians" to a confrontation with the larger world in which we live, and her growing stature as a writer made her explorations important to the world. And in the third phase of her career she is placing Canada and its literature on a level with the other literatures of the world.

Atwood has never turned her back on Canada, preferring to bring it along with her, making her country partake in the events of the world. This attribute, which led her to pen *Survival*, now leads her to speak of "strange things" from Canada at the University of Oxford and then to speak of Canada in the world at the University of Cambridge. More than thirty years ago, Atwood reflected on her own country:

> Canada, more than most countries, is a place you choose to live in. It's easy for us to leave, and many of us have. There's the U.S. and England, we've been taught more about their histories than our own, we can blend in, become permanent tourists. There's been a kind of standing invitation here to refuse authenticity to your actual experience, to think life can be meaningful or important only in "real" places like New York or London or Paris . . . The question is always, Why stay? and you have to answer that over and over.
>
> ("Travels Back," p. 48)

Then Atwood answers her own question, giving an answer for all writers who want to locate themselves in their own world:

> I don't think Canada is "better" than any other place, any more than I think Canadian literature is "better"; I live in one and read the other for a simple reason: they are mine, with all the sense of territory that implies. Refusing to acknowledge where you come from – and that must include the noodle man and his hostilities, the anti-nationalist lady and her doubts – is an act of

> amputation: you may become free floating, a citizen of the world (and in what other country is that an ambition?) but only at the cost of arms, legs or heart. By discovering your place you discover yourself. ("Travels Back," p. 48)

In discovering herself, Atwood has also discovered Canada's cultural traditions, and her writing has examined them, both their follies and their triumphs, in a relentless and ongoing attempt to make Canada a nation of the world and its literature a commanding presence on the world stage.

NOTES

1. Margaret Atwood, "Travels Back," *Maclean's* 86.1 (January 1973): p. 31.
2. "A Margaret Atwood Interview with Karla Hammond," *Concerning Poetry* 12.2 (Fall 1979): p. 73.
3. Joyce Carol Oates, "Margaret Atwood: Poems and Poet," *The New York Times Book Review*, 21 May 1978: p. 43.
4. Margaret Atwood, "Northrop Frye Observed," *Second Words* (Toronto: Anansi, 1982), p. 398.
5. Margaret Atwood, "Fifties Vic," *The CEA Critic* 42.1 (November 1979): p. 19.
6. Graeme Gibson, *Eleven Canadian Novelists* (Toronto: Anansi, 1973), pp. 11–12.
7. Joyce Carol Oates, "A Conversation with Margaret Atwood," *The Ontario Review* 9 (Fall–Winter 1978–79): p. 9.
8. Adele Freedman, "Happy Heroine and 'Freak' of CanLit," *Globe and Mail*, 25 October 1980: p. E1.
9. For Toye's place in publishing in Canada, see Roy MacSkimming, *The Perilous Trade* (Toronto: McClelland and Stewart, 2003), pp. 69–87.
10. Margaret Atwood, "Introduction," *Roughing It in the Bush; or, Life in Canada* (Boston: Beacon Press, 1987), p. vii.
11. Margaret Atwood, "Preface," *The Edible Woman* (London: Virago, 1980), p. 8.
12. Interview with Linda Sandler, *The Malahat Review* 41 (January 1977): p. 14.
13. Margaret Atwood, *Survival* (Toronto: Anansi, 1972), pp. 11–12.
14. For an analysis of the hostile reviews, see Rosemary Sullivan, *The Red Shoes: Margaret Atwood Starting Out* (Toronto: HarperFlamingoCanada, 1998), pp. 293–97.
15. Geoff Hancock, *Canadian Writers at Work* (Toronto: Oxford University Press, 1987), p. 258.
16. Margaret Atwood, "Canadian–American Relations: Surviving in the Eighties," *SW*, p. 386.
17. Northrop Frye, "Conclusion," *A Literary History of Canada*, ed. Carl F. Klinck (Toronto: University of Toronto Press, 1966), p. 821.
18. Margaret Atwood, *Bodily Harm* (London: Virago, 1983), p. 133.
19. Margaret Atwood, *The Handmaid's Tale* (London: Vintage, 1996), p. 49.
20. Marshall McLuhan, "Canada: The Borderline Case," *The Canadian Imagination: Dimensions of a Literary Culture*, ed. David Staines (Cambridge, MA: Harvard University Press, 1977), p. 227.
21. Margaret Atwood, *Eating Fire: Selected Poetry 1965–1995* (London: Virago, 1998), pp. 227, 256.

22. Margaret Atwood, "An End to Audience?" *Dalhousie Review* 60.3 (Autumn 1980): p. 424.
23. Margaret Atwood, "Writing the Male Character," *This Magazine* 16.4 (September 1982): p. 10.
24. Margaret Atwood, "*The Handmaid's Tale* and *Oryx and Crake* in Context," *PMLA* 119.3 (May 2004): p. 517.

2

LORRAINE YORK

Biography/autobiography

Margaret Atwood's relation to biography and autobiography has been the subject of much controversy. Like many writers, she steadfastly resists attempts to read her works as simple reflections of personal experiences; they are, as she constantly reminds her readers, artistic creations that may draw upon but not be reduced to observed experience. Another Canadian writer, Alice Munro, put the case memorably when she observed that writers often use a bit of starter dough from the real world, but the cake that rises from the pan is, of course, another confection altogether.[1] This chapter will not, therefore, consist of any such attempt to read Atwood's works biographically, as fictionalized autobiography. Instead, it will ponder representations of Atwood and her career, and it will use the notion of literary celebrity to do so.

There is no doubt that Atwood is the one Canadian writer who can, most unequivocally, be called a literary celebrity, and this chapter will assess not only how she has been represented as such, but how she has intervened as an active, canny agent to shape the discourses surrounding her celebrity. It may, at first glance, seem out of proportion to call any writer a celebrity, given the sort of attention that Hollywood A-list stars attract, but theorists of celebrity see it as a phenomenon that reaches across cultural institutions. As Christine Gledhill writes, the star "crosses disciplinary boundaries."[2] That means that the question of what sorts of public individuals qualify as stars is slightly beside the point. Stardom is, instead, one of the products of social exchange. That Margaret Atwood occupies this position of heightened visibility in her field of literary production is clear. Graham Huggan devotes a chapter of his book *The Post-colonial Exotic* to what he calls "Margaret Atwood, Inc.," the Atwood industry,[3] and there he offers several explanations for her remarkable success: first and foremost, hard work and productivity; her ability to function as a spokesperson on a wide range of topics both literary and political; the multiplication of her public roles as writer, feminist, environmentalist, nationalist; the "soundbite quality of many of her public utterances" and the "epigrammatic witticisms" found in her writing (in a word, she is media-friendly); and her launching of subversive attacks on social mores from the position of the middle class (Huggan, *Post-colonial Exotic*, pp. 214–17). Rather than trying to explain Atwood's celebrity in this fashion, however, this chapter will look at its manifestations: instead of asking *why* Atwood is a star, I will concentrate on *how* both she and her works are read in terms of celebrity, and how she, in turn, actively intervenes in these readings.

A central assumption of this chapter, and one that is particularly important to keep in mind when considering Atwood, is that stars are complex formations. One of the first systematic theorists of stardom, Richard Dyer, constructed the notion of the "star text" in order to capture that complexity. Dyer reasoned that one cannot ascribe a single "meaning" to a star; since individual consumers or groups of consumers may read a star differently, it is more useful, instead, to think of "star texts": a constellation of possible meanings and affects that audiences may attach to particular stars.[4] Accordingly, this chapter will not seek an authentic, verifiable biographical version of "the real" Margaret Atwood. Instead, it will examine how various, shifting, and compelling is the "star text" that is Margaret Atwood.

Literary celebrity and intervention

The production/consumption dialectic

A central point of debate in studies of celebrity is the way in which stars are formed: are they primarily constructs of large conglomerates who force their products upon an unsuspecting audience, or are they formed by powerful groundswells of popular feeling for particular individuals? One of the reasons why Richard Dyer felt compelled to theorize a star text was that he found theories of star formation that emphasized the former process, production, to be simplistic. Throughout his book *Stars* he emphasizes that he is not tempted by theories that depict the consumer as passive because there are so many ways that audiences can interact with stars. One of the virtues of Huggan's list of reasons why Atwood has become a literary star is its inclusion of forces both of production and of consumption: things Atwood or her literary agents did to promote her success (hard work, energetic media appearances) and affiliations that particular audiences formed with her work (feminists, environmentalists, nationalists, members of the middle class).

The star's relation to contradiction

In moving, as I have proposed, from a consideration of *why* Atwood has succeeded to a study of *how* she operates as a fully complex star text, it is crucial to note the role of contradiction in star images. Whereas Huggan tends to list the positive associations that readers have found in Atwood (e.g. Atwood = feminist; Atwood = nationalist), associations that, he argues, have underpinned her achievement of success, he tends to pay less attention to those attributes as sites of contestation. For some audience members, the equation "Atwood = feminist" is a powerful disabler of celebrity status, to name just one example. As Dyer argues, "star images function crucially in relation to contradictions within and between ideologies, which they seek variously to 'manage' or resolve" (*Stars*, p. 38). By "manage" Dyer appears not to mean "solve"; elsewhere in *Stars* he notes that the relation of the star to the contradictions in ideologies "may be one of displacement . . . or the suppression of one half of the contradiction and the foregrounding of the other . . . or else it may be that the star effects a 'magic' reconciliation" (p. 30). What sorts of ideologies might the star text Margaret Atwood thus work to "manage" or "resolve"?

To begin with: there is the relation between women and achievement. One characteristic of the star image of Atwood that has aroused equal measures of praise and disaffection is her uncompromising honesty about women's achievements, including her own. She has often spoken about how, when she began to think about writing in the 1950s, the predominant attitude in Canada towards women and writing was one of skepticism. Writing could be thought of as a viable pursuit for women only insofar as it could be reconciled with traditional, heterosexual domestic duties. That Atwood, after she gained success, refused to play this game, and has been fairly unblushing about her own hard work and talent, both wins over feminist supporters and alienates audiences with more conservative views. It also foregrounds the contested area: woman and achievement. As she once observed, "People still have a hard time coping with power of any kind in a woman, and power in a writer is uncanny anyway."[5]

Another example of a field of contradictions that Atwood's star image activates is the relation between women and satire. As I have noted elsewhere, Atwood's association with satire foregrounds the historical appropriation of the mode by male writers. As with the relations between women and achievement, Atwood's satire unleashes various, conflicting audience responses to the relation between women and social critique. Some readers or consumers of her star image (since those who respond to Atwood's star image do not necessarily read her books) find her satirical voice unsettling.

As I have written about a clasroom survey of student attitudes to Atwood's role as social satirist, "Satire does seem, in the minds of many readers, to be associated with unacceptable forms of female deportment: noncompliance, critique of sexual relations, barbed invective."[6] So a model of star formation that limits itself to examples of positive star-audience identification misses out on a complex dynamic of celebrity: audience controversy, contradiction, and discomfort. These forces – identification, attraction, discomfort, hostility, and every response in between – can all potentially be mobilized in star–audience relations. And this holds just as true for Margaret Atwood, the internationally celebrated author, as it does for any star of the screen.

The labor/leisure dichotomy

Another fundamental area of tension and contradiction in star images has to do with the relations between labor and leisure. Indeed, theorists of celebrity have seen this dichotomy as central to stardom itself. As Edgar Morin wrote over four decades ago, the star "proposes and imposes a new ethics of individuality, which is that of modern leisure."[7] And it is true that, as Dyer has pointed out, representations of the stars in magazines, during the golden era of Hollywood film, tended to reinforce this ethic, showing the stars at play, at parties, surrounded by luxury and entertainment (*Stars*, p. 39). Such a representation tends to undercut the role of labor, in this case the labor of making films. This mystification, in turn, increases the tension between the operations of luck and hard work in the formation of stars. Do stars achieve their stardom as the result of persistent hard work and dedication, or do they simply get lucky? Even so prodigious a worker as Margaret Atwood seems compelled to repeat, in interviews, that the key to her success is, to use the quotation from soprano Dame Joan Sutherland that is featured on Atwood's website, "Bloody hard work, duckie!"[8]

Fame as an adaptive response

Amidst these competing responses to stars, and the ongoing debate about stardom as top-down production or audience consumption, what often gets left out is, ironically, the star. What powers, if any, are left to celebrities to intervene in these forces? There are some indications that celebrities need not be the passive products they are often shown to be. As Barry King argues, "stardom is a strategy of performance that is an adaptive response to the limits and pressures exerted upon acting in the mainstream cinema."[9] King's comment is applicable to many more contexts than film, and in Margaret Atwood we have a particularly rich instance of the performance of celebrity as an "adaptive response." She appears as a chameleon of sorts; as she commented to Roy MacGregor, "The public has given me a personality of not having a public personality . . . Sometimes they make up things about it like Margaret the Monster and Margaret the Magician and Margaret the Mother. Romantic notions of what's really there keep getting in the way of people's actual view of you" (MacGregor, "Atwood's World," p. 66). That may be true, but Atwood herself has also aided and abetted this mythologizing process by being rather tightfisted with details of her personal life, as is, of course, her right. Restricting free access to her privacy has been one of those complex adaptive responses to her stardom. It has both allowed her to preserve some time to herself, her writing, and her family, and it has also, ironically, fed the publicity machines.

Once we grant the power of stars to fashion strategies for adapting to the performance that is their stardom, we open up the possibilities of their further interventions into their own star images. German Atwood scholar Susanne Becker has observed that Atwood "encounters – and uses – the publicity machine and the media business with superiority, dignity, and generosity."[10] She is, I think, right about this, but what I also find fascinating is the way in which any claim that a literary star is using the publicity machine has to be phrased in terms of care for others (and not, primarily, for the self). And yet, as Becker goes on to argue, at least some of Atwood's control over public discourse about her seems not entirely altruistic: "It is Atwood's strategy to address, summarize, and thus control much of the media imagery about her" ("Celebrity," p. 32). There is nothing particularly wrong with that; it can be a distinct advantage to control public discourses about oneself rather than be driven by them, particularly in the case of writers, for whom a constant mindfulness of the demands of an audience can be harmful.

One powerful example of Atwood's intervention into the making of her star image is her website. Stars and their publicity people often use websites as a means of disseminating counter-information about the star, particularly when scandal erupts or when an unflattering image of the star seems to have taken hold. In Atwood's case, the website provides some relief for her and for her assistants because it offers information that they would otherwise be asked to provide. One recent estimate figures that there are approximately 460 downloads from her website daily.[11] In addition to managing workload, the website also highlights Atwood's achievements (such as awards), thus confirming her literary star status, and it also appears to offer readers access to her, in spite of her assistant's warnings that, no, she cannot write book blurbs, she cannot find writers a publisher, and she will not read unpublished manuscripts. Playing off against this impression of the barricaded famous writer, fending off requests of all sorts, is the sort of access promised by the personal tone of some of the writings. There is also a feature called "From Margaret Atwood's desk" on the website, and it shows a roll-top desk where one can click on various drawers that will open and offer information (excerpts from speeches, etc). This invitational graphic seeks, I think, to balance out the regulatory, protective aspects of the website. At any rate, whether seeming to offer readers access or denying it, the website shows Margaret Atwood and her agents directly intervening in the flurry of media texts about her that are in circulation.

Atwood as a visual spectacle

Many Canadians, in particular, seem conscious of Atwood as a visual spectacle, not least among them Atwood herself. Canadians, of course, see her face printed frequently in magazines and newspapers, as a spokesperson for various causes or political positions, as an award-winning writer, and as a public personality generally. And since she first came to national prominence in the early 1970s, those media accounts have persistently focused on her personal appearance. By the 1980s, as Susanne Becker notes, Atwood became a frequent cover-girl for a number of Canadian national magazines. By that time, physical descriptions of Atwood had become such ready coinage that Canadian journalists were complaining that they were running out of adjectives. As Judith Timson wrote for the popular women's magazine *Chatelaine* in 1981, "writing about Margaret Atwood has become no easy task – all the descriptions for her hair have already been used up: that 'familiar wreath of disorganized hair,' that 'nimbus of crinkled curls,' that 'kinky flyaway hairstyle that is her trademark.'"[12] All of this intensive scrutiny of her personal appearance would suggest a vision of the literary superstar as media product. In the midst of all of this apparatus of star production, how can a celebrity intervene, fight back?

Atwood has found several ways in which to counter pervasive visual representations of herself. For one thing, she has proved herself to be adept at ridiculing such representations; she once noted that an enterprising critic had actually done a study of her book jacket photographs and had decided that there were "not enough smiles, in her opinion. Girls, like the peasants in eighteenth-century genre paintings, are supposed to smile a lot."[13] Such a verbal skewering reveals the ideological basis for the study: once again, that vexed relationship between women and success.

Another variety of humor, self-deprecation, also works to puncture the overblown spectacle of herself that she is confronted by in the media. As she commented to Adele Freedman interviewing her for the *Globe and Mail*,

"Now people say I'm beautiful; before I was famous, they just said 'Can't you do something with your hair?'"[14] In another medium, her comics, Atwood uses the same combination of self-deprecating humor and rapier-sharp verbal skewerings. She has had a long history of drawing comic strips, often devoted either to witty reflections on her own career or to current political affairs. On her website at this time of writing, she has included several comic strips depicting the pitfalls of going on book tours: being interviewed by bumptious, rude interviewers or, the classic situation, interviewers who have not read her book. In all of these comics she has depicted herself as a short woman with squiggles for hair, dressed in black boots, dress, and topped by a dramatic, "arty" black hat that bears an unsettling resemblance to a witch's cap. Many of the stock descriptions of her physical self are on full display here, and by co-opting and re-representing them, Atwood intervenes and recovers the power of representation. As Nathalie Cooke writes of some of the earlier comics in which Atwood represents herself parodically as "Survivalwoman," "Atwood presents Atwood as short and soft-spoken, buried under a mass of curls . . . These cartoon or stick figures are self-deprecating and funny, proof that Atwood takes her work seriously but does not take herself too seriously."[15] They are also proof of her ability to intervene in her own celebrity representation. Fittingly, then, when Atwood met a group of scholars and readers in the spring of 2004 at the University of Ottawa, to help celebrate an international conference on her works, "Margaret Atwood: The Open Eye," her presentation took the form of a slide show of personal photographs, another version of the autobiographical comic strip. These photos, arranged in chronological order, showed her typically quick, devastating wit as well as her use of self-deprecating representation ("This is me dressed up as a triangle," ran one terse commentary on a Hallowe'en photograph). But they were also, in places, movingly personal. She included, to my surprise, a photograph of her first marriage, a subject that she has persistently told interviewers is none of their business. And her photographs of her daughter Jess were offered with warmth and gentle humor. Her final photograph showed her shaking the hand of the Queen of England. Her dry reflection? "Only one of these women is the Queen of England." Again we have the same self-deprecation, meant to poke a hole in the image of her as an all-powerful icon. Of course, in typically Atwoodian fashion, it also reinforced it. At a large gathering of international critics, people devoted to delving into her work (and, in the case of some, into her private life), Atwood offered both an appearance of openness and a sly defensive maneuver. It is as though she declared that if she is to be a visual spectacle, she is, at least, fully capable of operating the light-and sound show. Like the desk graphic on her website, the slide show both opened some personal spaces and resolutely declared her right to keep others closed.

Fame as a deathly specter

Fiction is another space that Atwood can use to meditate on the processes and condition of stardom. This is not to suggest, of course, that the fiction becomes the simple reflection of her own experiences as a star; still, there are moments in a number of her fictions where she playfully draws on the "starter dough" of her personal knowledge of the subject. Susanne Becker has briefly traced some of these moments. She points to manifestations such as Atwood's wry play on literary celebrity in *Lady Oracle* (with a literary rising star, Joan Foster, who is noted for her flamboyant hair, no less), to the reflections of *Cat's Eye* which, in her view, "explores notions of artistic celebrity on a more serious note" ("Celebrity," p. 36), to *Alias Grace*, whose patchwork structure Becker says "pointedly mirror the workings of celebrity, sensationalism, and media hype in the late twentieth century" (p. 37).

In looking briefly at Atwood's fictions of fame, I want to add to Becker's analysis by noting the persistent concern with fame as deathly specter that runs through all of these works. In *Lady Oracle*, this motif is pervasive. The condition of fame is what Joan Foster finally finds a fate worse than death. When she goes on television talk shows and makes the mistake of being frank about her automatic writing experiences, then she is deluged with invasive questions about the spiritual realm. Her publishers, deaf to her pleas that she be spared this media circus, insist that everything is fine. And for them, it is: her notoriety has resulted in increased sales. Finally, Joan's thoughts take a deathly turn, one that speaks volumes about the dark correspondences between fame and death:

> I felt very visible. But it was as if someone with my name were out there in the real world, impersonating me, saying things I never said but which appeared in the newspapers, doing things for which I had to take the consequences: my dark twin, my funhouse-mirror reflection. She wanted to kill me and take my place, and by the time she did this no one would notice the difference because the media were in on the plot, they were helping her.[16]

This passage echoes things that Atwood herself has said about the effects of fame, both in interviews and in her more recent collection of essays on writing, *Negotiating with the Dead*, where she considers writing as a type of split personality syndrome. As she told a journalist from the *Guardian* in 2000, when she won the Booker Prize, the Margaret who is the "person on the big billboard . . . is sort of like having a twin who looks exactly like you, who is running around out of control."[17] From the earlier perspective of *Lady Oracle*, fame sounds eerily like a haunting.

In *Cat's Eye* it isn't so much that the perspective is that much more serious; the artist Elaine Risley has many funny wisecracks to offer about fame in the art world. But Becker is right in a sense, in that there is an aura of the autumnal about this representation of fame. The perspective, after all, is that of an artist who has been spirited away from her West Coast home to Toronto to attend a retrospective of her work. And if that isn't autumnal, not much is; as Elaine mordantly thinks, "first the retrospective, then the morgue."[18] There is a very real sense, in *Cat's Eye*, that Elaine's paintings have been placed in a morgue of sorts, though it more commonly goes by the name of an art gallery. Later in the novel, as she walks through the rooms of the gallery, it's as though she is bringing life back to these paintings in the act of reviving their moments of creation and of their inspiration in her past. In order to do that, however, Elaine needs to resuscitate her work from layers of critical explication that recall Joan Foster's experience of fame as "Lady Oracle." Of one painting, she notes that the gallery curator has had some trouble coming up with a trendy explication: "Risley continues her disconcerting deconstruction of perceived gender and its relation to perceived power . . . If I hold my breath and squint, I can see where she gets that" (*CE*, p. 547). Atwood is having fun with the language and posturing of academe, but she is also breathing her life back into the canvasses. What is frightening, though, is that this breathing stops; tired by her act of strolling through her own retrospective, Elaine admits, "I can no longer control these paintings, or tell them what to mean. Whatever energy they have came out of me. I'm what's left over." First the retrospective, then the morgue.

The morgue is exactly where Atwood's novel *Alias Grace* takes us, and Becker is right to note that the tissue of fabrications, multiple versions of truth, and lies is closely connected to fame. Grace Marks has achieved what Richard Ellmann, Oscar Wilde's biographer, once called "fame's wicked twin": notoriety.[19] We are back to twinning, fame, and destruction: a powerful constellation in the work of Margaret Atwood. In reading *Alias Grace* it is difficult to say, for instance, whether the death scene is the one that is investigated by the police or the one that Grace Marks lives out as an infamous woman, both in captivity and after her release. When she is about to be released from the Kingston penitentiary, she tells her friend Janet that because her "story is too well known" she is not likely to find employment; for Grace, "instead of seeming my passport to liberty, the Pardon appeared to me as a death sentence."[20]

This concern of Atwood's with the infamous woman as the evil twin of the famous star is one that is, I believe, linked to her perception of the hostility at the heart of celebrity. In *Lady Oracle*, Joan Foster's sense of her celebrity as a deathly, threatening specter is certainly helped on its way by the nasty machinations of the jealous journalist Fraser Buchanan. And Atwood herself is no stranger to professional jealousy and the hostility it can evoke. As early in her career as 1973, she complained to the Empire Club in Toronto that she had become a "Thing": "both icon and target, both worshipped and shot at."[21] In the early 1980s, journalist Judith Timson chronicled some of the nastier attacks on Atwood; one journalist, for instance, trashed Atwood for everything from riding in a limousine to breastfeeding her baby ("The Magnificent Margaret Atwood," p. 60). This hostility may seem puzzling, but to those who study the celebrity phenomenon, it is part of the territory. P. David Marshall notes that the celebrity houses a strange paradox; celebrated and given importance and cultural air time, he or she is nevertheless "viewed in the most antipathetic manner" as representing "success without . . . work."[22] We are back to the old labor–leisure celebrity dichotomy. But how could this dichotomy be at work in the case of a celebrity whose prodigious efforts are so apparent in something as basic as a list of works published? This question seems to have intrigued the German scholar Caroline Rosenthal, who conducted a comparative survey of instructors' responses to Atwood in various countries. She found that Canada has a "specific relationship to its most renowned author, who is proudly referred to as a superstar, on the one hand, and who is rejected for being one on the other."[23] In her domestic context, Atwood's fame discloses the dark underbelly of adulation: the hostility that she, in turn, transforms fictionally into a death-force.

Negotiating with the dead

Negotiating fame, for Atwood, becomes an act of negotiating with the dead. The title is, of course, that of Atwood's 2002 volume of essays based on the William Empson lectures that she delivered at Cambridge in 2000, but I read Atwood's musings about the writer's craft a bit differently. These six lively and erudite lectures trace a number of Atwood's characteristic concerns with writing, particularly her thesis that all writing involves and responds to a fascination with mortality, with descending into the realms of death and finding something of use to bring back to the surface.[24] I argue, though, that this is also a book that is haunted by the deathly specter that fame has become for Atwood.

First of all, Atwood very early on draws a distinction between the writer as writer and the writer as Public Personality that recalls comments she has made about her own fame. "Pay no attention to the facsimiles of the writer that appear on talkshows, in newspaper interviews, and the like," she warns. "They ought not to have anything to do with what goes on between you, the reader, and the page you are reading, where an invisible hand has previously left you some marks to decipher" (*NWD*, pp. 125–26). Fittingly, then, in *Negotiating with the Dead*, Atwood returns to her persistent concern with the writer as double, as split personality, but this split is exacerbated by the workings of celebrity. In her second essay, titled "Duplicity," Atwood poses the question, what is the connection between the two manifestations of the author, "the one who exists when no writing is going forward" and the "other, more shadowy and altogether more equivocal personage who shares the same body, and who, when no one is looking, takes it over and uses it to commit the actual writing" (*NWD*, p. 35)? Here Atwood mobilizes one of her favorite discourses: that of the tale of horror: writing becomes a verbal invasion of the body snatchers, writing a crime that is "committed." Welcome back to the playfully macabre vision of *Murder in the Dark*.

What especially interests me, though, in this passage, is the uncharacteristic break in the text that soon occurs; after posing this question, Atwood refers to a saying that she keeps tacked up on her bulletin board, "Wanting to meet an author because you like his work is like wanting to meet a duck because you like pâté." After offering the predictable interpretation of this saying, that meeting the famous is always disappointing, Atwood discloses that there's a "more sinister way" of reading it: "In order for the pâté to be made and then eaten, the duck must first be killed. And who is it that does the killing?" At this moment, the text breaks off, and another, calmer voice takes up the discussion, asking "Now, what disembodied hand or invisible monster just wrote that cold-blooded comment?" Clearly, we have Atwood's two writers jostling for textual ground here; the darker, shade-haunting presence poses a question about writing and reading as a species of death, as a feeding off the dead, and the calm voice of the author as everyday person, "a nice, cosy sort of person . . . a dab hand at cookies" interrupts to smoothe some nice, comforting batter over the gaping abyss (*NWD*, p. 35). Negotiating with the dead is more than an archetypal descent into the realms of mortality and knowledge, though for Atwood it is certainly and profoundly that. It's also negotiating with the living death that is fame.

Negotiating with biography

For the famous author, negotiating with those who want to delve into your life is, paradoxically, also an act of negotiating with the dead. When Rosemary Sullivan approached Atwood about writing a biography of her that would become her study *The Red Shoes*, Atwood's instant and emphatic response was "I'm not dead yet."[25] Biography is, par excellence, the making of pâté from the duck, so to speak. Given the fact that, as Atwood once mused of her fame, "You get to feel like the mechanical duck at the fun-fair shooting gallery, though no one has won the oversized panda yet, because I still seem to be quacking,"[26] then the making of pâté would seem to be a bit premature. But two works of biography have appeared, Sullivan's volume and Nathalie Cooke's *Margaret Atwood: A Biography*,[27] and so seeing how Atwood and her biographers have negotiated with the living death that is biography is fascinating to ponder.

First of all, both biographers have been clear as to what they did not wish their biographies to be: exposés. Cooke has noted that she did not want to produce what she calls a "lion biography," one that "places the biographical subject out of the ordinary domestic sphere and places her in the great mythic and wild beyond, as *literary lion*" (Cooke, "Lions, Tigers, and Pussycats," p. 22). Another term for this biography might be a celebrity biography. Sullivan claimed that what she was writing was, in fact, a "not-biography," if by biography one means a gossipy stroll through the subject's private life. Instead, she felt that she wanted to produce a study of what it was like to be a woman writer in Canada during the years that Atwood came to literary maturity. This is very much a social, contextual biography.

As a result, reviewers of these not-biographies have found themselves stymied; these books are not what they have expected, and very likely desired: a slice of pâté. As Elizabeth Renzetti, reviewing both biographies, notes "there's little contentious material in either one. If there is dirt under Atwood's carpet, it's not being swept up here."[28] One can almost hear the vacuum cleaner revving up. Reviewing Sullivan's *The Red Shoes*, Joan Givner offers a stronger critique; she argues that in a biography a "subject's voice should ring out, but it should not dominate the biographer's." She discerns in Sullivan's biography a "ventriloquism" of sorts, caused by the biographer's tentative approach to her powerful subject.[29] John Ayre follows a similar line, noting that Sullivan tended to interview mainly Atwood's friends and supporters; he argues that this "friendly focus" does not prove effective when analyzing the years of Atwood's critical and popular successes. Where, he wonders, are the voices of literary agents and publicists "who were very canny in exploiting Atwood's image in the 1970s?"[30] It seems as though, for many reviewers of these biographies, the living presence of Atwood dwarfed and enfeebled the biographer's attempts to shape a narrative of her life, a "retrospective" that is closer than one would like to think to the "morgue."

I close with one last attempt at biography, Michael Rubbo's 1984 Canadian National Film Board documentary, *Once in August*. Rubbo subscribes fully to the approach to Margaret Atwood and his works that I said at the beginning of this chapter would definitely not be my approach to the questions of biography and autobiography. He is determined to find, in Margaret Atwood's life, a magic key to the preoccupations of her fiction. Is it an unhappy childhood? An early trauma? The film is a wonderful treatment of the frustration of Rubbo's quest, and as Nathalie Cooke rightly points out, Rubbo "himself looks progressively more miserable" as the film goes on, frustrated at every turn by his subject ("Lions, Tigers, and Pussycats," p. 18). Atwood fields his autobiographical questions with the patience that a kindly soul gives to small dumb animals, but it is clear that she will give no encouragement to his quest to read her fiction in terms of her life. In the culminating comic sequence, Atwood and her family members take over the camera one evening, Atwood puts a paper bag with eyeholes cut into it over her head, and her family members take turns asking "Who is this woman?," providing jokey answers and generally laughing it up at Rubbo's expense. I read that film, and this sequence in particular, as emblematic of Margaret Atwood's negotiations with celebrity. Stars, as theorists of celebrity have commented, seem to offer access to some form of secret, private self – and yet, like Atwood in the film, paper mask firmly in place, they also rebuff that desire. As Christine Gledhill has perceptively noted, "the star promises what mass society and the human sciences – sociology, Marxism, psychoanalysis – throw into question: intimate access to the authentic self" (*Stardom*, p. xvii). In fact, historians of the star system, like Richard de Cordova, would suggest that such a promise was key in the formation of the celebrity system itself; as he observed, "With the emergence of the star, the question of the player's existence outside his or her work in film became the primary focus of discourse. The private lives of the players were constituted as a site of knowledge and truth."[31] With one swoop of a paper bag, Atwood negotiates those systems of celebrity that seek to define her and frustrates that long-standing desire for access to an authentic self. She has, in turning the camera-lens of the celebrity system back upon itself, found her own way of negotiating with the dead.

NOTES

1. Alice Munro, "What is Real?" *Making It New: Contemporary Canadian Stories*, ed. John Metcalf (Toronto: Methuen, 1982), p. 225.
2. Christine Gledhill, ed., *Stardom: Industry of Desire* (London: Routledge, 1991), p. xiii.

3. Graham Huggan, *The Post-colonial Exotic: Marketing the Margins* (London: Routledge, 2001), p. 208.
4. Richard Dyer, *Stars*, 2nd edition (London: British Film Institute, 1979, 1992), p. 3.
5. Roy MacGregor, "Atwood's World," *Maclean's*, 15 October 1979: p. 66.
6. Lorraine York, "Satire: The No-Woman's Land of Literary Modes," *Teaching Atwood's "The Handmaid's Tale" and Other Works*, eds. Sharon R.Wilson, Thomas B.Friedman, and Shannon Hengen (New York: Modern Language Association of America, 1996), p. 48.
7. Edgar Morin, *The Stars*, trans. Richard Howard (New York: Grove, 1960), p. 177.
8. www.owtoad.com. Accessed 2 August 2004.
9. Barry King, "Articulating Stardom," *Stardom: Industry of Desire*, ed. Christine Gledhill (London: Routledge, 1991), p. 167.
10. Susanne Becker, "Celebrity, or a Disneyland of the Soul: Margaret Atwood and the Media," *Margaret Atwood: Works and Impact*, ed. Reingard M. Nischik (Rochester, NY: Camden House, 2000), p. 29.
11. "Atwood Industry Goes Global," *Canadian Press Newswire*, 10 September 1996.
12. Judith Timson, "The Magnificent Margaret Atwood," *Chatelaine* (January 1981): pp. 60, 64.
13. Margaret Atwood, "If You Can't Say Something Nice, Don't Say Anything at All," *Language in her Eye: Views on Writing and Gender by Canadian Women Writing in English*, eds. Libby Scheier, Sarah Sheard, and Eleanor Wachtel (Toronto: Coach House, 1990), p. 20.
14. Adele Freedman, "Happy Heroine and 'Freak' of CanLit," *Globe and Mail*, 25 October 1980: p. E1.
15. Nathalie Cooke, "Lions, Tigers, and Pussycats: Margaret Atwood (Auto-Biographically)," *Margaret Atwood*, ed. Nischik, p. 22.
16. Margaret Atwood, *Lady Oracle* (Toronto: McClelland-Bantam, 1977), p. 252.
17. http://books.guardian.co.uk. Accessed 22 March 2002.
18. Margaret Atwood, *Cat's Eye* (Toronto: Seal Books, McClelland-Bantam, 1989), p. 19.
19. Richard Ellmann, *Oscar Wilde* (Harmondsworth: Penguin, 1987), p. 131.
20. Margaret Atwood, *Alias Grace* (Toronto: McClelland and Stewart, 1996), pp. 443–44.
21. William French, "Icon and Target: Atwood as Thing," *Globe and Mail*, 7 April 1973: p. 28.
22. P. David Marshall, *Celebrity and Power: Fame in Contemporary Culture* (Minneapolis: University of Minnesota Press, 1997), p. xi.
23. Caroline Rosenthal, "Canonizing Atwood: Her Impact on Teaching in the US, Canada, and Europe," *Margaret Atwood*, ed. Nischik, p. 43.
24. Margaret Atwood, *Negotiating with the Dead: A Writer on Writing* (Cambridge: Cambridge University Press, 2002), p. 178.
25. Rosemary Sullivan, *The Red Shoes: Margaret Atwood Starting Out* (Toronto: HarperFlamingoCanada, 1998), p. 3.
26. Margaret Atwood, "Survival, Then and Now," *Maclean's*, 1 July 1999: p. 55.
27. Nathalie Cooke, *Margaret Atwood: A Biography* (Toronto: ECW Press, 1998).

28. Elizabeth Renzetti, "New Books About, Not By, Atwood," *Globe and Mail*, 25 August 1998: p. C2.
29. Joan Givner, "Peggy Taking Charge," *Toronto Star*, 29 August 1998: p. M13.
30. John Ayre, "How a Gothic Girl Became Canada's Top Literary Star," *Globe and Mail*, 29 August 1998: p. D14.
31. Richard de Cordova, *Picture Personalities: The Emergence of the Star System in America* (Urbana: University of Illinois Press, 1990), p. 98.

3

PILAR SOMACARRERA

Power politics: power and identity

"The personal is political"

This well-known feminist slogan from the 1970s provides an adequate synopsis of Margaret Atwood's poetry collection *Power Politics* (1971). Atwood has always been concerned with the interface between the public and the personal worlds, and she has often referred to the blurry boundaries between them. In fact, as she explains, she chose this title for the collection because she saw this same phrase in a letter written to her by a friend and in a newspaper. For her the poems "exist between letter and newspaper, the so-called public world and the so-called personal world."[1] Coming at the beginning of her manifesto on power, "Notes on *Power Politics*" (1973), the following passage spells out the writer's attitude to this issue. According to Atwood, power circulates like a kind of energy and permeates all relations within a society:

> Power is our environment. We live surrounded by it: it pervades everything we are and do, invisible and soundless, like air . . .
>
> We would all like to have a private life that is sealed off from the public life and different from it, where there are no rulers and no ruled, no hierarchies, no politicians, only equals, free people. But because any culture is a closed system and our culture is one based and fed on power this is impossible, or at least very difficult . . . So many of the things we do in what we sadly think of as our personal lives are simply duplications of the external world of power games, power struggles. ("Notes on *Power Politics*," p. 7)

Atwood's well-known involvement with causes such as Amnesty International and the Canadian Writers' Union demonstrates that her interest in politics goes beyond her literary activity. In fact, the issue of sexual and national power politics is a wide-ranging and crucial topic in Margaret Atwood's work, which was articulated for the first time in the poems of *Power Politics*, and expanded to include the discourse of national and international politics in her novel *Surfacing* and in her book of criticism about

Canadian literature, *Survival*. Atwood's political preoccupations attain their highest point in her novels *Bodily Harm* and *The Handmaid's Tale* as well as in her poetry series *True Stories*, and resonate in her interviews and many of her essays, especially "Amnesty International: An Address," continuing in her recent novel *Oryx and Crake*. Starting from Atwood's definition of the word "political," this chapter will explore how power functions in the political and the personal domains, and will pay attention to the notions of authority, resistance, and dissent in the aforementioned selection of Atwood texts.

In an interview with Jo Brans, Margaret Atwood provides the following definition of politics, which, once again, links the political and the personal:

> Politics, for me, is everything that involves who gets to do what to whom . . . It's not just elections and what people say they are – little labels they put on themselves . . . Politics really has to do with how people order their societies, to whom power is ascribed, who is considered to have power. A lot of power is ascription. People have power because we think they have power, and that's all politics is. And politics also has to do with what kind of conversations you have with people, and what you feel free to say to someone, what you don't feel free to say.[2]

Atwood's definition of politics emphasizes the aspect of the ascription of power, and implies "who gets to do what to whom," which in the context of the texts analyzed in this chapter can be rendered as "who inflicts violence on whom," both in the political and sexual domains.

Atwood has confessed[3] that her ideas about power do not come from literary theory, but rather from reading Shakespeare and books about history and politics, as well as observing historical changes. Notwithstanding Atwood's declarations, the characteristics of invisibility, pervasiveness and presence in the private and public realms implied in Atwood's definition are also reflected in Michel Foucault's model of power. For Foucault, power should be seen as a verb rather than a noun, as it only exists in action: "Power in the substantive sense, '*le' pouvoir*, doesn't exist. The idea that there is either located at – or emanating from – a given point something which is a 'power' seems to me based on a misguided analysis . . . In reality power means relations, a more-or-less organised, hierarchical, co-ordinated cluster of relations."[4] In the same vein, Atwood does not believe that power emanates only from dictators. When the narrator of her novel *Surfacing* recounts her childhood years during the Second World War, she explains: "For us when we were small the origin was Hitler, he was the great evil . . . But Hitler was gone and the thing remained . . . It was like cutting up a tapeworm, the pieces grew."[5] For Atwood and Foucault power is unstable because it is diffused throughout all social relations rather than being imposed from above, and the Canadian writer even questions the reality of power: "power after all is not real, not really there: people give it to each other" ("Notes on *Power Politics*," p. 16). She has recently expanded this idea, saying that "give it to each other is somewhat limited" – they take from one another as well. "Political leaders," she adds, can't be so without followers, or enough followers."[6] As Silvia Caporale Bizzini argues, what seems to be clear in the Foucaldian example of power relations is that power does not appear anymore as something compact and unitary.[7] Foucault seems to echo Atwood's words when he states: "I hardly ever use the word power and if I do sometimes, it is always a short cut to the expression I always use: the relationships of power,"[8] and that political power is established "by the partial or total cession of the concrete power which every individual holds" (*Power/Knowledge*, p. 88).

"They are hostile nations": sexual politics

In *Survival*, Atwood develops the "basic victim positions," a hypothesis which, as Paul Goetsch observes, allows Atwood to deal with all kinds of power relationships that move easily from political and social violence to gender relationships:[9]

> *Position One: To deny the fact that you are a victim . . .*
> *Position Two:*
> *To acknowledge the fact that you are a victim, but to explain this as an act of Fate, the Will of God, the dictates of Biology (in the case of women, for instance), the necessity decreed by History, or Economics, or the Unconscious, or any other large general powerful idea . . .*
> *Position Three:*
> *To acknowledge the fact that you are a victim but to refuse to accept the assumption that the role is inevitable . . .*
> *Position Four: To be a creative non-victim.*[10]

Atwood illustrates her victim hypothesis in *Power Politics*, where heterosexual relationships are seen as a Foucaldian struggle for power. She sees the collection as a sequence which deals with female–male power relationships at three levels: individual, political, and mythological,[11] each of which is developed in one of the three sections of the book. For Gloria Onley,[12] these poems present men and women as political prisoners of the sexist society, trapped as victor/victims in their own reflections of the world and of each other. Although the early feminist readings[13] of the book interpreted it as sexist realism, that is, considering the woman as the only victim and the man as aggressor, the male and female subjects of the poems alternate the positions of victor and victim. The relationship between them is perfectly illustrated by the drawing, conceived by Margaret Atwood, which appears on the cover of the first edition of the collection. The illustration is a parody of the Hanged Man card of the Tarot, representing a woman, covered in bandages like a mummy and hanging upside down, tied to the arm of a knight in armour. The woman is the apparent victim, yet he is also suffering from the pain caused by her dangling weight. Furthermore, she has certain advantages over him: her position upside down can be interpreted as the yoga posture on the head (*sirshasana*) which allows better concentration of the mind, and her eyes are open, whereas he has no eyes. This "open eye" which could be "the third eye" or inner eye of oriental philosophies closes the most emblematic poem in the collection:[14]

> you fit into me
> like a hook into an eye
>
> a fish hook
> an open eye[15]

The poem's effectiveness is based on the contrast between the simile of the first two lines and the surprise metaphor of the last two. The simile for the romantic cliché of perfect lovemaking, which relies on the domestic image of "hook" and "eye" as complementary clothing fasteners, is suddenly transformed into a nightmarish vision of horror. Atwood has revealed that it was suggested to her by a scene from the surrealist film *Chien Andalou*, by Luis Buñuel, in which a razor blade enters an eye.[16] The ambiguity provoked by the pun "eye"/"I" suggests that the woman is aware of the aggression and accepts it, thus turning the poem into a caustic comment on sadomasochistic relationships. The hook can also be associated with the colloquial expression "being hooked." Many of the women in *Power Politics* and in Atwood's novels are addicted to negative relationships. In another poem from the collection, the female voice admits, "Have to face it I'm / finally an addict" (*PP*, p. 3), and in *Surfacing* the nameless narrator makes a similar statement: "When you can't tell the difference between your own pleasure and your pain then you're an addict" (*S*, p. 78). In *Bodily Harm*, Rennie, the protagonist, feels "hooked like a junkie"[17] to her relationship with her surgeon Daniel.

In the humorous poems which follow the initial epigram in *Power Politics*, romantic love continues to be the target of Atwood's satire. She reproduces stereotypical romantic encounters, in which the lovers go to the cinema or to a restaurant, absorbed in powerful or powerless roles. In "They eat out," the woman becomes a sorceress who touches her lover with fork transformed into a magic wand. The man is turned into a Superman to whom the narrator and the rest of the guests remain indifferent. From this pathetic Superman, he is transformed into a suffering Christ who lies drunk and helpless in the arms of the woman, who assumes the role of the Virgin Mary in a parody of Michelangelo's famous sculpture *La Pietà*. The female subject also becomes a soothsayer, foretelling the man's death in several poems (pp. 16, 30), and in "Their attitudes differ," she has the power as the spy scientist, the analyst, and the writer who, once again, requests the man's death "so [she] can write about it" (*PP*, p. 10) A rhetorical analysis of the poems[18] also demonstrates the powerful nature of the female subject, who is in control of the discursive situation. The dialogic relationship between an "I" and a "you" is the quintessential topic of love poetry. According to Jan Montefiore, in the great tradition of Petrarch and Shakespeare, the lover-poet is principally concerned with defining his own self through his desire for the image of his beloved.[19] However, the poems in *Power Politics* offer a new version of the unrequited love of the courtly tradition, in which the "I" projects a monstrous other. In most of the poems, the "I" is deprecatory and authoritarian, scolding and insulting the "you":

> It was you who started the countdown
>
> . . .
>
> and it was you whose skin
> fell off bubbling
>
> . . .
>
> You attempt merely power
> you accomplish merely suffering
>
> (*PP*, p. 32)

The male figures in the poems "My beautiful wooden leader" and "Imperialist" also appear ridiculous in their desire to invest themselves with power. The "beautiful wooden leader" is, in fact, unreal and scorned. As Atwood herself has noted, "this knight is of course incomplete without a maiden to rescue" ("Notes on *Power Politics*," p. 8). The "hordes" of women he has rescued follow him in a parodic procession, but his attempt to impose his authority is ineffective, because "the people all / ride off in the other direction" (*PP*, p. 7).

Even when the "you" is qualified as "Imperialist," he cannot face the fact that he has power and clumsily "walks backwards" immersed in his own narcissism. This is one of the first poems of the collection in which international and sexual politics are interconnected, and it resonates with Atwood's views about Canada as a colony:

Imperialist, keep off
the trees, I said

No use: you walk backwards,
admiring your own footprints.
(*PP*, p. 15)

The male and the female subjects in this poem could also represent the United States and Canada. In fact, as Katherine E. Waters suggests, sexual politics is a microcosm of the wider political reality of imperialism,[20] a connection which Atwood also perceives when she remarks that "man must conquer. He must conquer other men, or women, or nature itself" ("Notes on *Power Politics*," p. 14). The woman's body becomes "a foreign country [he] would like to invade"[21] and "cover / with flags" (*PP*, p. 49), a line which is echoed by the narrator of *Surfacing* when she confesses that her aim in the sexual battles with her partner is to obtain "a victory, some flag I can wave" (*S*, p. 81).

The war of the sexes is a central topic in the works published in the 1970s, with continuities in Atwood's recent writings. In "Notes on *Power Politics*," she suggests that this war is perhaps more than a metaphor, as "there is more than one way of dying" (p. 13). One of the texts in which this metaphor reaches an emotional peak is the poem which gives the title to this section of my chapter. Glossing this poem, Alicia Suskin Ostriker comments that the lovers are indeed hostile nations mapping each other's weaknesses, not because their hostility has a rational basis but because they cannot stop.[22] The opening verses present an apocalyptic vision of the relationship, in which Atwood's ecological concerns are also evident:

In view of the fading animals
the proliferation of sewers and fears
the sea clogging, the air
nearing extinction

we should be kind, we should
take warning, we should forgive each other

Instead we are opposite, we
touch as though attacking . . .
(*PP*, p. 37)

In this poem, which Sherrill Grace describes as "a plea for disarmament before destruction is final,"[23] the "I" presents the "you" with logical arguments in order to persuade him to achieve reconciliation. The appeal, however, seems to be ignored, and even the caresses are interpreted as aggression. In the third part of the poem, she continues trying to convince her interlocutor that this is a private relationship in which political and economical power should not interfere: "Here there are no armies / here there is no money" (*PP*, p. 38), adding that "surviving / is the only war / [they]can afford." In *Surfacing*, which can be considered a companion novel to *Power Politics*, Anna and David are also involved in the war of the sexes: "her body was her only weapon and she was fighting for her life, he was her life, her life was the fight: she was fighting him because if she ever surrendered the balance of power would be broken and he would go elsewhere. To continue the war" (*S*, pp. 147–48). This confrontation functions in the same way as the natural survival of the species: logic and civilization do not help, and only the strongest survives. In "The Accident has occurred" Atwood uses wilderness images to represent this Darwinian struggle, which concludes with a final dilemma: "Which of us will survive / which of us will survive the other" (*PP*, p. 23).

In addition to the vision of the heterosexual relationship as warfare, *Surfacing* and *Power Politics* also share the depiction of sexual intercourse as a painful experience, a view which is already anticipated in the initial epigram about the "hook" and the "eye." In "They travel by air" (*PP*, p. 11) the sexual encounter is portrayed as a collision of mirrors. In the [illegible] poem in which the "I" experiences pleasure, orgasm is described as "a kick in the head, orange / and brutal" with an impact of "sharp jewels" (*PP*, p. 22). In another poem which tries to provide a definition for sexual love, the male lover is represented as a wounded animal trying to liberate itself from a trap, whereas the female is reduced to the ground which is trodden, where he feels compelled to project his identity: "you move / into me as though I / am (wrenching / your way through, this is / urgent, it is your / life) the / last chance for freedom" (p. 46). In *Surfacing* we find a similar image when the narrator hears David and Anna, who are making love, and she thinks "of an animal at the moment the trap closes," concluding that sex is "like death" (*S*, p. 76). The deadly aspect of sexual relationships is certainly emphasised in *Power Politics*, in which some of poems resound with connotations of gender violence, as when a female voice ominously announces that "nothing remembers / you but the bruises on my thighs and the inside of my skull" (*PP*, p. 13). In "Small tactics," another title which resonates with war metaphors, the infliction of violence resembles a game:

> These days my fingers bleed
> Even before I bite them
> Can't play it safe, can't play
> At all any more
>
> (*PP*, p. 17)

Similarly, in *Bodily Harm*, Rennie cannot distinguish any more between her lover's sadomasochistic game and real aggression:

> Jake liked to pin her hands down, he liked to hold her so she couldn't move. He liked that, he liked thinking of sex as something he could win at. Sometimes he really hurt her, once he put his arms across her throat and she really did stop breathing. Danger turns you on, he says. Admit it. It was a game, they both knew that. (*BH*, p. 207)

In this novel, Atwood takes the violence of sadomasochistic sexual games as a starting point and expands it into the wider sphere of political torture and national and international power struggles, which will be the focus of the next section of this chapter.

"Nobody is exempt from anything": national and international politics

Bodily Harm, whose plot concerns a lifestyles journalist who involuntarily becomes involved in the violent manipulation of the elections in a former British Caribbean colony, is Atwood's most politically committed novel. In it the integration of sexual and political themes is evident from the beginning. Sexual politics are patent in the opening episode of Rennie's coming home to discover that a stranger has left a coiled rope on her bed. Moreover, the policemen who are investigating the case "wanted it to be [her] fault" because of her "indiscretion" and "provocation" (*BH*, p. 15). At the crossroads between the political and the personal is the novel's discussion of pornography, a phenomenon defined by Alison Assiter as "the representation of the eroticisation of relations of power between the sexes."[24] Rennie's journalistic assignment to write about pornography is what makes her aware of the potential danger of Jake's sadomasochistic games. Several critics[25] have noted how the fusion of sexual and political violence becomes explicit at the end of the novel when Rennie contemplates the beating up of prisoners sadistically tortured by the guards from the window of the cell where she herself is imprisoned:

> It's indecent, it's not done with ketchup, nothing is inconceivable here, no rats in the vagina but only because they haven't thought of it yet, they're still amateurs. She's afraid of men and it's simple, it's rational, she's afraid of men because men are frightening. She's seen the man with the rope, now she knows what he looks like . . . Rennie understands for the first time that this is not necessarily a place she will get out of, ever. She is not exempt. Nobody is exempt from anything. (*BH*, p. 290)

Rennie's last thought ("Nobody is exempt from anything") appears as a paradoxical conclusion for someone who had been promised that the article she had to write about the Caribbean island would be "Nothing political" (*BH*, p. 16). When she reaches her destination, she is confronted with contradictory views. Paul, the American drug dealer and gun runner with whom she becomes sentimentally involved, tells her that what goes on in the island is "local politics" and "has nothing to do with her" (*BH*, pp. 150–51). Dr. Minnow, a Canadian-educated citizen of the fictional island of St. Antoine, warns her of the way everyone in his world is involved: "Everyone is in politics here, my friend," says Dr. Minnow. "All the time. Not like the sweet Canadians" (*BH*, p. 124). As Helen Tiffin notes,[26] Dr. Minnow's is the one voice in the narrative which could be considered disruptive, with his perspicacious comments on British colonialism in the Caribbean and on the neo-colonialism[27] of the United States and Canada in the area. In a novel which does not present us with a very positive view of politicians, Dr. Minnow is the only character who believes in democracy and shares Atwood's utopian view that it is necessary to "change things" (*BH*, p. 133) in a country where "nothing is inconceivable." In fact, as Paul points out, in an island like St. Antoine concepts like democracy, and even human rights, are permanently at stake (*BH*, p. 240).

The fictional portrait of this former British colony allows Atwood to lay bare the crudest dimensions of power. Firstly, power is ascription, as political leaders are given power at elections. However, it is not always the honest politicians who are elected, as elections can be manipulated. Secondly, following Foucault, she shows that the historical *raison d'etre* of political power is to be found in the economy (*Power/Knowledge*, p. 89). In her Amnesty International Address of 1981, Atwood gives an extended version of her definition of politics which adds the economic factor: "By 'politics' . . . I mean who is entitled to do what to whom, with impunity; who profits by it; and who therefore eats what."[28] Thirdly, as Atwood herself has remarked, the aim of absolute power is to silence *the voice*, to abolish the words, so that the only voices and words left are those of the ones in power,[29] who, as suggested in *Power Politics*, often remain silent: "We hear nothing these days / from the ones in power / . . . Language, the fist / proclaims by squeezing / is for the weak only" (*PP*, p. 31). In *Bodily Harm*, Ellis, the local oligarch supported by the United States, keeps getting elected because of his fraudulent practices during the elections ("The only votes Ellis is getting are the ones he buys" [*BH*, p. 228]). In addition, he controls the economy of the island. When his re-election is threatened by other candidates, he silences the opposition and the potentially subversive voices by killing Minnow and presumably Prince, and having Rennie and Lora imprisoned. In accord with the lines from *Power Politics* I have just quoted, we never hear Ellis's words in the novel, we just contemplate his acts of oppression.

Dealing also with political oppression and torture, "Notes Towards a Poem That Can Never Be Written" is a companion piece to *Bodily Harm* which was published in *True Stories* in the same year as the novel. Both texts, fictional and poetic, are manifestos concerning the materiality of power in contrast with what Atwood calls "our affluent way of thinking . . . worry[ing] about our personal health, our fitness and our personal romances."[30] As Foucault notes, nothing is more material, physical and corporal than the exercise of power (*Power/Knowledge*, pp. 57–58), and nowhere is power more material than in torture. In the section "Torture" of "Notes Towards a Poem . . . ," which echoes the beating up of Lora in *Bodily Harm*, Atwood declares that "power / like this is not abstract, it's not concerned / with politics and free will, it's beyond slogans."[31] In view of so many acts of political oppression, nobody can exempt oneself, nobody is innocent, for "innocence is merely / not to act" (*SP*, p. 258). Especially called to act is the writer who is "an observer, a witness" (*SW*, p. 394), and the poem ends urging him or her to accept this political responsibility ("Elsewhere you must write this poem / because there is nothing more to do" [*SP*, p. 259]), because, as Atwood writes in her Amnesty International Address: "Placing politics and poetics in two watertight compartments is a luxury . . . and it is possible only in a society where such luxuries abound. Most countries in the world cannot afford such luxuries" (*SW*, p. 394).

Atwood's next novel, *The Handmaid's Tale*, explores the consequences which ignoring acts of political repression can have in its portrait of American society during a fundamentalist dictatorship, known as the Republic of Gilead, where women, forced into servitude as Handmaids, are ordered into producing babies for the governing elite. The changes that lead to the establishment of the Republic of Gilead are subtle but progressive, and thus ignored by most people, as Offred, the protagonist, explains: "We lived, as usual, by ignoring . . . Nothing changes instantaneously . . . There were stories in the newspapers, of course, corpses in ditches or the woods . . . but they were about other women, and the men who did such things were other men."[32] The Gileadean regime, which aims to be ubiquitous and internalized by the population ("The Republic of Gilead, said Aunt Lydia, knows no bounds. Gilead is within you" *HT*, p. 33), imposes its power through brainwashing and strict surveillance undertaken by security forces: the Angels (army), the Eyes ("invisible" police), and the Guardians. The role of an invisible police in the creation of the panoptic state is discussed by Foucault in *Discipline and Punish*: "a centralised police, exerci[se]s a permanent, exhaustive surveillance which makes all things visible by becoming itself invisible."[33] Given that *The Handmaid's Tale* depicts the quintessential disciplinary society where power is brought to the most minute and distant elements, Foucault's model can be applied to almost all of its aspects.

In the highly stratified society of Gilead, all the different social strata are obsessed with obtaining some power, even in a menial form, because "when power is scarce, a little of it is tempting" (*HT*, p. 320). The most powerful figure in the novel is the Commander, who, as the Historical Notes at the end of the novel clarify (*HT*, p. 318), probably belongs to an organization who provided the ideological bases for the Gileadean regime. However, contrary to common belief, in this patriarchal dictatorship it is not only the men who have power, as Atwood herself has remarked:

> Some people mistakenly think that the society in *The Handmaid's Tale* is one in which all men have power, and all women don't. That is not true, because it is a true totalitarianism: therefore a true hierarchy. Those at the top have power, those at the bottom, don't. And those at the bottom include men, and those at the top include women. The women at the top have different kinds of power from the men at the top, but they have power nonetheless, and some of the power they have is power over other women. Like Serena Joy, like the Aunts . . .[34]

The function of the Aunts in this totalitarian regime is to disseminate the doctrine among women, exercising a matriarchal power which is disguised as a spirit of camaraderie, similar to that of the army. In fact, the disciplinarian organization of the Handmaids' collective resembles that of the military forces, as Aunt Lydia announces at the beginning of the novel: "Think of it as being in the army" (*HT*, p. 17). Nevertheless, the development of the plot is slightly at odds with the author's statement that "those at the bottom don't have power," as the typically Atwoodian powerful/powerless dyad constituted by Offred, the Handmaid who narrates the story, and Serena Joy, the Commander's Wife, illustrates. Serena Joy has power over Offred because she "is in control, of the [birth-giving] process and thus of the product" (*HT*, p. 104). However, being the Commander's mistress gives Offred a kind of sexual power over Serena Joy. Since the personal and the political domains are always interacting in Gilead as everywhere, power relations change continuously, a Foucaldian view which is spelled out by Paul in *Bodily Harm*: "There's only people with power and people without power. Sometimes they change places, that's all" (*BH*, p. 240).

Directly related to Atwood's definition of power, reiterated in *The Handmaid's Tale* as "who can do what to whom and get away with it, even as far as death" (*HT*, p. 144), is the power that Doctors have in the Gileadean regime. Doctors can send the Handmaids to the feared colonies if they report them for infertility, and they use this power to obtain their sexual favors. They are very important in this kind of regime because, as Foucault has it, medicine is concerned with the conservation of the "labor force" (*Power/Knowledge*, p. 171), or in this case "the reproduction force." One of the pillars of the Gileadean regime is the control of reproduction, which Foucault has also identified as one of the objectives of power.[35] The other pillar underpinning it is public torture, which is the subject of a whole chapter in *Discipline and Punish*, explaining that all public executions are political operations. (Foucault, *Discipline and Punish*, p. 53). Accordingly, the Gileadean regime makes ample use of repressive devices like the Salvagings and the Particicution, public executions which serve to eliminate "political enemies" (*HT*, p. 319).

Capable of the crudest forms of torture for political dissenters, this dictatorship also endorses Foucault's view that there is no power without resistance: "the latter [resistances] are all the more real and effective because they are formed right at the point where relations of power are exercised; resistance to power . . . exists all the more by being in the same place as power; hence, like power, resistance is multiple" (*Power/Knoweledge*, p. 142). Ironically, in *The Handmaid's Tale*, resistance to the rules of the Gileadean regime is provided by the regime itself in the existence of clubs like Jezebel's, where the Commanders entertain themselves with "loose" women. There are also external resistance groups, like Mayday and Underground Femaleroad, as well as many types of personal resistance exercised secretly, for as Offred says, "There is something powerful in the whispering of obscenities, about those in power" (*HT*, p. 234).

Due to its manifold tensions and contradictions, the Republic of Gilead is a society which lives in a permanent state of war, which "[was] going on in many places at once" (*HT*, p. 92). For Atwood war is the most obvious and visible form of the exercise of power, of men attempting to dominate each other ("Notes on *Power Politics*," p. 13). When asked about the pervasiveness of wars in her works, she responds: "it's in my books because it's in life."[36] In all wars, "the lust for power will prevail," observes Tony, the war historian of *The Robber Bride*.[37] The continuities between power and war have also been perceived by Foucault: "It may be that war as strategy is a continuation of politics. But it must not be forgotten that 'politics' has been conceived as a continuation, if not exactly and directly of war, at least of the military model as a fundamental means of preventing civil disorder" (*Discipline and Punish*, p. 53). Following the Foucaldian notion, in wars "people tak[e] and los[e] power over other people" (*S*, p. 91). In a poem from *Power Politics* which resembles a newsreel, Atwood traces the history of the world from the point of view of a woman who relates the succession of wars from the Crusades until the two World Wars of the first half of the twentieth century. The episodes do not appear to differ much except in the rise of violence, which leads the female voice to exclaim: "and I can scarcely kiss you goodbye / before you run into the street and they shoot" (*PP*, p. 28).

CorpSeCorps/Corporate power

In her recent novel, *Oryx and Crake*, Atwood takes a humorous turn on her preoccupation with war and defines it as "misplaced sexual energy."[38] Humor apart, our writer's nightmares about the abuses of power culminate in the dystopian vision of society in this novel, where power no longer centers in the state – there is no mention of government at all in the novel – but is spread through the social system via the corporate power of global capitalism. In *Bodily Harm*, Atwood was already anticipating the effects of globalization, when she had Dr. Minnow say that "There is no place that is not of general interest" (*BH*, p. 135). More than twenty years later in *Oryx and Crake*, the aim of the Corporations is "to be global," launching their product not just "on society as a whole . . . but on the planet" (*O&C*, p. 294). The disciplinary control is perpetuated by the private security forces, the "CorpSeCorps," which imply one step further in the Foucaldian police state. Hierarchy is also present in a society which, as Ronald Wright observes, is divided in two: a techno-elite who lives in fortified company compounds, and the dangerous "Pleeblands," an urban jungle where the masses live.[39] Power is invisible but more tangible than ever, as, again following Foucault, it is multiple and comes from many locations: "it wasn't just one side you had to watch out for. Other companies, other countries, various factions and plotters" (*O&C*, p. 27).

In her fictions to come, Margaret Atwood will no doubt continue exploring the workings of power, which is usually conceptualized as the capacity of powerful agents to realize their will over the will of powerless people. This is only one of the three kinds of power distinguished by Atwood, amply illustrated in *Power Politics, Bodily Harm*, and *The Handmaid's Tale*. The second one is "the desire for power over the physical universe through experiment and the intellect" ("Notes on *Power Politics*," p. 18), explored in *Oryx and Crake*. The third one, "the hardest form of power to acquire . . . is power over oneself," the search for which concerns most of Atwood's characters and, indeed, most of us. She has also stated that "to renounce power . . . has its dangers" ("Notes on *Power Politics*," p. 16). As this inter-generic itinerary through her works demonstrates, Atwood's approach to the topic of this chapter is complex and multi-dimensional, and like Foucault's, it focuses on how our identity is always determined by a net of relations of power.

NOTES

1. Margaret Atwood, "Notes on *Power Politics*," *Acta Victoriana* 97.2 (1973): p. 7.
2. Interview with Jo Brans ("Using What You're Given"), *Margaret Atwood: Conversations*, ed. Earl G. Ingersoll (London: Virago, 1992), p. 149.
3. Private email correspondence with the author of this chapter.
4. Michel Foucault, *Power/Knowledge. Selected Interviews and Other Writings 1972–1977*, ed. Colin Gordon (New York: Pantheon Books, 1980), p. 198.
5. Margaret Atwood, *Surfacing* (London: Virago, 1996), p. 123.
6. Private email correspondence with the author of this chapter.
7. Silvia Caporale Bizzini, "Power Politics: Literature and Foucaldian Analysis," *In-Between: Essays and Studies in Literary Criticism* 5.1 (1995): p. 24.
8. Michel Foucault, "The Ethic of Care for the Self and a Practice of Freedom," *The Final Foucault*, eds. James Bernauer and David Ramussen (Cambridge, MA: MIT Press, 1988), p. 11.
9. Paul Goetsch, "Margaret Atwood: A Canadian Nationalist," *Margaret Atwood: Works and Impact*, ed. Reingard M. Nischik (Rochester, NY: Camden House, 2000), p. 173.
10. Margaret Atwood, *Survival* (Toronto: Anansi, 1972), pp. 36–38.
11. Margaret Atwood Papers, Manuscript Collections. Thomas Fisher Rare Book Library, University of Toronto, Box 90: Folder 2.
12. Gloria Onley, "Power Politics in Bluebeard's Castle," *Canadian Literature* 60 (1974): p. 25.
13. In fact, as Karen F. Stein rightly argues, the book can be considered a response to Kate Millett's book *Sexual Politics* (1970), in which the concept of heterosexual relationships as political was first articulated. See Karen F. Stein, *Margaret Atwood Revisited* (New York: Twayne, 1999), p. 30.
14. This poem is one of the most commented-on poetic texts in Canadian literature. See for example, George Bowering, "Atwood's Hook," *Open Letter* (Winter 1990): pp. 81–90. In addition, it has given title to the first international conference about Margaret Atwood ("Margaret Atwood: The Open Eye," University of Ottawa, April 2004).
15. Margaret Atwood, *Power Politics* (Toronto: Anansi, 1996), p. 1.
16. Private conversation with the author of this chapter.
17. Margaret Awood, *Bodily Harm* (Toronto: McClelland-Bantam, 1982), p. 134.
18. For the rhetorical analysis of *Power Politics*, see Pilar Somacarrera, "'Barometer Couple': Balance and Parallelism in Margaret Atwood's *Power Politics*," *Language and Literature* 9.2 (2000): pp. 135–49.
19. See Jan Montefiore, *Feminism and Poetry. Language, Experience and Identity in Women's Writing* (London: Pandora, 1987), p. 98.
20. Katherine E. Waters, "Margaret Atwood: Love on the Dark Side of the Moon," *Mother Was Not a Person*, ed. Margaret Andersen (Montreal: Black Rose Books, 1972), p. 102.
21. Unpublished poem, Margaret Atwood Papers, Box 12: Folder 14.
22. Alicia Suskin Ostriker, *Stealing the Language. The Emergence of Women's Poetry in America* (Boston: Beacon Press, 1974), p. 152.
23. Sherrill Grace, *Violent Duality: A Study of Margaret Atwood* (Montreal: Véhicule Press, 1980), p. 59.

24. Alison Assiter. "Romance Fiction: Porn for Women," *Perspectives on Pornography: Sexuality in Film and Literature*, eds. Gary Day and Guy Bloom (New York: St. Martin's Press, 1988), p. 103. For a discussion of pornography in *Bodily Harm*, see Coral Ann Howells, *Margaret Atwood* (Basingstoke: Macmillan, 1996), pp. 105–25, and J. Brooks Bouson, *Brutal Choreographies. Oppositional Strategies and Narrative Design in the Novels of Margaret Atwood* (Amherst: University of Massachusetts Press, 1993), pp. 111–34.
25. Howells, *Margaret Atwood*, p. 123, and Jennifer Strauss, "'Everyone is in Politics': Margaret Atwood's *Bodily Harm* and Blanche d'Alpuget's *Turtle Beach*," *Australian/Canadian Literatures in English. Comparative Perspectives*, eds. Russell McDougall and Gillian Whitlock (Melbourne: Methuen Australia, 1987), p. 118.
26. Helen Tiffin, "Voice and Form," *Australian/Canadian Literatures in English*, eds. McDougall and Whitlock, p. 123.
27. For an exploration of Atwood's postcolonial concerns in the novel, see Diana Brydon, "Atwood's Postcolonial Imagination: Rereading *Bodily Harm*," *Various Atwoods. Essays on the Later Poems, Short Fiction, and Novels*, ed. Lorraine York (Toronto: Anansi, 1995), pp. 89–116.
28. Margaret Atwood, *Second Words. Selected Critical Prose* (Toronto: Anansi, 1982), p. 394.
29. Margaret Atwood, "An End to Audience?" *Dalhousie Review* 60.3 (Autumn 1980): p. 427.
30. Interview with Jo Brans, *Margaret Atwood: Conversations*, ed. Ingersoll, p. 148.
31. Margaret Atwood, *Selected Poems 1966–1984* (Toronto: Oxford University Press, 1990), p. 259.
32. Margaret Atwood, *The Handmaid's Tale* (London: Vintage, 1996), p. 66.
33. Michel Foucault, *Discipline and Punish. The Birth of the Prison* (New York: Vintage Books, 1979), p. 40.
34. Interview with Margaret Atwood in Margaret Reynolds and Jonathan Noakes, *Margaret Atwood: The Essential Guide* (London: Vintage, 2002), pp. 12–13.
35. About the importance of medicine and the control of reproduction, see Foucault, *Power/Knowledge*, pp. 171–72.
36. Unpublished interview with the author of this chapter.
37. Margaret Atwood, *The Robber Bride* (London: Virago, 1994), p. 30.
38. Margaret Atwood, *Oryx and Crake* (London: Bloomsbury, 2003), p. 293.
39. Ronald Wright, "All Hooked Up to Monkey Brains," *The Times Literary Supplement*, 16 May 2003: p. 18.

4

MADELEINE DAVIES

Margaret Atwood's female bodies

By writing her self, woman will return to the body which has been more than confiscated from her, which has been turned into the uncanny stranger on display.[1]

Margaret Atwood's female protagonists show marked signs of bodily unease. From Marian's socio-political anorexia in *The Edible Woman*, to Elaine's shape-shifting in *Cat's Eye*, through Joan's aggressive consumption in *Lady Oracle*, and towards Iris's vicious verbal annihilations of her aging body in *The Blind Assassin*, Atwood's fictional female bodies become battlefields where anxieties relating to wider power structures are written onto female flesh. This chapter explores Atwood's writing of the female body, which in turn opens up debates relating to her analysis of power politics within a lived socio-culture. In addition, her writing of the female body (which often belongs to female writers or artists) raises dominant critical issues within women's writing and these issues refract back on Atwood's novels and cast new light upon them.

No reader could miss Atwood's preoccupation with the female body and nor could the reader fail to be aware of the various ways in which the body becomes associated with shape-shifting, masquerade, crisis, or play in these novels. Often Atwood dips into Gothic parody or carnivalesque grotesquerie in her writing of the female body; repeatedly it is written in terms of surveillance and hiddenness and it is connected with ideas of incarceration; it is linked with metaphors of disembodiment, a failure to be completely *there*, or with the occupation of liminal territories which mark uneasy gaps between "real" and "other"; the relationship between mind and body is stressed constantly so that fractured or disrupted psyches result in alienated bodies that become sinister enemies even to their inhabitants; the body is the site of diseases of the breast and the womb, of bad hearts and evil eyes; it is the site on which political power is exercised and the site on which abuse is practiced and in turn rehearsed. Atwood's female bodies are socio-cultural documents, psychological maps, comedy turns, dark doubles or sinister twins, treacherous strangers waiting in the wings, and always they are unmistakable signs of key energies at work within the novel to hand. In Atwood's body of work the bodies at work are never neutral sites but are always active articulations of territorial disputes; to understand Atwood's writing fully we have to understand how these disputes are figured and what the terms of combat are.

L'écriture féminine

To place these emphases within a critical framework it is worth intersecting them with ideas raised by feminist writer Hélène Cixous in her seminal essay, "The Laugh of the Medusa" (1975). This essay outlines Cixous's agenda for *l'écriture féminine*, a specifically female discourse in which the female body and female difference are inscribed in language and text. Cixous's ecstatic war-cry celebrates the semi-mystical nature of femaleness and calls on women to reject male, rule-bound language in favor of a language connecting body with text. "Woman must write herself: must write about women and bring women to writing, from which they have been driven away as violently as from their bodies" ("Medusa," p. 334), she argues: it is men who have "driven away" women from writing and it is men who have confiscated their bodies, their voices, and thus their writing in order to defend patriarchal order, which they fail to realize crushes them equally. In insisting "Text: my body" ("Medusa," p. 339), Cixous suggests that only when women inhabit their bodies fully and write from them can they produce a female language and female texts capable of challenging historical and political constructions, of subverting the dominant linguistic order, and of representing them*selves*.

Cixous is necessarily vague when it comes to solid definitions of a "*féminine*" practice of writing, "for this practice can never be theorized, enclosed, coded – which doesn't mean that it doesn't exist" ("Medusa," p. 340). However, within these limits, flow, multiplicity, rejection of boundaries, and connection between the female gestation drive and female writing feature strongly in her highly metaphorical essay, which acts as a blueprint for the type of writing she is advocating. Obviously there are major problems with *l'écriture féminine* as it is outlined by Cixous in this essay: feminist critic Elaine Showalter is by no means alone in noting that Cixous "describes a Utopian possibility rather than a literary practice," while her emphasis on female anatomy "risks a return to the crude essentialism, the phallic and ovarian theories of art, that oppressed women in the past."[2] Further, Cixous's celebration of the female body risks making of it "too unproblematic, pleasurable and totalized an entity," so that we may feel bullied into endorsing claims we feel are more feminist fantasy than lived reality.[3] In addition, Atwood's response to Cixous's essay is not hard to anticipate: her suspicion of political or literary hard lines is registered repeatedly in interviews, usually in irritated responses to the vexed question of her feminist allegiance. The following statement, for example, draws attention to her resistance to those very totalizing impulses that Cixous strays towards: "As for Woman, capital W, we got stuck with that for centuries. Eternal woman. But really 'Woman' is the sum of women. It doesn't exist apart from that, except as an abstracted idea."[4] A more grumpy equivalent of this view finds its way into *Cat's Eye* in Elaine's defensive response to rallying feminist rhetoric: "I am not Woman, and I'm damned if I'll be shoved into it."[5]

So much for Cixous's "Woman." However, despite the manifest problems with the notion of *l'écriture féminine*, and despite the likelihood of Atwood's ambivalent response to it, "The Laugh of the Medusa" does offer a potential blueprint for women's textual self-representation and a strategy for challenging male-inscribed discourses. It also offers a lens through which Atwood's writing of her female protagonists can be productively interpreted. Atwood differs from Cixous in refusing idealizing totalities and insisting on writing the realities of women operating within a historically specific socio-culture, but the bodies she writes are nevertheless subversive carriers of a female language and thus of coded meanings. In the fictive autobiographies discussed in this chapter, *Lady Oracle, Cat's Eye*, and *The Blind Assassin*, Atwood's female writers or artists are engaged in acts of self-representation. Joan, Elaine, and Iris simultaneously write and rewrite their own stories using their bodies as primary text and constant referent. Their bodies *are* their stories and to write one they must write the other in a language capable of expressing both. Thus Atwood's strategies and those advocated by Cixous may not be as far removed as it may at first seem since both forge profound connections between body and text.

Coding the body

It is clear that Atwood repeatedly writes the female body in terms of the culture that determines it, simultaneously throwing light on that body and on that cultural process which is always and inescapably political. Gayatri Spivak argues that "there is no such thing as an uncoded body," drawing attention to ways in which the body is always marked by "codes" that bear witness to wider cultural and political forces acting upon it.[6] As such, Atwood's female bodies are inevitably coded bodies that tell the story of the subject's experience within a political economy that seeks to consume them, convert them into consumers in turn, shrink them, neutralize them, silence them, and contain them physically or metaphorically. Hence Marian's peculiar anorexia in Atwood's first novel, the subversive anti-comedy, *The Edible Woman*, where the protagonist's loss of appetite marks a resistance to pre-designated roles as both consumed and consumer. (It is no coincidence that Marian works for a market research company.) In this case, Marian's body shows no signs of physical change so that the only "code" betrayed by her body is an increasingly severe loss of appetite, yet this is itself a "code" since, as Susie Orbach explains, any form of anorexia (literally "loss of appetite") "speaks" volumes: the starving woman's "body is a statement about her and the world and her statement about her position in the world ... She speaks with her body."[7] Marian's protest is silent: it is manifested in terms of her body and we have to decode that body if we are to understand the language of its protest.

This provides an early example of Atwood's emphasis upon the body as figurative text in fictional life stories concerned with women's position within power structures that seek to contain them. As Dorothy Jones notes, Atwood's novels are consistently concerned with the stories of women (and occasionally of men) who are "powerless people caught in traps devised by the powerful": here, "power" relates to those traps set either at the macro level (*The Handmaid's Tale* and arguably *Alias Grace*) or at the micro level (as in *Cat's Eye, Lady Oracle, The Blind Assassin*, and numerous others).[8] In this sense "power" becomes entwined with Atwood's use of the word "political," which she interprets as meaning "how people relate to a power struture and vice versa ... How do the forces of society interact with this person?" (*Conversations*, p. 185).

Atwood's writing of power relationships find one expression in her writing of the various female bodies who tell their tales. Iris Chase in *The Blind Assassin*, for example, discusses the bruises left on her body by her sexually abusive husband in terms of "a kind of code, which blossomed, then faded, like invisible ink held to a candle. But if they were a code, who held the key to it?"[9] Here the flesh is literally made word as the bruises become a type of writing that offers a figurative testimony. Iris then speaks of the sense of obliteration she experienced as a result of her husband's abuse: "I was sand, I was snow – written on, rewritten, smoothed over" (*BA*, p. 271). Here bodily harm is figured in terms of text so that Iris represents herself as a blank space or page encoded by others: with no autonomy over her own body she has no rights over the words written onto it and no access to them anyway since they are inscribed in a code to which she does not hold the key. Iris emerges from her sexual and textual abuse "smoothed over" and thus effectively erased: she is the disempowered victim of wider forces and it is significant that the means through which she expresses her sense of radical disempowerment involves an image that situates the body as figurative text.

Images of erasure litter Atwood's fictive autobiographies of women struggling to write their stories of powerless lives. Ideas of nullity, void, and absence often dominate symbolic activity in these stories as if these images and symbols alone attest to the storyteller's deletion from the body politic.

Images of erasure and void also testify to the crises of identity suffered by Atwood's protagonists, whose uncertain sense of subjectivity repeatedly produces split selves, doppelgängers, counterparts, and complements, as well as several cases of mistaken identity. With their bodies "written on, rewritten, smoothed over" by others these protagonists' sense of presence and fixed identity becomes tenuous to the point of crisis. With no power within the political economy Atwood's women fight to reclaim authorship of their own identities via a rewriting and reclaiming of their bodies and of the old codes: Iris's memoir, detailing past abuse and in so doing connecting text with body, provides just one example of this reclamation.

The recurrent emphasis on erasure and void becomes conjoined with ideas relating to incarceration and surveillance in Atwood's writing of the female body. Again, this is manifested at both macro and micro levels in these novels, so that the state imprisonment of Offred in *The Handmaid's Tale* and Grace Marks in *Alias Grace* is matched by the metaphorical imprisonment of Elaine, Joan, and Iris. Certainly the level of surveillance to which they are all subject is equal, as Atwood demonstrates the extent to which the female subject and her body are contained and closely watched within a patriarchy that considers their very existence an attack or departure waiting to happen. The idea is made explicit in Atwood's short piece, "The Female Body," where the speaker advises: "Quick, stick a leash on it, a lock, a chain, some pain, settle it down, so it can never get away from you again."[10]

Atwood's narratives of female resistance evade the bodily containment of the subject and break free to articulate the experience of incarceration and surveillance in a culture where women are trained in both self-surveillance and in exercising the surveillant gaze over other women. In so doing the narratives repeatedly illustrate how women's bodies become "disputed territories" and even what Hélène Cixous terms the "uncanny stranger on display" ("Medusa," p. 337). Repeated examples are offered of how women learn to see themselves and other women through men's eyes, thereby becoming accidental policemen of the very power structure that excludes them. The casualties are the protagonists themselves, who find that they are reduced to a "space that defines itself by not being there at all" (*BA*, p. 409), and alienated from the very bodies by which they have been trapped.

The starved, transformed, beaten, diseased, abused, and incarcerated female bodies that litter Atwood's novels should therefore be seen in the context of a concern to draw attention to women's position within a culture that plays numerous dirty tricks on them. Atwood herself would not resist the connection between "politics" and "art" in her writing (within the defined limits of the word "politics" given above), stating: "What art does is, it takes what society deals out and makes it visible, right? So you can see it."[11] Connection with Cixous is clear here since the latter insists on the politically transformative potential of women's writing: "writing is precisely *the very possibility of change*, the space that can serve as a springboard for subversive thought, the precursory movement of a transformation of social and cultural structures" ("Medusa," p. 337). They may disagree on the vocabulary but Atwood and Cixous appear to agree on the revelatory capacity of writing, and potentially even on the subversive capacity of a woman who writes.

In writing at all the passive role of silent spectator is actively refused. Women's writing is an assertion of the right to be heard and it is a rejection of cultural myths that position women writers as "unhappy ladies" who are doomed to be "killed by a surfeit of words."[12] All of Atwood's female tellers of their own stories are emerging from a lifetime of enforced or self-imposed silence (the aural equivalent of void) and this in part accounts for the repeated images and metaphors connected with muteness, secrecy, and tonguelessness in the novels discussed here. Each of these fictive autobiographers are examples of Cixous's voiceless women who have been "muffled throughout their history" and who have "lived in dreams, in bodies (though muted), in silences" ("Medusa," p. 343). Furthermore, each novel offers active demonstrations of the refusal or retreat from "the word": in *Cat's Eye*, for example, the retrospective narrative features an episode where the traumatized Elaine vomits her lunch of alphabet soup onto fresh snow. With her nascent painter's eye the young Elaine notes how colorful the half-digested soup looks against its pure white backdrop as she detects "here and there a ruined letter" (*CE*, p. 137). In this episode we find an image figuratively representing Elaine's retreat from language which eventually results in her refuge in painting, a non-verbal mode of communication. Her body has rejected the word, her body increasingly becomes to her "the uncanny stranger on display," and only when body and word reconnect can Elaine write her story. Similar episodes involving active metaphors of word-rejection litter Atwood's fictive autobiographies and each attests to the curiously voiceless life of its storyteller.

Ultimately these storytellers find their voices and "*seize* the occasion to *speak*" ("Medusa," p. 338) as Cixous implores women to do, having wandered around in circles, confined to the narrow room in which they've been given a "deadly brainwashing" ("Medusa," p. 336). The emphasis upon incarceration is common to both Cixous and Atwood. Atwood's narrators write their lives in terms which call attention to their roles as silent witnesses to event. Their autobiographies seem to emerge in a gush as though the strain of repression has burst forth in a torrent of words reconnecting body and text. All have felt driven away from the world of words, the male discourse, as from their bodies throughout their lives, but they have finally broken their silence and in doing so they produce subversive and even dangerous narrative confessions. Their stories may be small scale in terms of public event (though each constitutes a socio-cultural document) but even so Elaine, Joan, and Iris "draw their stories into history" by intersecting their stories with received versions of history ("Medusa," p. 338). Further, they all write not in the "white ink" of the mother's milk ("Medusa," p. 339), but in the blood-red ink of the body. The latter is more visible.

Writing the body

The Blind Assassin offers a literal example of this blood-soaked inscription when Iris recalls a daydream in which the body writes itself in graphically physical terms. Winifred has stated that pregnant women were said to have used the rollercoaster ride at Sunnyside to induce miscarriages: asked whether this really worked Winifred responds, "*Of course it didn't work . . . and if it had, what would they have done? With all the blood, I mean? Way up in the air like that?*" (*BA*, p. 325). This triggers Iris's speculation about the visual nature of this scene and she imagines the womb-blood as "long thick lines of red, scrolling out . . . Like skywriting" (p. 325). The older Iris, who is consistently preoccupied with questions of language now extends her speculation into the world of words: "but if writing, what kind of writing? Diaries, novels, autobiographies?" (p. 325). Here, in Iris's imagination, the woman's text literally emanates from her body (somewhat over-fulfilling Cixous's recommendation, "Text: my body") and those texts take traditionally female forms. "Diaries, novels, autobiographies" become products of the female body in this formula and they come to us written in the red ink of female blood.

Iris's imaginary novelists, diarists, and autobiographers who literally write with their bodies are effectively articulating the right to tell their own story and to express their own history. Iris Chase even aligns herself *with* history (her bones, she states, "ache like history" *BA*, p. 56), and the alignment is entirely justified since her body not only contains her history but *is* her history. When she writes her memoir she cannot help but write the story of her body in which she has lived it. Iris is prepared to go one stage further in repeatedly suggesting that it is her *body* writing independently of her as she reiterates the notion that her hand (or "the other hand"), a synedoche for the body since it is a part standing for the whole, is scribbling away of its own volition.[13] Iris seems to suggest at such points that her text has been produced by a type of automatic writing and this naturally recalls a previous "hand writing" exercise in another of Atwood's guilt-soaked confessionals, *Lady Oracle*.

This earlier memoir is an anti-Gothic narrative infused with carnivalesque play. Locked in a vicious silent war with her mother where Joan's weapon of choice is fat, Joan's aggressively bloated body is a subversive text, a figure of speech in its own right. Quite what the war is about is unclear even to Joan, though she senses it involves issues of bodily ownership ("the disputed territory was my body," *LO*, p. 69). She also senses that her mother's notions of femininity fail to accord with her own, which derive less from ideologically inscribed cultural edicts (which are always more about prescribing behaviour than about prescribing appearance, as Naomi Wolf points out) than from an instinctive recognition of Aunt Lou's essential femaleness defined by rolls of soft, billowing, befurred flesh.[14] It is no coincidence that Joan's most eloquent battle tactics involve subversions of the very cultural signs in which her mother places so much faith: Joan's "fashion show in reverse," for example, is a carnivalesque parody of a display designed to celebrate and enforce the values of encoded femininity as combined with the principles of consumption (*LO*, p. 71). Joan's fashion show ironizes "consumption" and rewrites femininity in fleshy terms: here her inflated body speaks volumes and it does so without saying a word.

Only when Joan stops filling her mouth with food does she begin writing, and this raises further questions concerning the links Atwood forges between "body" and "text." Joan is still at the stage where her range of secrets and alternative identities thwart direct speech but she does now manage to produce written text. What we find here is, in Maud Ellmann's terms, a "secular version of the Eucharist" where fat is "transubstantiated into prose." The exchange between food and text makes logical sense since "reading and writing mime the processes of eating and excreting" so that the former "provide a kind of methadone" for the latter.[15] Thus Joan's fat melts away to reappear magically as another kind of text, this one written down, though the exchange less body and more text does in this case produce a deeply evasive form of words in the Gothic bodice-rippers she produces. Not only do these texts offer formulaic fantasy but they also encourage perilous Gothic thinking of the kind that traps Joan herself.

A more positive text emanates from Joan's experiments in automatic writing which produce her Lady Oracle poems and which involve a sideways step into liminal territory between dream and waking. Joan's experiments in automatic writing constitute a springing forth of what Cixous describes as "the immense resources of the unconscious" resulting from a writing of the self in which the body insists on being heard ("Medusa," p. 338). "Unconscious" the writing certainly is, since the words Joan writes fail to make any sense to her when she emerges from her trance state: if this is her body she is hearing she cannot understand a word of it. Possibly, in this parodic Gothic context of astral bodies and spirits, it is someone else's body she is writing; after all, as Coral Ann Howells points out, "the most significant thing about an Oracle is that it is a voice which comes out of a woman's body and is associated with hidden dangerous knowledge, but that it is not her own voice."[16] Joan's mother is the prime suspect here, especially as, in a neat irony, she seems more tangible as an astral body than in corporeal form. However, regardless of who the "voice" that Joan transcribes actually belongs to, the significant point here is that is emanating from unconscious territories through which Joan travels during her liminal waltz. The most important aspect of Joan's automatic writing lies in the fact that the language she produces sidesteps "the language of men and their grammar" because it emanates from the unconscious rather than from the conscious mind ("Medusa," p. 343). In these terms Joan's automatic writing constitutes an example of Cixous's *écriture féminine* in distilled form because it springs from a place where cultural and linguistic constraints fail to hold ground. Little wonder then that the words themselves "knock the wind out of the codes," just as Cixous envisions ("Medusa," p. 339).

Elaine's paintings in *Cat's Eye* offer yet another version of automatic writing where this time images write the fractured history lodged in the fictive autobiographer's unconscious mind. Joan's inability to understand the words she has written when in a trance is matched by Elaine's inability for much of her narrative to read the images she produces. As before, Elaine is uneasy in the world of words and Atwood ensures that this is made clear via the number of mistakes she makes when using them (one example being her confusion over the term "fallen women," which she muddles with "falling women"). Elaine knows that language is duplicitous, unlike mathematics which means what it says and unlike art (or so she thinks), which tells stories in non-verbal versions. In addition art offers a further attraction to Elaine since, as Molly Hite points out, the painter is "a professionalized embodiment of the one-way gaze": thus, when Elaine paints, she is appropriating the very "non-reciprocal" surveillant gaze to which she has so traumatically been subjected as a girl.[17]

Elaine's traumatic childhood has resulted in serious memory-gaps and in a propensity for metamorphosis, disguise, and identity shifts. It is significant that the reader is unable to formulate any fixed idea of what Elaine actually looks like, so frequently does she redesign her appearance. It is significant also that in this Gothic tale of twins, mirrors, and witches, the few glimpses of Elaine that solidify into physical images are snatched from her reflection in a smoke-glass elevator mirror, once with Josef when she is in a pre-Raphaelite phase, and again with Jon upon their reunion in the present-tense narrative. The latter is more reliable for less costume is involved but the image suggests nebulousness as Elaine notes whilst looking at her reflection, "I could be any age" (*CE*, p. 367). This essentially formless self-figuring accounts for the reader's inability to pin Elaine down to a clear image since her taste for disguise and shape-shifting leads her permanently to draw attention to her own hazy form: "I vary. I am transitional" (p. 5); "I could be a businesswoman out jogging, I could be a bank manager, on her day off" (p. 19). Elaine is her own "uncanny stranger" for much of her narrative and what began as adolescent self-protection ends as mature self-alienation.

Each image or disguise adopted by Elaine in her life as in her art constitutes an attempt to write a new self in a retreat from subjectivity. In this sense her body, like those of Joan and Iris, is a type of palimpsest, a manuscript on which old "writing" has been erased to make way for the new: the old "writing," however, may still be discernible if it is looked for closely enough. Only at the end of the narrative when Elaine has reconnected with her memory and faced down her ghosts can she peer through her writings and rewritings of herself, understand what each "text" means, drop the disguises and assert: "I will have to do . . . I will come as I am" (p. 403). At this point she is finally able to read her pictures accurately and she is simultaneously able to remove her disguises in an acceptance of her body, her retrospective text, and her self.

The aging body

Cat's Eye concludes with the bittersweet image of two raucous old ladies on a plane whom Elaine notes with considerable envy. These old ladies convert their bodies' various infirmities into topics of bawdy humor and revel in the freedom from responsibility that their age has conferred upon them. This is a gleeful image of the aging female body (a stubborn taboo in Western culture) and one that is at the polar extreme to that offered by Iris Chase in *The Blind Assassin*. Here the aging body is yet another form of Cixous's "uncanny stranger on display" since Iris repeatedly states that the face and body she sees in her mirror do not seem to belong to her. This body irritates her with its disabling infirmities, and the vicious language Iris uses in relation to it is often marked by ugly images of decay and putrefaction.

Iris's ancient body bores and frustrates her and it also has the potential to halt the verbal unpacking of her long-locked steamer trunk in the form of her memoir. A race between her body and her text develops early in the novel and the reader realizes that time is running out for both. In these terms her memoir is, as Coral Ann Howells notes, "a kind of bleeding to death" (the words are soaked in blood once more) and Iris only just manages to complete her narrative before her death.[18] As Iris's body gradually decomposes, it simultaneously composes her text, and her narrative can thus be seen in terms of a writing down of the body before it ceases to be. Iris empties her body of all its words, memories, sensations, and secrets, just as she imagines in her analysis of the phrase "spilling the beans," where the removal of the guilt-soaked story leaves the bean-spiller "depleted," "like an empty sack flapping in the wind" (*BA*, p. 448). Without the body there is no text, but here it is also true that without the text there is no body.

Iris's body language may be soaked in frustrated self-disgust, but both this language and the text into which it is poured are also marked with wry parodic play. Iris's aging body allows her to indulge in one of her favorite identities as a sinister witch or malevolent fairy godmother. She is careful to avoid giving her neighbors the impression that she is either of these things (the stereotypes of age appal her as much as they give her malicious delight) but Iris repeatedly refers to herself in terms which owe much to grim fairy-tale visions.[19] When, for example, Iris fantasizes about the long-lost Sabrina's return just prior to her death, she warns her granddaughter away, drawing on the image of the sinister fairy-tale crone: "an old woman, an older woman, living alone in a fossilized cottage, with hair like burning spiderwebs and a weedy garden full of God knows what. There's a whiff of brimstone about such creatures" (*BA*, p. 521). There is a type of burlesque relish in such constructions of the witch-like old woman but at the same time there is a horror of them, and Iris both inhabits the construction in aligning herself with it and resists it by occupying an objective viewpoint ("such creatures" suggests "they" rather than "me"). Nevertheless the "whiff of brimstone" hangs over Iris throughout her narrative. Her acts of writing have a history of wreaking havoc and the memoir she is finishing has the capacity for posthumous wreckage too. The haunted and witch-like Iris wielding her blood-soaked pen surely demonstrates E. L. Doctorow's claim, as quoted by Atwood herself, that "there is no one more dangerous than the storyteller."[20] And this storyteller who is locked away in her "fossilized cottage" is especially dangerous since she surpasses Cixous's call for a language that "will wreck partitions, classes, and rhetorics, regulations and codes" ("Medusa," p. 342). Iris's text knows no bounds because it can at best only be completed by the words "The End," which refer equally to her text in spidery scrawl and to her life. Under these terminal circumstances, why not use language as a wrecking-ball?

The witch figure is connected not just with the aged Iris but with Atwood's younger protagonists too: Elaine in *Cat's Eye* and especially Joan in *Lady Oracle*, who is not only prophetess, oracle, and alleged communicator with the dead but also a "trickster" and "her own Triple Goddess," have witch-like associations woven into their narratives (see also *The Handmaid's Tale, The Robber Bride*, and *Alias Grace*).[21] In part this contributes to the Gothic texture of these novels, but these associations also plug into constructions of the female writer herself. In telling tales at all, Atwood's "I-women, escapees" ("Medusa," p. 337) have wandered into dangerous territory where the woman's text speaks the unspeakable, reveals the secrets of the living and the dead, subverts received notions of "history," and undoes "the work of death" ("Medusa," p. 340). In addition, each Atwoodian autobiographer discussed here knows herself to be essentially duplicitous, constantly inviting doubt around the veracity of her own shady narrative and repeatedly drawing attention to textual adventures in bad faith even in the act of composition. Little wonder, then, that each protagonist casts herself or is cast by others in the traditionally gendered role of witch, since they are all dangerously deceitful holders, and spillers of secret beans.

But above all, each of Atwood's protagonists discussed here tells a tale of survival and resistance. *Lady Oracle, Cat's Eye*, and *The Blind Assassin* are each survival narratives in that their fictive autobiographers are veterans of power struggles fought on socio-political and interpersonal battlefields. In each case their bodies have offered coded versions of these struggles, which write their stories in alternative terms. In each text discussed here, the body that Atwood writes offers a figurative commentary on the framing narrative and forges provocative connections between the two.

Like Atwood, we should tread carefully around any blueprint or theoretical hard line: "I tend to be shy of theories because I know their limits," she states as she draws attention to the potentially disabling parameters of critical practice (*Conversations*, p. 52). The limitations of Cixous's notion of *l'écriture féminine* have been indicated earlier in this chapter, and Atwood would no doubt be keen to add more. However, the patterns Cixous celebrates in her essay calling for a female discourse written from the body and inscribing difference are certainly circulating in Atwood's fictive autobiographies discussed here, where "text" and "body" are locked together in mutual expression. This is not to claim that Atwood's novels are in any sense a demonstration of Cixous's *écriture féminine*, because they most certainly are not. It is, however, to claim that Cixous's vision of female inscription is usefully intersected with Atwood's writing practice and that analysis of Atwood's body of writing must pay close attention to her writing of the body where the fight for autonomy and articulation is figuratively written in permanent ink.

NOTES

1. Hélène Cixous, "The Laugh of the Medusa" (1975), *Feminisms: An Anthology of Literary Theory and Criticism*, eds. Robyn R. Warhol and Diane Price Herndl (New Brunswick, NJ: Rutgers University Press, 1991), p. 337.
2. Elaine Showalter, "Feminist Criticism in the Wilderness," *Modern Criticism and Theory: A Reader*, ed. David Lodge (London: Longman, 1988), pp. 335–36, p. 337.
3. Ann Rosalind Jones, "Writing the Body: Toward an Understanding of *l'écriture féminine*," *Feminisms*, eds. Warhol and Herndl, p. 363.
4. Earl G. Ingersoll, ed., *Margaret Atwood: Conversations* (London: Virago, 1992), p. 201.
5. Margaret Atwood, *Cat's Eye* (London: Virago, 1990), p. 379.
6. Gayatri Spivak in Lukas Barr, "An Interview with Gayatri Chakravorty Spivak," *BLAST unLtd* (Summer 1989): p. 12.
7. Susie Orbach, *Hunger Strike: The Anorectic's Struggle as a Metaphor for our Age* (London: Penguin, 1986), p. 28.
8. Dorothy Jones, "Narrative Enclosures," *Margaret Atwood: Entering the Labyrinth: The Blind Assassin*, ed. Gerry Turcotte (Wollongong, NSW: University of Wollongong Press, 2003), p. 48.
9. Margaret Atwood, *The Blind Assassin* (London: Bloomsbury, 2000), p. 371.
10. Margaret Atwood, "The Female Body," *Good Bones* (London: Virago, 1993), p. 46.
11. Margaret Atwood, *Bodily Harm* (London: Virago, 1983), p. 208.
12. Margaret Atwood, *Lady Oracle* (London: Virago, 1982), p. 313.
13. This is by no means the only occasion where Iris's body is said to write of its own volition: when Iris thinks of the abandoned laundry on her cellar steps, she describes the clothes as "blank pages my body's been scrawling on, leaving its cryptic evidence" (*BA*, p. 368). Here, the body is guilty of involuntary, coded inscription onto the "blank pages" of the clothes. Atwood's preoccupation with the idea of the "other hand" is explored in her discussion, *Negotiating with the Dead*, which can in many ways be read as an explanation of the energies involved in the working out of this idea in *The Blind Assassin*. See *Negotiating with the Dead: A Writer on Writing* (London: Virago, 2003), pp. 25–50.
14. Naomi Wolf, *The Beauty Myth* (London: Vintage, 1991), p. 14.
15. Maud Ellmann, *The Hunger Artists: Starving, Writing & Imprisonment* (London: Virago,1993), p. 23.
16. Coral Ann Howells, *Margaret Atwood* (Basingstoke: Macmillan, 1996), p. 67.
17. Molly Hite, "An Eye for an I: The Disciplinary Society in *Cat's Eye*," *Various Atwoods: Essays on the Later Poems, Short Fiction, and Novels*, ed. Lorraine M. York (Toronto: Anansi, 1995), pp. 196–97.
18. Coral Ann Howells, *Contemporary Canadian Women's Fiction: Refiguring Identities* (New York and Basingstoke: Palgrave, 2003), p. 42.

19. A further example of Iris's self-construction as witch is offered in Iris's description of herself as the granny of "Little Red Riding Hood"; here an evocative inversion occurs when Iris states that the granny is not in the wolf but that the wolf is in the granny (see *BA*, p. 366).
20. E. L. Doctorow, *City of God*, quoted in Atwood, *Negotiating with the Dead*, p. 34.
21. Sharon R. Wilson, "Mythological Intertexts in Margaret Atwood's Works," *Margaret Atwood: Works and Impact*, ed. Reingard M. Nischik (Rochester, NY: Camden House, 2000), p. 220.

5

SHANNON HENGEN

Margaret Atwood and environmentalism

"What is a human being?" This question, among others, constitutes what Atwood calls the "sub-sub-subtext" of her lecture delivered at Carleton University (Ottawa, Canada) in January of 2004, "Scientific Romancing: The Kesterton Lecture." Primarily a lecture on science fiction, it also touches on themes that have informed her writing for several decades – despotism versus decency; obsessive control versus the spectrum of human desire; science and art; reason and the imagination – all of which contribute to her sense of the environment. How much imbalance in these pairs of terms can we tolerate? Or, as she says in her lecture, "How far can we go in the alteration department and still have a human being?"[1]

The present is a turning point for Atwood. She states in the Kesterton Lecture and in her very short piece entitled "Writing *Oryx and Crake*" that, until now, the human animal has not changed. "What we want has not changed for thousands of years, because, as far as we can tell, human nature hasn't changed either" ("Kesterton Lecture," n.p.); and, "*homo sapiens* remains at heart what he's been for tens of thousands of years – the same emotions, the same preoccupations."[2] Her view of the animal itself up to this turning point will emerge in analysis of her work. For now, keep in mind that given current scientific research we are able, for the first time, to alter that animal beyond recognition. According to biologist Edward Wilson in his book, *The Future of Life*, all naturally occurring species are capable of great adaptation. But without the will to adapt mutually, and "if present trends continue," by the year 2100 scientists will be challenged "to create new kinds of plants and animals by genetic engineering and somehow fit them together into free-living artificial ecosystems."[3] In other words, what we now know as natural, however stressed, will have disappeared. He continues in this passage, which is an imagined address to those future scientists, that "if you go ahead and succeed in the attempt, we regret that what you manufacture can never be as satisfying as the original creation" (*The Future of Life*, p. 78). In another section of the book, Wilson suggests that the rampant technophilia of our age forces us to ask, "What, after all, in the long term does it mean to be human?" (p. 129). The adaptation and co-evolution that have characterized the naturally occurring environment, and so the very basis of survival among organisms, is being tampered with by current technologies. And while Wilson refuses to imagine what genetically modified humans might become, Atwood does not.

In an interview with Evan Solomon for the CBC television program, *Hot Type* (12 October 2003), on the subject of her novel, *Oryx and Crake*, Atwood recommends that viewers read Wilson's book as background to the novel. We therefore need to consider Wilson's arguments further. Essentially, he asks that we broaden our definition of environmentalism in order to move away from viewing it as a kind of "special-interest lobby" (*The Future of Life*, p. 39). At the core of the term is acknowledgment that we co-evolved among countless species and across millions of years "as one organic miracle linked to others" (p. 40). Biology has not yet succeeded in creating a vocabulary that promotes broad environmentalism, according to Wilson, and although he does not explicitly look to imaginative writers to do so, he might.

A female biologist whose work resonates with Atwood's on the subject of the environment is Donna Haraway who, unlike Wilson, openly declares in the introduction to *The Haraway Reader* her "love of words."[4] A kind of bridge between technical and creative writers, Haraway explicitly advocates the use of figures of speech in scientific writing as a way of "swerving around a death-defying and death-worshiping culture bent on total war" (*Reader*, p. 2). Hers is then a more poetic logic than Wilson's but nonetheless powerful. Not posing the question that both Atwood and Wilson do concerning what it means to be human, she declares that in fact "we have never been human" (Introduction, p. 2), have never been "self-made, autocthonous, or self-sufficient" (p. 317). Instead we have been one of many "companion species" who complicate one another's being. "Human" to Haraway falsely implies a creature presumed to inhabit only the culture side of what is itself a false dichotomy between culture and nature. She writes: "There is no border where evolution ends and history begins, where genes stop and environment takes up, where culture rules and nature submits, or vice versa" (p. 2). Imagining or figuring an environment in which we celebrate our role not as conquerors but as companion species will, she believes, lead us to "a more livable place, one that in the spirit of science fiction I have called 'elsewhere'" (p. 1).

Haraway has moved from her eloquent defense of the cyborg as a potentially revolutionary figure to articulation of the larger body of companion species who will emerge "after departure of possessive individuals and hermetically sealed objects" (p. 303). Always compelled by "entities that are neither nature, nor culture" (p. 332), she has argued for a kind of imaginative and affective environmentalism wherein we delight in our interdependencies: "Companion species take shape in interaction. They more than change each other; they co-constitute each other, at least partly . . . And the ontology of companion species makes room for odd bedfellows – machines; molecules; scientists; hunter-gatherers; garbage dumps; puppies" (p. 307).[5]

Environmentalism in the works of Atwood and the biologists becomes a concern with the urgent preservation of a human place in a natural world in which the term "human" does not imply "superior," or "alone," and in which what is fabricated or artificial is less satisfying than what has originally occurred. But Atwood's own imaginative writing has evolved over time. Her recent novel, *Oryx and Crake*, begins to consider what a genetically engineered human might be in the form of the Crakers, and there she dares to look beyond her own repeated belief that human nature cannot change. Consider Atwood's comment in her Clarendon Lectures in English Literature at Oxford University, published under the title *Strange Things*: "the desire to be superhuman results in the loss of whatever small amount of humanity you may still retain."[6] Being human to Atwood clearly implies acceptance of the whole range of our physical, emotional, spiritual, and intellectual state. To deny or splice out any of that state is to amputate the self as it has been known so far, and so to stress nature perilously.

Non-fiction prose

Before turning to her imaginative renderings of the human in her poetry and fiction, further attention should be given to the views expounded in the non-fiction prose already noted. Each of the chapters in *Strange Things* develops the book's subtitle, "The Malevolent North in Canadian Literature," for the Canadian North has inspired a range of deep feelings in the country's authors. The first chapter concerns the failed exploration of the far Canadian north by nineteenth-century British navigator Sir John Franklin and 135 other men, all of whom died there as a result of lead poisoning. Atwood argues that had the British explorers relied upon local technologies such as hunting and fishing practiced by the indigenous inhabitants of the Canadian Arctic but considered "primitive" by the explorers, and not upon the state-of-the-art European technology that produced lead-soldered food cans, they could have survived (*Strange Things*, p. 14). Ignoring a sense of shared place thus contributes to our dehumanization.

In her chapter on the desire of some Canadians throughout the country over time to become Native inhabitants, "The Grey Owl Syndrome," Atwood develops the theme of Euro-Aboriginal relations. She concludes that "the first Europeans in Canada literally could not have survived without the help of the Native peoples, which was frequently offered out of a spirit of generosity and honour and at considerable cost to the Natives themselves" (p. 39). In the twentieth century, some non-Native Canadians have claimed Native ancestry in order to feel close to their adopted land (p. 37). The groundwork for that claim is the writing of some nineteenth-century Canadian authors whom Atwood describes as the unacknowledged parents of "the Canadian environmental movement of the 1980s and 1990s" (p. 45). Gradually, from the time of early exploration to the late 1800s, "living like the Natives in order to survive in the wilderness was translated into living like the Natives in the wilderness in order to survive. Survive what? The advancing decadence, greed, and rapacious cruelty of white civilization" (p. 44). Native people can in fact, in the view of the authors she discusses, represent "a cure for their [non-Natives'] over-civilized ills" (p. 46), a cure, in other words, for willful imbalance.

The Canadian North and wilderness in general serve as witness that we have not yet fully understood much less subdued the natural world of which we are a part. At the end of the second chapter of *Strange Things*, Atwood suggests that Canadians should perhaps take the historical "white-into-Indian project" and adapt it to environmental (and therefore human) ends. She writes: "If white Canadians would adopt a more traditionally Native attitude towards the natural world, a less exploitative and more respectful attitude, they might be able to reverse the galloping environmental carnage of the late twentieth century and salvage for themselves some of that wilderness they keep saying they identify with and need" (p. 60). The "Malevolent North" of her subtitle is malevolent only when we believe we must conquer it. Instead we can invoke the cooperative stewardship advocated by the biologists not to subdue but to preserve our wildernesses. Without doing so, the North "will be neither fearful nor health-giving, because it will be dead," Atwood states in the final lines of the last chapter (p. 116).

Atwood's Kesterton Lecture reminds us of the importance of the imagination and so of the arts as companions to science. To separate them, or to ignore and degrade the arts altogether, is to threaten our very being as humans, for "our technological inventiveness is generated by our emotions, not our minds" ("Kesterton Lecture," n.p.). The arts express the emotions that guide scientific research. Specifically,

> Literature is an uttering, or outering, of the human imagination. It lets its shadowy forms of thought and feeling – Heaven, Hell, monsters, angels and all – out into the light, where we can . . . perhaps come to a better understanding of who we are and what we want, and what the limits to those wants might be . . . If we can imagine it, we'll be able to do it. (n.p.)

Science without the arts undermines humanity, as witnessed in her speculative novel of 2003, on the writing of which she claims as a basic axiom these questions: "What are our saving graces? Who's got the will to stop us?" ("Writing *Oryx and Crake*," p. 6). In the *Hot Type* interview she describes the imagination as a form of insurance, allowing us to ponder, before taking action, that vital query about what kind of a world we want.

Poetry

Because it is to the arts, especially literature, that we must turn to "come to a better understanding" of human desire, we need to study carefully Atwood's creative work, her figurings (to borrow Donna Haraway's term once again). In the interests of discussing the movement of her work over time, we will consider briefly some early and middle poetry before turning to fiction: *Procedures for Underground* (1970)[7] and *Interlunar* (1984).[8] We should expect to see "Heaven, Hell, monsters, angels and all," for, never idealistic, Atwood seems to probe what is really human, equally real and human, as though to summon understanding. She seems to suggest that we should accept both what ties us to nature and what produces the successes and excesses of culture, including science.

Procedures for Underground introduces the theme of the machine intruding into the psyche, or what Haraway might call the making of cyborgs. The setting of these poems is similar to that of Atwood's novel *Surfacing* from the same period, a northern Quebec bush. The titles of the opening poems – "Dream: Bluejay or Archeopteryx," "The Small Cabin," "Two Gardens," "The Shrunken Forest," and "Midwinter, Presolstice," for example – point towards the non-urban and also to the "underground" or inarticulate side of the human psyche, that which is made conscious only through poetic figures and dream logic. A naive point of view in the early poems states that "the invaders are coming nearer" ("A Dialogue," *Procedures*, p. 12), but we will eventually know that such points of view, because naive, are dangerous. We remember that the imagination must help us confront all the products of the human heart and mind: the invaders can be us. Part of accepting who we are is knowing that we exist between nature and culture, and that we can escape neither.

Childhood may figure for Atwood as a place in which we were closer to the real, closer to an intuition that we are as much composed of greed and aggression as we are of kindness. Returning there is as difficult as touching the non-conscious mind or expressing the nuances of the heart, and yet we attempt to in, for example, "Return Trips West."

Recalling Atwood's claim in the non-fiction prose that the human psyche has never changed, the speaker in "A Soul, Geologically," muses about her companion soul that it has presumably always been in awe of the workings of the natural world, at best viewing them as "gifts" ("Chrysanthemums," *Procedures*, p. 61) and at worst (as often in our own time) willing mastery over them. The early humans spoke "the earliest language" ("Fishing for Eel Totems," *Procedures*, p. 69) but we have lost the ability to articulate respect for nature. Nevertheless, a kind of reverential awe of natural phenomena persists in us, the speaker feels in "For Archeologists," despite our inability to accept it. Such primitive faith might in fact be one of the "saving graces" Atwood referred to in her piece on the writing of *Oryx and Crake*; we will see that it is clearly so in the novel *Surfacing*.

In *Interlunar*, "The Burned House" pursues the theme of nature's very slow but very certain power to self-renew. The cabin of the speaker's childhood burns on from this volume to *Morning in the Burned House* more than ten years later. An earlier speaker asserts that "each thing / burns over and over and we will / too, even the lake's / on fire now" ("The Sidewalk," *Interlunar*, p. 88). And in "The Burned House" the adult speaker says, "I stretch my new hands into the flames / which burned here and are still burning / slowly and unseen" (p. 93). Against the implied belief of current techno-science that we can extend human life indefinitely with prostheses of various kinds, the constant cycle of death and renewal that we witness in nature is a more trustworthy guide. *Morning in the Burned House* ends with the ever-burning cabin, the "burned house," and its promise of eternal rebirth.

Nature always renews, as the biologists concur. The earlier volume is suffused with interlunar half-light where human love and the aspirations of the soul mix with nature's other great powers. The speaker in "A Blazed Trail" acknowledges her deep bond with her lover; the poem ends on "the sound / the earth will make for itself / without us" (*Interlunar*, p. 101). The volume ends with the title poem and "the musty fresh yeast smell / of trees rotting, earth returning / itself to itself" (p. 102) in that never-ending cycle of which humans have always been a part. These inarticulate sights, sounds, and smells can bring us to ourselves in ways that the language of viciousness and greed alone never can.

Atwood's work, like all art, shows us what we want, the limits to which we can go to achieve what we want and remain human, and how we prevent ourselves from overreaching those limits. Wisdom, insight, love, mercy, and compassion – a sense of one another and the rest of nature as companion species – describe the human as much as heedless lust, arrogance, greed, viciousness, thoughtlessness, and ignorance, a sense that we are superior, that we deserve more and better and will have it at any cost. Her fiction pursues similar themes though with different figurings.

Fiction

Atwood's novel *Surfacing* (1972)[9] hints at the search for faith in primitive gods as antidote to current psychic malaise, that faith being one of humankind's "saving graces." The unnamed narrator of the novel journeys back home to a childhood place representing her more real self, regaining her life story en route. Storytelling, getting the story right, becomes another of our most basic human needs in the three works of fiction discussed here: *Surfacing, Life Before Man* (1979),[10] and *Oryx and Crake* (2003).[11] The most natural version of the self must often be discovered under layers of culture and then the split halves of the self are rejoined in these tales.

The narrator of *Surfacing* travels with three other people to the site of her family's cabin in the northern Quebec bush to attempt to solve the mystery of her father's disappearance. She has not returned to this site for many years and so she must face nearly forgotten memories; the story becomes that of the narrator's accepting her own complicity in the kind of naivety and mindless causing of pain that we see as dangerous in Atwood's poetry of the same period. Having repressed her youthful unwillingness to free the creatures that her brother trapped for pointless experiments, and more importantly having failed to tell the truth about her own unhappy affair with a married man and subsequent abortion, the narrator has lost touch with herself, her feelings.

The inability of characters in this novel to connect emotionally with one another makes obvious the absence of such saving graces as compassion and love that emerge in Atwood's later poetry. And the lack of connection between people transfers to an indifference to the natural world that has resulted in the "dying white birches" (*S*, p. 9) of the work's opening pages, the "fished out" lake (p. 32), and most obviously in the mutilated and hanged blue heron (pp. 137–38). The environment of *Surfacing* is not one in which the companionship and stewardship advocated by biologists figures significantly. But by the novel's closing pages the narrator is able "To prefer life"

(p. 220) and to suggest her love for Joe, the man with whom she has been living but not communicating, and with whom she has probably conceived a child. In an early reverie about her previous, married lover she had stated bluntly that "I'll never trust that word [love] again" (p. 55). Clearly she undergoes a recasting of her story.

At the beginning of the novel the narrator, when noting a roadside crucifix, refers to "the alien god, mysterious to me as ever" (p. 17) and so starts to recall the spirit of her childhood home. As the narrator prepares to dive into the lake that pervades this novel's imagery, in her attempt to see the underwater petroglyphs that she believes her father was replicating before he disappeared, she enters fully into a meditation that will eventually free and renew her: "Anything that suffers and dies instead of us is Christ . . . Canned Spam, canned Jesus, even the plants must be Christ. But we refuse to worship; the body worships with blood and muscle but the thing in the knob head will not, wills not to, the head is greedy, it consumes but does not give thanks" (pp. 164–65).

Her starting to admit a truer story about the abortion and end of the affair occurs simultaneously with her search for her father and ultimately for her forgotten memories of both of her parents. Lamenting not "granting it sanctuary" (p. 170), she later feels "her lost child surfacing within me, forgiving me" (p. 191). She wants to thank the gods of that place for taking her on a journey back to herself and the "feeling" that was "beginning to seep back into" her (p. 171): "These gods, here on the shore or in the water, unacknowledged or forgotten, were the only ones who had ever given me anything I needed" (p. 170). Although she "didn't know the names of the ones I was making the offering to . . . they were there, they had power" (p. 171), and they guide her towards "salvation."

Evocative descriptions of the wild natural setting of this novel serve as counterpoint to the empty and often hurtful exchanges between human characters. The narrator's current lover, Joe, is silent, bitter, and unkind; the other couple, David and Anna, are held together by mutual scorn and fake jollity. In contrast, the setting seems to offer a kind of grace: "The wind starts again, brushing over us, the air warm-cool and fluid, the trees behind us moving their leaves, the sound ripples; the water gives off icy light, zinc moon breaking on small waves. Loon voice . . . the echoes deflect from all sides, surrounding us, here everything echoes" (p. 47). Communion with this original place leaves the narrator "clean" (p. 208) whereas the other humans, the ones who rescue her when she escapes her traveling companions, "are evolving, they are halfway to machine, the left-over flesh atrophied and diseased, porous like an appendix" (p. 215). In the novel's final sentence, "The lake is quiet, the trees surround me, asking and giving nothing" (p. 224).

The narrator has apparently found that rare human place where nature and culture merge.

Having found her parents' gifts to her – their deep understanding of the natural world – and also having moved beyond what she describes as their "perilous innocence" (p. 169) during her journey, she feels open to "begin" and to "trust" (p. 224). Her parents were "from another age, prehistoric" (p. 169) but she and her generation, in her view, are turning into what she and her friends refer to as "Americans" but what are in fact "the happy killers" of either Canada or the US: "There is nothing inside the happy killers to restrain them, no conscience or piety; for them the only things worthy of life were human, their own kind of human, framed in proper clothes and gimmicks, laminated" (p. 151).

The unnamed narrator has just undergone a rebirth through accepting her own guilty cruelties, and she surfaces with "the primeval one who will have to learn, shape of a goldfish now in my belly, undergoing its watery changes" (p. 223). She and the father of her child "can no longer live in spurious peace by avoiding each other . . . and we will probably fail" (p. 224). And yet this novel stands as a powerful testament to the sacredness of all life forms: "Anything we could do to the animals we could do to each other" (p. 143). Presumably also any care we can take with the animals and other life forms in our environment will preserve what remains of our humanity.

What remains of our humanity can seem slim indeed in *Life Before Man*. A tale of marriages, affairs, divorces, suicides, and other deaths in the center of the city of Toronto, this novel contrasts with *Surfacing* in both setting and characterization. No main figure here journeys back to a more real past to gain insight into how to act in future. No reclamation of a truer story occurs. Yet Atwood's ongoing concern with how humans fit into the environment persists. The four principal adults who interact – Elizabeth, Nate, Lesje, and William – will approach their most basic nature, and Lesje, the paleontologist, often explicitly states her views on the natural world. Uneasy and awkward in Toronto's social milieu, Lesje takes refuge in that of the dinosaurs whose lives she studies in her job at the Royal Ontario Museum. Her partner William, whom she abandons for Elizabeth's partner Nate, is "a specialist in environmental engineering" (*LBM*, p. 19) and yet seems removed from any basic understanding of human nature and so of the natural environment. Foolishly optimistic in Lesje's view (p. 19), William is also incapable of seeing even his lover as what Donna Haraway would call a companion species: "William . . . finds her [Lesje] impossibly exotic . . . He bites her on the neck when they make love. Lesje doesn't think he'd let himself go like that with a woman of, as she once caught him putting it, his own kind" (p. 20). Partly Jewish and of Ukrainian and Lithuanian background,

Lesje remains somewhat outside the mainstream Toronto of this novel and so keeps a perspective on it. Primitive drives and potential violence underlie the behaviour of the main characters, combined with a failure to feel – familiar Atwoodian psychic terrain.

Early in the novel, Lesje wonders: "Does she care whether the human race survives or not? She doesn't know. The dinosaurs didn't survive and it wasn't the end of the world. In her bleaker moments . . . she feels the human race has it coming. Nature will think up something else. Or not, as the case may be" (p. 19). Having become pregnant in order to force Nate to choose between his former family and her, she feels no guilt although she believes she might give birth to "a throwback, a reptile" for having conceived in "rage" (p. 270). Once she has accepted her own potential for vengeance, Lesje seems to be learning survival in the culture of late twentieth-century Ontario, discarding her fantasies of natural prehistoric life. In the process, Lesje also finally comes to see that her conflict with Nate's wife, Elizabeth, is affecting Nate's and Elizabeth's children; she in fact comes to see Elizabeth herself not as the unscrupulous, fickle, and dominating figure she has been throughout the novel, but "shorter, worn, ordinary; mortal" (p. 285). Elizabeth herself must relinquish her need to win in human relationships, the heartlessness that has resulted in the most recent of her many, many lovers having killed himself. She moves from her opening reverie – "I don't know how I should live" (p. 3) – to comforting her hated Aunt Muriel on the aunt's deathbed, and then to the final scene in which she "blinks back tears": "She can't remember the last time anyone other than her children helped her to do something" (p. 291). Highly cultured, Elizabeth must acknowledge her ties to nature and inevitable decline.

Nate, the lawyer turned wooden toy maker turned lawyer again, seems ineffective and uncertain while having frequent fantasies of a kind of return to nature, culminating in a breakaway run from his mother's house. William similarly and more frighteningly sheds his too civilized veneer in a moment of frenzy and attempts to rape Lesje as she leaves him. And so in *Life Before Man* as in the fiction and poetry that comes before it, human nature is figured as dangerous to itself and other life forms except when knowledge of our own power to destroy is tempered with those traits that are also essentially human – forgiveness, compassion, stewardship, and simple kindness. Lesje's sense of how the human animal fits into the environment seems clear and compelling: "without the past she would not exist," she realizes (p. 284). And elsewhere: "All the molecular materials now present in the earth and its atmosphere were present at the creation of the earth itself. . . . She is only a pattern" (p. 153). Also, "Everything that's gone before has left its bones for you and you'll leave yours in turn" (p. 141).

This novel's environmental engineer, William, predicts that the "next age . . . will be the age of insects" (p. 111), and as if to prove him right, Atwood notes in the opening paragraphs of her post-catastrophe novel, *Oryx and Crake*, the spiders and grasshoppers that the main character, Snowman, encounters on awakening. His location is coastal and as he emerges from sleep at the novel's beginning he does so "listening to the tide coming in, wave after wave sloshing over the various barricades, wish-wash, wish-wash, the rhythm of heartbeat" (*O&C*, p. 3). Like other Atwoodian figures, Jimmy/Snowman must retune himself to his own heartbeat, to his own heart, to understand the term "human." And in this case he must do so alone in natural surroundings, for the human race has been destroyed, he believes, and what remains is a colony of humanlike creatures called Crakers, whom he has been chosen to oversee. Despite the destruction of people, the world continues to be "beautiful," he observes in the final chapter, one that opens with the same lines as the first, describing Jimmy "listening to the tide coming in" (p. 371). As biologists argue, the natural environment in its profound resourcefulness will outlast human abuse of it and continue to be beautiful.

The humans in this novel are driven by greed. Crake, a gifted specialist in transgenics, creates two simultaneous projects that he thinks will solve the environmental challenges of our century, particularly overpopulation. One is the BlyssPluss pill that promises renewed libido, prolonged youth, and protection against sexually transmitted diseases. The other is the formation of the humanlike creatures who will replace humans on earth when BlyssPluss wipes us out, for unknown to its worldwide consumers, this pill contains the virus for a "rogue hemorrhagic" (p. 325). Crake makes Jimmy immune to the hemorrhagic, without Jimmy knowing, so that Jimmy will survive to monitor the Crakers. Crake also enlists the help of the novel's love interest, Oryx, a handsome and mysterious Asian woman with a past of horrific abuse who believes in Crake's vision to improve the human race. Oryx will market the BlyssPluss pills and Jimmy will do the ad campaign. In this milieu lacking any restraint on free enterprise, humanity's refusal to accept the natural aging process results in huge profits for corporations that produce the illusion of invulnerability. The body has overcome "the mind and soul" (p. 85), Snowman muses: "[the body] must have got tired of the soul's constant nagging and whining and the anxiety-driven intellectual web-spinning of the mind . . . It had dumped the other two back there somewhere, leaving them stranded in some damp sanctuary or stuffy lecture hall" (p. 85).

Jimmy's references to the life of the mind and particularly the soul recall other moments in Atwood's fiction and poetry that promote appeal to and acceptance of the natural powers. Jimmy's mother in this novel, a woman who abandons him for a life of resistance to the status quo, describes the experiments with reproduction and replacement of human organs, including the neocortex, that Jimmy's father is conducting as "immoral" and "sacrilegious" (p. 57). Her language here recalls a lost ethics and spirituality, what we have traded for "a second kick at the sexual can" (p. 55). Significantly, when Jimmy finds a shortwave radio on his desperate foray back into one of the gated Compounds for food, he "prays" to hear another human voice (p. 273). Oryx and Crake share a cynicism about what is real. Not believing in God, Crake goes further: "I don't believe in Nature either," he states. "Or not with a capital N" (p. 206). When what has always been real about being human is denied – the facts of our having strong aggressive drives that can nevertheless be tempered with such qualities as compassion and forgiveness, and our aging, infirmities, and death – then we are free to redefine our nature. Crake is suspicious of love, for example, calling it "a hormonally induced delusional state" (p. 193). He opts to redesign "the ancient primate brain" itself: "Gone were its destructive features, the features responsible for the world's current illnesses. For instance, racism . . . the Paradice people simply did not register skin colour. Hierarchy could not exist among them" (p. 305). But Jimmy is unnerved by the Crakers in the post-catastrophic world, for they lack a sense of humor or ambiguity or loss, and they cannot read.

Having lived his life coldly since abandonment by his mother, Jimmy lets himself be led into a career in what he calls "well-paid window-dressing" (p. 188), ultimately for Crake's large and powerful corporation. Jimmy genuinely loves words but, in line with a long series of affairs and heavy drinking, his passions seem misdirected. He acknowledges that, before the catastrophe and the several months since that he has spent alone or in the presence of the Crakers, he never grew up (p. 251). We imagine that a more courageous Jimmy might have functioned like the bold artists who, as Atwood claims in her non-fiction prose, are capable of showing science its heart, of revealing the motives behind, for example, current transgenic research. However, the arts and humanities as we have known them no longer exist in *Oryx and Crake*; they are "no longer central to anything" (p. 187). The dominant human feeling in this milieu is greed, despite the persistence of people like Jimmy's lovers, classmates at his training academy, whom he describes post-catastrophe as "Generous, caring, idealistic women" (p. 189).

We come to the end of this novel not knowing how greatly Jimmy has changed, how willing he has become to acknowledge both human vulnerability and its antidotes – compassion, faith, mercy, among them – and the potential for destructiveness. Will he tell "his tale" or listen to those of the humans he finally discovers, or will he kill them, or they him (p. 374)? Should only the Crakers survive, what remains of being human?

Conclusion

Nature – physical or human – seen as a commodity always represents betrayal in Atwood's work, and betrayal has consequences. In her recent and very short prose pieces entitled *Bottle*,[12] she retraces the environmental theme that has compelled her consistently, here, for example, in "King Log in Exile." A fanciful legend about a log who rules ineffectively over a kingdom of frogs, the legend explains how King Log had signed a trade deal that benefited him financially through "a sharp upturn in exports, the chief commodity being frogs' legs" (*Bottle*, p. 21), and how through his "benevolent inertia" a new king, King Stork, had been put in place by "foreign powers." King Log escapes the ire of his subjects to "a villa in the Alps" (p. 22). "Meanwhile the Stork King has eaten all the frogs and sold the tadpoles into sexual slavery. Now he is draining the pool. Soon it will be turned into desirable residential estates" (p. 23). Thus the theme of predation of nature motivated by financial gain and the illusion of ease becomes legendary in Atwood's short performance pieces.

The human soul makes an appearance in these pieces, too, however. In "Faster," we learn that "Walking was not fast enough so we ran. Running was not fast enough, so we galloped," and so on up to flying. "Flying isn't fast enough, not fast enough for us . . . But a human soul can go only as fast as a man can walk, they used to say. In that case, where are all the souls? Left behind" (p. 41). When we attempt to outpace our souls, we betray and trample our nature. Not considered a spiritual writer, Atwood nevertheless points towards the soul as a repository of important values, among them a sense of awe at nature's power. The human heart also figures significantly throughout her work, as do instinctual drives. Human nature is made as much of reverence, compassion, and the capacity to forgive, as of lust, greed, arrogance, and cruelty. To deny any part is to lessen the whole. As whole creatures we both affect and are affected by the larger environment in which we evolve, and her work asks us to bear that interconnectedness firmly in mind.

NOTES

1. Margaret Atwood, "Scientific Romancing: The Kesterton Lecture," Carleton University, Ottawa, Canada, 22 January 2004, n.p.
2. Margaret Atwood, "Writing *Oryx and Crake* and *The Handmaid's Tale*: From Novel to Opera," booklet distributed by the Canadian Opera Company on the occasion of COC's production of *The Handmaid's Tale*, 23, 26, 29 September and 1, 5, 9 October 2004, at the Hummingbird Centre for the Performing Arts, Toronto, p. 6.

3. Edward O. Wilson, *The Future of Life* (New York: Knopf, 2002), p. 77.
4. Donna Haraway, *The Haraway Reader* (New York: Routledge, 2004), p. 2.
5. Michelle Lacombe investigates connections between Haraway's and Atwood's ideas in her paper "Resistance in Futility: The Cyborg Identities in *Oryx and Crake*" delivered at "Margaret Atwood: The Open Eye" Symposium, University of Ottawa, April 2004; to appear in the forthcoming conference publication, ed. John Moss.
6. Margaret Atwood, "Eyes of Blood," *Strange Things: The Malevolent North in Canadian Literature*, Clarendon Lectures in English Literature 1991 (Oxford: Clarendon Press, 1995), p. 84.
7. Margaret Atwood, *Procedures for Underground* (Boston: Little, Brown and Company, 1970).
8. Margaret Atwood, *Interlunar* (Toronto: Oxford University Press, 1984).
9. Margaret Atwood, *Surfacing* (New York: Fawcett, 1979).
10. Margaret Atwood, *Life Before Man* (New York: Fawcett, 1979).
11. Margaret Atwood, *Oryx and Crake* (Toronto: McClelland and Stewart, 2003).
12. Margaret Atwood, *Bottle* (Hay, UK: Hay Festival Press, 2004).

6

COOMI S. VEVAINA

Margaret Atwood and history

What does the past tell us? In and of itself, it tells us nothing. We have to be listening first, before it will say a word; and even so, listening means telling, and then re-telling.[1]

History was once a substantial edifice, with pillars of wisdom and an altar to the goddess Memory, the mother of all nine muses. Now the acid rain and the terrorist bombs and the termites have been at it, and it's looking less and less like a temple and more and more like a pile of rubble, but it once had a meaningful structure.[2]

Unraveling history

These two quotations, one from Atwood's lecture on her first historical novel, *Alias Grace*, and the other from *The Robber Bride* and spoken by her female military historian Antonia Fremont, signal Atwood's interest in postmodern debates over history, which have been going on since the 1960s. Historians, cultural theorists, and literary critics have argued over the traditional claims of history to represent the objective truth about the past, in a context of general skepticism where the "master narratives" of history, religion, and nation have lost much of their authority, so that these "substantial edifices" are in danger of being reduced to "a pile of rubble."[3] Of course this is not to deny that the real past existed, but simply to point out that any historical account is only a reconstruction from fragments of the past which are available to us, and that any historical narrative is largely governed by the perspective adopted by a particular historian; telling history is always a question of interpretation.[4] Moreover, there has been a shift away from macro-history to micro-history, where the story is told by marginalized voices or eyewitness accounts which were frequently omitted from official historical records. This forces us to acknowledge the fact that official histories only endorse the "truths" of the dominant power groups or as Michel Foucault has argued, "systems of discourse are often synonymous with systems of power."[5] The end result of this process of challenging traditional authority is that the totalizing narratives of "History" have now given way to the pluralist notion of "histories" – or even "herstories" in many of Atwood's novels, which are told from a female character's perspective.

In all her works, Atwood reveals a distinctly postmodern engagement with history. Like the military historian Antonia (Tony) Fremont in *The Robber Bride*, she too has her doubts about historical truth; like Tony she is not a "proof addict" (*RB*, p. 49) for she knows that "History is a construct" and that "any point of entry is possible" (p. 4). All one needs to do is to "*Pick any strand and snip, and history comes unravelled*" (p. 3). Once it gets unraveled, it is easy to see that the "truths" of history depend on whoever is doing the chronicling. After the death of the beautiful, smart and "hungry" Zenia, (the robber bride of the title), Tony knows that, as an historian, she is free to play fast and loose with the quixotic truths of Zenia's personal history – about which she admittedly knows next to nothing. All she has is a vague impression of the dead woman because "so much has been erased, so much bandaged over, so much deliberately snarled, that Tony isn't sure any longer which of Zenia's accounts of herself was true" (p. 3). The fact also remains that Tony is the one who has the authority to tell Zenia's story and that Zenia will only be history "if Tony chooses to shape her into history. At the moment she is formless, a broken mosaic; the fragments of her are in Tony's hands, because she is dead, and all of the dead are in the hands of the living" (p. 461).

With the dead in the hands of the living, any amount of conscious or unconscious manipulation is possible. In the "Historical Notes" at the end of Atwood's feminist dystopia *The Handmaid's Tale*, for instance, the Cambridge Professor James Darcy Pieixoto is seen to be brazenly playing with the historical "facts" of Offred's life in the Republic of Gilead, two hundred years after the fall of the regime. Basing his conference keynote address entitled "Problems of Authentication in Reference to *The Handmaid's Tale*," on the thirty tape cassettes found within a metal footlocker, he makes light of the terrorism and dehumanization endured by nearly all the women and most of the men in Gilead. The tapes made by Offred are regarded as mere artifacts which exude "a whiff of emotion recollected, if not in tranquillity, at least *post facto*."[6] Offred becomes an elocutionary act and her narrative status diminishes considerably in Pieixoto's reconstruction of her story. Worse still, her narrative warning against moral dictatorship and atrocity is summarily dismissed in an "editorial aside" by the male professional historian who is interested in reconstructing his grand impersonal narrative of a vanished nation's history. It is interesting to note that though Offred's anguish and her description of daily life in the Republic of Gilead seem to be truthful, she herself does not pretend to be giving us the objective truth simply because, as Atwood tells us in *True Stories*, "The true story is vicious / and multiple and untrue / after all."[7] In a self-reflexive manner, Offred admits that her entire narrative is a reconstruction from memory, and that any retelling is always selective, and so possibly a reduction and a distortion of what really happened: "there are too many parts, sides, cross-currents, nuances; too many gestures, which could mean this or that, too many shapes which can never be fully described, too many flavours, in the air or on the tongue, half-colours, too many" (*HT*, p. 144). Aware of the fictive nature of her narrative, Offred calls it a "tale" rather than a "report" or a "diary." However, it must also be noted that Offred's anguished existence in "the long parentheses of nothing" (p. 79) in Gilead would have remained unknown to future generations had Professor Pieixoto not "chosen" to usher her into history.

It is a truth universally acknowledged that historians often choose to immortalize the strangest of events and people. The life of the most notorious Canadian woman of the 1840s, Grace Marks, was extensively written about not only in Canadian but also in American and British newspapers, for having been convicted of murder at the age of sixteen. "The combination of sex, violence, and the deplorable insubordination of the lower classes was most attractive to the journalists of the day."[8] In the "Author's Afterword" at the end of *Alias Grace*, Atwood says that having found three different versions of the Kinnear–Montgomery murder given by Grace herself and numerous, often contradictory, accounts of the "facts" of Grace's life, she has "fictionalized historical events (as did many commentators on this case who claimed to be writing history)" (*AG*, p. 466) and where mere hints and outright gaps exist in the records, has felt free to invent. The novel depicts Grace as an unreliable narrator who, like the legendary storyteller Scheherazade (to whom she is likened by her lawyer Kenneth MacKenzie), escapes death and survives merely by telling wonderful stories with "a composure that a duchess might envy" (p. 132). Her unreliability is repeatedly foregrounded in the novel for, acutely aware of power politics, she seems to be telling people not the truth about herself but what they wish to hear. Consequently people react to her in diverse ways, providing readers with multiple perspectives on her motives and on events themselves. In his book *Narrative Logic* F. R. Ankersmith emphasizes the importance of multiple points of view and says that "if one view of the past prevails, there is *no* view of the past because only a multiple play of perspectives provided by a variety of narrations can enable us to 'see' at all the contours and specificity of each view of the past."[9] As readers we are forced to forego the satisfaction of narrative closure and are left wondering about the actual events in Grace's life, as well as the authority of any official historical account.

Our desire for sensationalism causes women like Grace Marks to find their way into the essentially male bastion of history, but others with equally interesting pasts disappear without a trace. Highlighting this issue of selection, the narrator of Salman Rushdie's *Shame* sharply observes:

> History is natural selection. Mutant versions of the past struggle for dominance; new species of fact arise, and old, saurian truths go to the wall, blindfolded and smoking last cigarettes. Only the mutations of the strong survive. The weak, the anonymous, the defeated leave few marks . . . History loves only those who dominate her: it is a relationship of mutual enslavement.[10]

Though this is largely true, often even the "strong" get left out due to the ideological positions of those who do the chronicling. Atwood's interest in the past of the formerly excluded "ex-centrics" (as both off-center and decentered) leads her to contribute to the body of knowledge which Linda Hutcheon has called "archival women's history" (*A Poetics of Postmodernism*, p. 110). In a poem entitled "Half-Hanged Mary" in *Morning in the Burned House*, Atwood talks about her ancestor Mary Webster (one of the two people to whom she dedicates *The Handmaid's Tale*) who was accused of witchcraft in the 1680s in a Puritan town in Connecticut and was hanged from a tree.[11] In the poem Mary tells us,

> I was hanged for living alone,
> for having blue eyes and a sunburned skin,
> tattered skirts, few buttons,
> a weedy farm in my own name,
> and a surefire cure for warts;
>
> Oh yes, and breasts,
> and a sweet pear hidden in my body.
> Whenever there's talk of demons
> These come in handy.[12]

A submissive, dependent poor woman would have seemed normal, but a granite-spirited, independent woman is seen as abnormal – not unlike Hester Prynne in Hawthorne's *The Scarlet Letter*. The men of the town cast their personal and collective Shadow (in the Jungian sense of the term) on her and rush to witness the hanging, "excited by their show of hate, / their own evil turned inside out like a glove, / and me wearing it" (pp. 59–60). Their womenfolk are fearful of that same hatred and suspicion turned against themselves, and so they do not dare to speak in her defense though they have often been helped by Mary with their secret female troubles and know that she is just another ordinary woman like themselves. All night while she is hanging from the tree, alone in the dark, Mary continues her quarrel with God about free will. She reworks the Cartesian dictum of "I think, therefore I am," to "*I hurt, therefore I am*" (*Morning in the Burned House*, p. 62), asserting that she is still alive, though she finds little respite in the "three dead angels" Faith, Charity, and Hope. Instead, affirming her innocence in the eye of God, "I call / on you as witness I did / no crime" (p. 65), she resolutely bites down on despair and the temptation to give up, for this is a tortured woman's survival narrative. The next morning, when the men come to "harvest" her body and find her still alive, they feel certain that she is in fact a witch but are unable to act contrary to the law of double jeopardy and cannot hang her a second time for the same "offense." Before the hanging, Mary was an ordinary woman but, as the last section of the poem reveals, the horrific event seems to have empowered her during the last fourteen years of her life after the hanging. She now appears to be a mythic figure who has transcended dichotomies for she is spiritual and earthly, holy and blasphemous, and has become the embodiment of paradox, as she herself says, "The cosmos unravels from my mouth, / All fullness, all vacancy" (p. 69).

Surely history ought not to have failed to mention such an extraordinary woman. By writing Mary Webster into being, Atwood reveals the way in which history creates reality and reality creates history. These constructs are brought into being through language. Thus, in all her works, the critique of the epistemology of mimesis prompts her to be profoundly skeptical of the "picture theory" of language which sees language as depicting reality. Her belief in the artifice of fictional representation underlies her preference for the "game theory" which regards language as a serious game between the reader and the writer. Better still, the concept of "play," which resists even the necessary rules of the game, seems attractive to her. Atwood's comments in her obituary on her friend and fellow writer, Angela Carter, would seem to apply to her as well: "Perhaps *play* is the operative word – not as in *trivial activity*, but as in word-play, play of thought, or play of light."[13] The paradoxes and ambivalence in her writing also valorize the notion that women's discourse, which challenges the authority of a discourse of reason while working from within it, is necessarily "double-voiced" and even "multi-voiced." In "Sorties" Hélène Cixous says: "Woman un-thinks the unifying, regulating history that homogenizes and channels forces, herding contradictions into a single battlefield."[14] Language thus becomes a tool to lay bare the fact that reality is essentially surreal, absurd, inchoate and ambiguous: "What can you do with reality but chase it around? . . . Picture me then, butterfly net or popgun in hand, flapping over the fields with the elusive subject flitting away into the distance."[15]

Our riotous, cacophonic, quixotic selves

In *Midnight's Children* Rushdie says that a human being is "anything but a whole, anything but homogeneous; all kinds of everywhichthing are jumbled up inside him, and he is one person one minute and another the next."[16] Rushdie is sketching a postmodern concept of individual identity which owes much to psychoanalysis, where traditional notions of a unified self are displaced by a recognition of all the unconscious processes which influence our thoughts, feelings, and behavior. This emphasis on the importance of the unconscious might be summed up in the following comments, which provide an explanation for Rushdie's statement: "The erratic and devious presence of the unconscious, without which the position of the subject cannot be understood, insists on heterogeneity and contradictions within the subject itself."[17] Those contradictory forces within the subject, owing to the presence of the unconscious, complicate the issue of representation when it comes to writing fiction, especially contemporary autobiographical fiction and postmodern historical novels. Atwood's writing reveals an interesting movement from the modernist notion of the "self" to the postmodernist concept of a destabilized "subject." In her second novel *Surfacing*, (1972), her view of the self seems distinctly modernist. During her mystic quest on the island, the unnamed narrator of the novel discards the numerous false selves which she has acquired since her childhood and arrives at a glimpse of her true self. The dive into the wreck of her fragmented self results in a spiritual awakening and a feeling of wholeness. She despairs of not being able to help her friends, particularly David, who is so "infested" and "garbled" that "it would take such time to heal, unearth him, scrape him down to where he was true."[18] Four years later, in her comic Gothic *Lady Oracle*, Atwood emphasizes the postmodern view of the self as she playfully insists that there is no single Joan Foster but many Joans.

In the most absorbing of her "psychohistories," Atwood focuses on "the other voice" of the first nineteenth-century Canadian female literary celebrity, Susanna Moodie. What impressed Atwood about Mrs. Moodie "was not her conscious voice but the other voice running like a counterpoint through her work."[19] In the "Afterword" Atwood talks about the split in Mrs. Moodie's personality, which is observable in her contradictory responses to the Canadian landscape, to the settlers who are already there, and indeed to the whole ethos of colonization in which she herself was participating:

> she preaches progress and the march of civilization while brooding elegiacally upon the destruction of the wilderness; she delivers optimistic sermons while showing herself to be fascinated with deaths, murders, the criminals in Kingston Penitentiary and the incurably insane in the Toronto lunatic asylum. She claims to be an ardent Canadian patriot while all the time she is standing back from the country and criticizing it as though she were a detached observer, a stranger. (*JSM*, p. 62)

By reconstructing and renegotiating Moodie's historical past imaginatively, Atwood pays homage to her as a literary foremother who, though dead, continues to live on.

It may be argued that it was Mrs. Moodie's repressed awareness of the division within her own identity which lured her to the multiplicity displayed by "the celebrated murderess," Grace Marks. In her book *Life in the Clearings* (1853) she talks about her meeting with Grace in the Kingston Penitentiary in 1851. According to Mrs. Moodie's interpretation, the motive behind the double murder was Grace's passion for Thomas Kinnear her employer, and her frenzied jealousy of his housekeeper and mistress, Nancy Montgomery. As Atwood has commented, "Moodie portrays Grace as the driving engine of the affair – a scowling, sullen teenage temptress – with the co-murderer, the manservant James McDermott, shown as a mere dupe, driven on by his own lust for Grace as well as by her taunts and blandishments" ("In Search of *Alias Grace*," p. 223). Later when Mrs. Moodie saw her in the violent ward of the Lunatic Asylum in Toronto, she revised her earlier opinion as she came to believe that Grace must have been deranged all along. Atwood says that when she first read the book in the sixties, she accepted Mrs. Moodie's account uncritically till years later when she began serious research on Grace's life. She then realized that not only had Mrs. Moodie got the locations and names of the participants wrong, but that there were as many reactions to Grace as there were people, primarily because, being "human," Grace too had multiple selves.

Like the trickster in traditional mythologies who embodies contradictions, we thus witness Grace slipping with supreme ease from one role into another and are left wondering if she was "a sham" as a lunatic, "an accomplished actress," "a most practised liar," "a Siren" devoid of moral scruples (*AG*, p. 71), "a female fiend and temptress, the instigator of the crime and the real murderer of Nancy Montgomery, or . . . an unwilling victim, forced to keep silent by McDermott's threats and by fear for her own life" (pp. 463–64). Does she genuinely suffer from amnesia or is she faking it? Could she have prevented the murders or was the situation beyond her control? Was she truly a victim of double consciousness (which is also called disassociation of personality), or was she merely play-acting and speaking in Mary Whitney's voice during the neuro-hypnotic trance session conducted by Dr. Jerome Dupont (actually her old friend Jeremiah, the peddler)? Like us, Dr. Simon Jordan looks for certainties but Grace continues to outwit him in a provoking game of hide and seek: "She glides ahead of him, just out of his grasp, turning her head to see if he is still following" (p. 407).

Like Grace, the other characters in the novel have multiple or at least dual selves, but while those on the lower rungs of the social ladder get branded as liars and anti-social elements, others on the higher rungs escape censure altogether. In the novel, the Governor's wife, her daughter Lydia, Mrs. Quennell, and Reverend Verringer appear to be well-intentioned, "normal" people, trying their level best to get Grace released from the Penitentiary. Atwood however, is deeply skeptical of the motives of do-gooders and refuses to let us see them as simple and straightforward. In her first novel, *The Edible Woman*, Duncan suggests that people like Florence Nightingale were cannibals, feeding on chunks of other people's egos. True to his assessment, the Governor's wife is obsessed by criminals and even has a scrapbook with all their details, which Grace consults surreptitiously from time to time. Others, like Mrs Quennell, delight in the illusion of power that occult practices seem to give them. While working with Grace, Dr. Jordan, an American psychiatric doctor expert in matters concerning amnesia, is horrified by the darkness unleashed from his personal Pandora's box and almost has a nervous breakdown. (In the end he flees Canada and never finds out the truth of Grace's innocence or guilt.) The power politics within society however, will not permit *respectable* people like him to be regarded as abnormal and institutionalized for their mental condition. Instead, as a member of the medical profession, it is he who has the power to institutionalize others. With characteristic shrewdness, Grace observes that "a good portion of the women in the Asylum were no madder than the Queen of England" (p. 31).

In *The Robber Bride*, we likewise hear of the demonic Zenia from three "normal" women – Tony, Roz, and Charis – but, as readers, we cannot help but wonder if Zenia is real or imaginary. Coral Ann Howells suggests that she is both: "Zenia is the archetypal nomad, migrating from one story to another, operating on the borders between the real and the supernatural, so that all three protagonists see very different versions of Zenia . . . and we as readers can never decide how to interpret this shape-shifting figure with her multiple identities."[20] The cover design on the Bloomsbury hardback edition of the novel, which features Leonora Carrington's "Portrait of the Late Mrs. Partridge" reinforces this interpretation, for the woman's appearance seems disproportioned and bizarre. The hair which bristles out of her head against the backdrop of clouds gives her a witch-like appearance but she seems also to have a nurturing aspect to her personality for, in the picture, she is feeding a big bird. (It is, in fact, a partridge.) Does this mean that though Zenia has traumatized the three women, she has also done them some good? The first epigraph to the novel is instructive here: "A rattlesnake that doesn't bite teaches you nothing." Evidently she is their Shadow figure or doppelgänger, representing the numerous repressed, rejected selves within their own carefully constructed personalities. She is repeatedly depicted as a psychic externalization of the deepest hopes and fears of the three women. Tony concludes the novel wondering if Zenia was "in any way like us? . . . Or, to put it the other way around: Are we in any way like her?" (*RB*, p. 470). In Jungian psychology, an encounter with the Shadow figure, though extremely painful, can also prove to be enriching. Going back to the cover design, is Zenia then both a taker and a giver, a destroyer and an instructor? Also, since the Shadow cannot be rejected and permanently annihilated, Zenia, though physically dead, will continue to live on in the minds and hearts of Tony, Roz, and Charis.

Since "There is never only one of anyone,"[21] neither the characters nor the author can be anything but multiple. Refusing to let reviewers and critics confine her to literary ghettos, Atwood impishly asserted at the International Literary Festival, "WORD," in London in 1999, "there are too many of me." True to this statement, though her engagement with history seems distinctly postmodernist, she casts her vision in a modernist mold, thereby eluding both the labels. With one foot in modernism and the other in postmodernism Atwood, like Elaine in *Cat's Eye*, seems to say that the trick is "to walk in the spaces between" the words (*CE*, p. 238). Thus, while her novels fracture accepted notions of reality and self, unlike other postmodern texts they do not emerge as what Ihab Hassan calls "a riotous cacophony of conflicting discourses."[22] This is largely due to the fact that like Grace, Atwood too reveals herself to be an expert seamstress for, when (re)creating the fluid past of her characters, she quilts the disparate bits and pieces into an aesthetic whole. While quilting, her stitches are so small that the seams are barely visible. In order to make her narrative credible, the writer-historian must demonstrate supreme expertise in manipulating words and not behave like the bumbling fool-heroine, Joan, who clumsily weaves together her motley self "out of bright patches with all the crooked seams showing"[23] in her popular Gothic bodice-rippers.

Why do we need such lying truth-tellers?

The plural nature of both external reality and the human self make the word, whether written or spoken, seem completely unreliable. Can the visual image be trusted more than the word? As readers, when we first look at the novel *Alias Grace*, we assume the picture on the jacket of the Canadian and British hardback editions (from McClelland and Stewart and Bloomsbury) to be that of Grace, but soon find out that it is a painting by Dante Gabriel Rossetti called "Head of a Girl in a Green Dress." We later find Grace's engraved portrait as it appeared in the Toronto *Star and Transcript* reproduced in the novel, but we suspect that it is of no real help. Like Dr. Simon Jordan all we can say is that Grace's appearance is such that she "could easily pass for the heroine of a sentimental novel" (*AG*, p. 58). Photographs have long been associated with realism in the belief that "the camera never lies," but recently (and even before the manipulations of digital photography) we have begun to see in photography, as in fiction, "the patterns on the window,"[24] where photographs are seen not merely as unreliable but often as duplicitous and deceitful. In *The Blind Assassin*, photographs are often described as not being true to life. Laura, the sister of the narrator Iris Chase Griffin, plays trickster with photographs. Having learned the craft of hand-tinting photographs, she first of all steals the negative from her employer and then reworks a photograph of herself and Iris with Alex Thomas, the young man they both loved, sitting between them. She cuts her own picture out of the photograph she gives Iris and Iris's picture out of the photograph she keeps for herself. The only part of herself that remains in the photograph she gives her sister is her own hand, painted a pale yellow. Likewise, she tampers with Iris's wedding photos and paints Iris's husband Richard Griffen such a dark gray that his features are barely visible. In another photograph Winifred, Richard's sister, is colored a lurid green, Iris is given a wash of aqua blue, and Laura herself is painted in brilliant yellow. The colours undoubtedly reflect what she thinks of each of them. Richard is painted in that sinister gray, indicating that Laura sees him as the lord of the underworld, Pluto, raping the young Persephone-like maiden, herself. (Incidentally, this is a coded message which Iris only understands when it is too late.) Winifred, an older woman who strongly resembles the Aunts in *The Handmaid's Tale*, is painted in green because Laura sees her as the sinister arm of Richard. Laura explains to Iris that she has painted her in blue because she is asleep. As the novel unfolds, we realize that this may be true, for Iris's blindness to the reality around her and her refusal to nurture younger women, make her the blind assassin of Laura and also of her daughter Aimee.

Both the word and the visual image are unreliable, but we obsessively continue to re-create the past and refuse to let bygones be bygones. The compulsion to narrativize is due to the unfailing potential of narrative to make sense out of the chaos of lived experience and present it in a form that seems natural. As Hans Kellner says, "This is the 'mythic' aspect of narrativity itself, both in the Aristotelian sense that narrative always gives things a plot (*muthos*) of some sort, but also in Barthes' sense that narrative turns the chaos of history into an illusion of the immediacy and order of nature" ("Narrativity in History," p. 24). In the Atwood canon the most extreme examples of narrators who cannot escape the compulsion to narrativize are the eighty-two-year-old woman Iris and the sole survivor of a genetic experiment gone wrong, Snowman, in *Oryx and Crake*. Both Iris and Snowman are unsure of who their audience will be, but they tell their stories all the same. The issue gets further complicated because, in a bizarrely Gothic manner, the dead themselves refuse to be ignored and forgotten. Past events do not disappear, because historical time is not a solidified crystal but "a series of liquid transparencies, one laid on top of another. You don't look back along time but down through it, like water. Sometimes this comes to the surface, sometimes that, sometimes nothing. Nothing goes away" (*CE*, p. 3). These strange truths compel us to narrativize both our individual and collective pasts in both fiction and history.

"The Circle Game"

"The past belongs to us, because we are the ones who need it" (Atwood, "In Search of *Alias Grace*," p. 229), but does our obsession with the historical past indicate that we learn useful lessons from history and move upwards on the evolutionary ladder? The intertextual and intratextual echoes in Atwood's writing emphatically deny this possibility. Though a historian herself, Tony feels that we learn almost nothing from history (*RB*, p. 462). The numerous historical and literary allusions in *The Handmaid's Tale* indicate that, under the veneer of civilization, we human beings have remained much the same.[25] In the "Historical Notes" Professor Pieixoto's "sophomoric, smutty puns and jokes at the expense of women like Offred who endured the religious extremism of Gilead, strike the reader as ominous signs that little has really changed. Offred is still a victim of the patriarchal world view" (Garretts-Petts, "Reading, Writing and the Postmodern Condition," p. 82). In *The Blind Assassin*, the communist agitator on the run (who is a character in the novel-within-a-novel also entitled "The Blind Assassin"), tells his beloved who finds his story needlessly gory that he is ready to take it back and change it, but he adds that he would then have to rewrite history,[26] for his science-fictional Planet Zycron with its ruined city of Sakiel-Norn, though "located in another dimension of space" (*BA*, p. 9), is essentially true to history. Besides critiquing the Anglo-Canadian social system in the 1930s, with its ruthless capitalism as symbolized by Richard Griffen on home territory and the blinding of young carpet weavers in Bihar, India, the dystopian narrative harks back to the Code of Hammurabi, Herodotus, the laws of the Hittites, the conquest of Mexico, the destruction of the city of Kerman, the Renaissance, Jacobean and Restoration periods in English history, as well as slave trades in different parts of the world and, most importantly, the brutality to which women have been subjected in almost every part of the world at all periods of history. The science fiction writer in "The Blind Assassin" knows that in order to sell his pulp fiction he does not have to dream up sensational elements, for history has them all. Sakiel-Norn with its Snilfards and Ygnirods and its laws prohibiting reading is like the terrifying Republic of Gilead in many ways but its name is roughly translatable as "The Pearl of Destiny" (*BA*, p. 15). Perhaps it is the destiny of humans to destroy themselves and all forms of life with their "cleverness" and reduce civilization to a pile of rubble.

According to Darko Suvin, the best science fiction is about "clairvoyance – literally, clear seeing – of what's hidden yet advancing upon us."[27] This seems to be true not only of the science fiction created by the man in *The Blind Assassin* but of all that Atwood has written. In March 1988, soon after the publication of *The Handmaid's Tale*, she said during an interview with me that she had made a rule to herself that she would not put anything in the book "that hasn't already been done in some form or another, that isn't happening now or for which we don't have the technology."[28] The ironic vision of the narrators, their wry, laconic tone and dark humor, poignantly bring out the Swiftean social satire in her writing. In recent years she seems to be getting increasingly pessimistic but is still very conscious of her role as a writer. As a visionary writer, she regards art as not for "art's sake" or for "morality's sake" but for "survival's sake" and regards her own writing as a legitimate way of participating in struggle. Atwood sees the human race as tied like the mythical Ixion to a fiery wheel of endless repetition, though she hopes that by creating social and political awareness through her writing, she can prod us into breaking free of such fetters. Like the narrator of *The Circle Game* she seems to be telling the reader that she wants to break the "prisoning rhythms"[29] that we, in our "normal" anaesthetized state, are barely aware of.

By taking us back into the past through her fictive reconstructions of history, Atwood seeks to make her readers aware of our present state and lead us into the future with the hope that we will learn to act responsibly in ways which will make our rapidly shrinking and increasingly threatened world a better place for ourselves and for the generations to come.

NOTES

1. Margaret Atwood, "In Search of *Alias Grace*: On Writing Canadian Historical Fiction," *Curious Pursuits: Occasional Writing, 1970–2005* (London: Virago, 2005), p. 228.
2. Margaret Atwood, *The Robber Bride* (London: Bloomsbury, 1993), p. 462.
3. Linda Hutcheon, "Incredulity Toward Metanarrative: Negotiating Postmodernism and Feminisms," *Postmodernism and Feminism: Canadian Contexts*, ed. Shirin Kudchedkar (New Delhi: Pencraft International, 1995), p. 75.
4. Linda Hutcheon, "Historicising The Postmodern: The Problematising of History," *A Poetics of Postmodernism: History, Theory, Fiction* (New York: Routledge, 1996), p. 90.
5. Quoted in W. F. Garretts-Petts, "Reading, Writing and the Postmodern Condition: Interpreting Margaret Atwood's *The Handmaid's Tale*," *Open Letter*, Seventh series 1 (Spring 1988): p. 83.
6. Margaret Atwood, *The Handmaid's Tale* (London: Vintage, 1996), p. 315.
7. Margaret Atwood, *True Stories* (Toronto: Oxford University Press, 1981), p. 11.
8. Margaret Atwood, *Alias Grace* (Toronto: McClelland and Stewart, 1996), p. 463.
9. F. R. Ankersmith, quoted by Hans Kellner in "Narrativity in History: Poststructuralism and Since," *History and Theory* 26.4 (1987): p. 21.
10. Salman Rushdie, *Shame* (London: Picador, 1983), p. 124.
11. Atwood tells Mary Webster's story in her essay on "Witches," *Second Words: Selected Critical Prose* (Toronto: Anansi, 1982), pp. 329–33.
12. Margaret Atwood, "Half-Hanged Mary," *Morning in the Burned House* (Toronto: McClelland and Stewart, 1995*)*, pp. 58–59.
13. Atwood, "Angela Carter: 1940–1992," in *Curious Pursuits*, p. 156.
14. Hélène Cixous, "Sorties," *New French Feminisms: An Anthology*, eds. E. Marks and I. de Courtivron. (Amherst: University of Massachusetts Press, 1980), p. 252.
15. Atwood, General Introduction to *Curious Pursuits*, p. xv.
16. Salman Rushdie, *Midnight's Children* (London: Picador, 1981), pp. 236–37.
17. Rosalind Coward and John Ellis, *Language and Materialism: Developments in Semiology and the Theory of the Theory of the Subject* quoted in Hutcheon, *Poetics*, p. 160.
18. Margaret Atwood, *Surfacing* (London: Virago Press, 1984), p. 152.
19. Margaret Atwood, *The Journals of Susanna Moodie* (Toronto: Oxford University Press, 1970), p. 63.
20. Coral Ann Howells, "Margaret Atwood: Twenty-Five Years of Gothic Tales," *Littcrit* 28.1, issue 53 (June 2002): pp. 10–27.
21. Margaret Atwood, *Cat's Eye* (Toronto: McClelland and Stewart, 1988), p. 6.
22. Ihab Hassan, *The Dismemberment of Orpheus: Towards a Postmodern Literature* (New York: Oxford University Press, 1971).
23. Le Anne Schreiber, "Motley with Method," *Time* 108 (11 October 1976): p. 54.
24. Lorraine York, "'Violent Stillness: Photography and Postmodernism in Canadian Fiction," *Mosaic* 21/23 (Spring 1988): pp. 193–201.
25. For a detailed discussion of this aspect of Atwood's vision, see "Wastelanders in this New Gilead" in my book *Re/Membering Selves: Alienation and Survival in the Novels of Margaret Atwood and Margaret Laurence* (New Delhi: Creative Books, 1996), pp. 87–88.

26. Margaret Atwood, *The Blind Assassin* (London: Bloomsbury, 2000), p. 30.
27. Darko Suvin, "Afterword: With Sober, Estranged Eyes," *Learning from Other Worlds: Estrangement, Cognition and the Politics of Science Fiction and Utopia*, ed. Patrick Parrinder (Liverpool: Liverpool University Press, 2002), pp. 272–90.
28. Coomi S. Vevaina, "Daring to be Human: A Conversation with Margaret Atwood," *Margaret Atwood: The Shape-Shifter*, eds. Coomi S. Vevaina and Coral Ann Howells (New Delhi: Creative Books, 1998), p. 152.
29. Margaret Atwood, *The Circle Game* (Toronto: Anansi, 1966), p. 44.

7

ELEONORA RAO

Home and nation in Margaret Atwood's later fiction

"No place like home"

My opening phrase, taken from *The Blind Assassin* is, in its turn, a well-known quotation from *The Wizard of Oz*. In Atwood's novel, it relates to an episode from the Chase sisters' adolescence, where it is irreverent, odd, loony Laura who rewrites the sentence she heard many times from Reenie, the family housekeeper, whose language floods over with common sense, folk sayings, and popular wisdom. Laura's rewriting of "There's no place like home" – a stupid statement in her opinion – goes like this: "She wrote it out as an equation. *No place = home. Therefore, home = no place. Therefore home does not exist.*"[1] *The Blind Assassin* destabilizes received notions of home, with their conventional meanings of comfort, security, and custom. The Chase family estate – Avilion – acts as a refuge for the whole family; it functions as a bastion to keep the world outside at bay. In this novel, however, homes are also represented as provisional; they are unstable entities, like the patrimony of the Chase family. The sense of security, stability, and reassurance that Avilion has provided for Iris and Laura crumbles at one point in the narrative. Such a precarious figuration of home parallels the representation of nation and issues of national identity. Contemporary Canada, seen through Iris's eyes, appears, much to her astonishment, an odd assortment, a multicultural mosaic of ethnicities and languages with an elusive identity, which for people of Iris's generation and background comes very much as a surprise. Crucial also in this novel is the presence of an outsider, here embodied by Laura.[2] Iris's condition, on the other hand, is one of a beleaguered present and an excruciatingly painful past; her tale is one of place and displacement, constantly shifting between a now and a then. This tale underscores her dislocation and her dream of an elsewhere (both as a young and as an old woman).

Over the past ten years Atwood has argued against the importance commonly attributed to national identity for writers in postcolonial contexts, maintaining that "we gave up a long time ago trying to isolate the gene for Canadianness."[3] In line with her postnationalist phase, which we could place around 1991 with the publication of *Wilderness Tips*, Atwood has developed such a stance further in *The Robber Bride, The Blind Assassin*, and *Oryx and Crake*, challenging dominant discourses of home and homeland. However, in my discussion I have chosen one novel from the 1980s, *Cat's Eye*, before treating one from the 1990s, *The Robber Bride*, and *Oryx and Crake* (2003). All three novels problematize concepts of home and homelessness, in order to show how discourses of home are an extension of discourses of nation and national belonging, and how these are based on exclusion and oppression. In addition I would like to show how in these texts home as a repository of containment and safety shifts into "a discourse of insecurity."[4] In *Cat's Eye*, the visual artist Elaine Risley travels from Vancouver, where she lives in exile from her past, back to Toronto for a retrospective of her work. She starts to remember other journeys that belong to her adolescence, when her family moved from the wilderness to the city. At the time the experience of crossing the border on the way back to Toronto coincided with a movement from happiness, security, freedom, and peace to a sense of loss, pain, loneliness, humiliation, and the threat of more pain. As she recalls: "until we moved to Toronto I was happy."[5] Notwithstanding the passing of time, Elaine still considers Toronto to be the wrong place. The city seems to her oppressive and small, because of its intolerant and puritanical attitudes. In addition she feels constantly threatened by it: "their watchful, calculating windows. Malicious, grudging, vindictive, implacable" (*CE*, p. 14). Toronto represents an abhorrent world, as opposed to Vancouver, a place of refuge where she imagined she would be free of the past and would find happiness by starting afresh. Moving to Vancouver becomes an escape, a flight from the familiar, but also an act of amputation, of erasure which is also a denial of her previous life.

The representation of Elaine as a misfit, a victim of her girlfriends' tyranny, especially that of Cordelia, and ultimately as a stranger and an outsider can be connected with the novel's postcolonial implications. Elaine's first schoolteacher, Miss Lumley, is a proponent of English rule and British Empire:

> "The sun never sets on the British Empire" . . . Before the British Empire there were no railroads or postal services in India, and Africa was full of tribal warfare, with spears, and had no proper clothing. The Indians in Canada did not have the wheel or telephones, and ate the hearts of their enemies . . . The British Empire changed all that. It brought in electric lights. (p. 79)

Miss Lumley advocates the conventional ordering of an imperial center and subsidiary margin. But something is not quite right, and Elaine, albeit unintentionally, undermines her teacher's teaching: "Because we are Britons," she muses one morning after class has sung "God Save the King" and "Rule Britannia," "we will never be slaves. But we aren't real Britons because we are also Canadians. This isn't quite as good, although it has its own song . . . *The Maple Leaf Forever*" (p. 80). The position Elaine occupies with respect to Cordelia and the other girlfriends who bully her unmercifully – seeing her as on the margin and not quite measuring up – has obvious colonial (and thus also religious and racial) analogies in the text. She is, for example, impressed by how much the difficulties of Mr Banerj, her father's postgraduate student from India, are similar to her own. Likewise, she is attracted to Mrs Finestein, for whom she works as a baby-sitter, because this Jewish woman can happily ignore the prevailing Christian conception of what a wife and a mother should be.

Other considerations on who rules and to what end run throughout the novel. Carol Osborne has remarked on how Elaine's resistance to Cordelia is "associated with blackness," while Cordelia and her friends are "associated with white images." The usual symbolism of black and white is thereby reversed, and Elaine "aligns herself with minorities, both literally and figuratively, in order to overcome the oppression of white middle class Canadian society,"[6] an oppression which mirrors others, like Canada's subjection to both British and American imperialism. Indeed, Burnham High School, with its official school plaid, crest, and Gaelic motto, and with a picture of Dame Flora MacLeod, the head of the MacLeod clan, hanging next to the portrait of the Queen, underscores just that. A number of displaced persons show up in Elaine's paintings. Even at the end, during her show, Elaine still feels displaced in Toronto: "I shouldn't have come back here, to this city that has it in for me" (p. 410).[7]

Atwood's subsequent novel *The Robber Bride* is set in an early 1990s Toronto still dominated by a white elite, though in fact it provides a problematic representation of Toronto as a global multiethnic city. A preoccupation with questions of home and estrangement, national identity and belonging runs through this novel, which is populated by characters who experience a literal or metaphorical exile. It is accompanied, however, by the recognition that such a displaced condition is different for "those from other countries,"[8] that there is an "us" (white Anglophones) and a "them" (the immigrants) (*RB*, p. 99). In *The Robber Bride* the attention to visible minorities foregrounds difference, but the kind of difference highlighted in the novel is not simply multiculturalism, difference among cultures. It is also difference within culture and within the self.[9] In this novel each one of the protagonists – Tony, Roz, and Charis – feels estranged and foreign from her community, her family, her home country, like Zenia, who is the foreigner par excellence. I wish to draw a connection between the representations of home, mother country, and community in this novel, since as Benedict Anderson has argued, home, nation, and family operate within the same mythic metaphorical field.[10] I want also to show how the very notion of home country is called into question.

In *Cat's Eye*, for the protagonist, "'home' is a foreign word in a place [Toronto] where [she] feels like a foreigner, where she felt and still feels out of place, isolated and excluded as if she were a member of a different culture or race."[11] When Elaine comes back to her birthplace for an exhibition of her paintings, she wanders through the streets like a transient, nomad stranger: "In my dreams of this city I am always lost" (*CE*, p. 8). The questioning of the importance commonly attributed to a place called home is not altogether absent from Margaret Atwood's earlier fiction. In *Bodily Harm* (1981) Rennie muses over the meaning of roots:

> Rennie is from Griswold, Ontario. Griswold is what they call her background. Though it's less like a background . . . than a subground, something that can't be seen but is nevertheless there, full of gritty old rocks and buried stumps, worms and bones; nothing you'd want to go into. Those who'd lately been clamouring for roots had never seen a root up close, Rennie used to say. She had, and she'd rather be some other part of the plant.[12]

To come back to *The Robber Bride*, the rootlessness motif is central: the protagonists feel like foreigners in their home country.[13] Such a theme of estrangement allows the text to probe further into the characters' experiences of a sense of "being at home" and "not being at home." In so far as Tony, Roz, and Charis are represented as outsiders and homeless strangers, the novel brings into focus notions of home. To look into even metaphorical exile means to look into what or where it is to be at home, the place of inheritance, where one belongs as if of right. It requires a reflection on the meanings of home and a sense of place, with their implications of stability and security. It means also to look into dispossession, into what has been lost, and into what the three women try to re-create.

It is the homeless wanderer Zenia who shatters the sense of comfort, safety, and sanctuary attained by Roz, Charis, and Tony in their homes. Like exiles they experience a feeling of discontinuity within themselves. Like exiles they are double, split into a "now" and a "then," a "here" and a "there"; this self-division is reinstated by their doubled or tripled names: Charis/Karen, Roz Andrews/Rosalind Greenwood/Roz Grunwald, Tony Fremont/Tnomerf Ynot – names that represent a part of the self they wish either to ignore or suppress. The three of them have tried to gloss over their own discontinuity, to forget their past as homeless "orphans." In their adult lives they all try to create a sense of home, to achieve a sense of stability and safety. However, they are forced to renegotiate such feelings as Zenia bursts into their lives and shatters them, showing how precarious and provisional that security was. They are forced to face chaos and instability both inside and outside, and are pushed into "perennial borders" (*RB*, p. 49), shifted into disorder.

During childhood and adolescence Tony, Roz, and Charis feel like strangers and/or homeless outsiders. "Tony spent her first days motherless. Nor – in the long run – did things improve" (p. 136). Tony's mother, who is English, has never fully accepted her new situation in Canada nor her Canadian husband, whom in the end, she leaves.

> She was forced . . . to this too-cramped, two-storey, fake Tudor, half-timbered, half-baked house, in this tedious neighbourhood, in this narrow-minded provincial city, in this too-large, too-small, too-cold, too-hot country that she hates . . . *Don't talk like that!* she hisses at Tony. She means the accent . . .
>
> So Tony is a foreigner, to her own mother; and to her father also, because, although she talks the same way he does, she is – and he has made this clear – not a boy. Like a foreigner, she listens carefully, interpreting. Like a foreigner she keeps an eye out for sudden hostile gestures. Like a foreigner she makes mistakes. (pp. 144–45)

Tony is represented as a homeless outsider, alien to the world of her contemporaries. At college she stays "by herself" (p. 115), not having "much in common" with the other girls, and not having a "warm homely home" (p. 159) to return to during vacations. With time things do not change a great deal. As an historian and a female expert on war, Tony feels like an interloper; she is remote and aloof from her colleagues and from academic life. Tony's sense of non-belonging is expressed also by her habit of writing words backwards; she feels at home only in the other world of her own creation where she is no longer Antonia Fremont but "TNOMERF YNOT. This name had a Russian or Martian sound to it, which pleased her. It was the name of an alien, or a spy" (p. 137).

Through the story of Roz the novel highlights two social problems of contemporary Canada: the phenomenon of mass displacement and the presence of DPs (Displaced Persons) in Canada. Roz's immigrant background (her father is a DP of Jewish origin) contributes to the "undercurrent of exile" around her (p. 63). Roz feels foreign to Canadian culture and like a foreigner she tries to assimilate: "She wasn't like the others, she was among them but she wasn't part of them. So she would push and shove, trying to break her way in" (p. 322). During her adolescence Roz would continue to feel an "interloper" (p. 341), and in her adult life, in spite of her financial success, she never feels at ease in her own community. She fears to appear as a foreigner to her own children, obsolete and archaic: "She spent the first half of her life feeling less and less like an immigrant, and now she's spending the second half feeling more and more like one. A refugee from the land of middle age, stranded in the country of the young" (p. 77).

The other character, Charis, is virtually an orphan, without a home or family. Hers is a story of isolation, pain, and sexual abuse. Her perennial feeling of being dis-anchored is well rendered by the narrator's comment: "Charis meandered: Tony saw her sometimes on the way to and from classes, wandering slantways across the street" (p. 118).

The novel presents recurring and conflicting notions of home through the three main characters. For them home connotes, in the first instance, safety, refuge, and protection from the outside world, be it Roz's Rosedale mansion, Charis's cottage on the Island, or Tony's "turretted fortress" (p. 387). Roz has a clear perception of what Tony's home represents for her, the "red–brick Gothic folly. Perfect for Tony though, what with the turret. She can hole herself up in there and pretend she's invulnerable" (p. 288). Roz herself as an adult tries to build the sense of home and family she did not have as a child. She wishes to secure feelings of permanence, adherence, and stability for her children. "*Secure*, is what she wants them to feel; and they do feel secure, she is certain of it. They know this is a safe house, they know she is *there*, planted solidly, two feet on the ground" (p. 301). Tony's own perception of her home place undergoes major shifts and restructuring. The sense of protection she feels in "her armoured house" (p. 409) is disrupted by Zenia's intrusion in her life. The events will prove the provisionality of such feelings, and, as a result, the identity of Tony's home will prove to be unfixed. "In the waning light the house is no longer thick, solid, incontrovertible. Instead it looks provisional, as if it's about to be sold, or to set sail" (p. 37). Similarly, Roz's mansion will eventually fail to provide the sense of bounded assurance, solidity, and refuge. It will no longer function as an oasis, as a harbor. In her fantasies her own bathtub becomes full of "sharks" (p. 105) or, in turn, her kitchen is transformed into a gloomy forest in which Roz finds herself "Wandering lost in the dark wood" (p. 389). With the help of Roz and Tony, Charis manages to "exorcise" her house from the "fragments" of Billy and Zenia, and to reclaim it. "*Her* house . . . her fragile but steady house, her flimsy house that is still standing" (p. 283).

Zenia's reiterated and predatory actions force Tony, Roz, and Charis back into feeling not at home, estranged from themselves and from their familiar places: "Tony felt safe this morning, safe enough. But she doesn't feel safe now. Everything has been called into question . . . Menace, chaos, cities aflame, towers crashing down, the anarchy of deep water" (p. 35). Biddy Martin and Chandra Mohanty, in their influential essay, "Feminist Politics: What's Home Got to Do with It?" have exploded the received notions of "home" and the ambience of safety, security, and individualism that the word has gathered around itself. As they argue, the notion of "home" is constructed on the tension between two specific modalities, "being home" and "not being home": "Being 'home' refers to the place where one lives within familiar, safe, protected boundaries; 'not being home' is a matter of realizing that home was an illusion of coherence and safety based on the exclusion of specific histories of oppression and resistance, the repression of differences even within oneself."[14] In the novel such a fracture within the self is opened up by Zenia's invasion into the other women's lives.

It has earlier been argued here that home, nation, and family belong to the same mythic metaphorical field. As Roger Rouse suggests, "the old paradigms within which we used to situate ourselves (via such concepts as 'mother tongues,' 'fatherland,' 'cultural identity,' or 'home') are becoming inoperative. Yet this does not mean that we have simply lost what formerly held us in place, that we are homeless migrants."[15] He argues that the terms which define who, what, and where we are must be reformulated in the light of the new social and psychological spaces we create for ourselves. In addition, the shifting notions of home in the novel suggest that home partakes in a logic of inclusion and exclusion. Home is not a neutral place: it is a political concept, like nation. As Rosemary George Marangoly has so forcefully argued:

> Homes are built on select inclusions . . . grounded in a learned (or thought) sense of kinship . . . Membership is maintained by bonds of love, fear, power, desire and control . . . Homes are not about inclusions and wide open arms as much as they are places carved out of closed doors, closed borders and screening apparatuses . . . Imagining a home is as political an act as is imagining a nation. Establishing either is a display of hegemonic power.[16]

In *The Robber Bride* the seemingly conflictual qualities of comfort and terror, of power and violence are suggested by this refashioned perspective that Tony has of her own place: "She takes off her glasses . . . From the street her room must look like a lighthouse, a beacon. Warm and cheerful and safe. But towers have other uses. She could empty oil out the left–hand window, get a dead hit on anyone standing at the front door" (*RB*, p. 188).

The dividing line between the inside and the outside begins to falter: closed borders do not hold. By way of analogy, shifting borders come into play when the novel looks into questions pertaining to national, ethnic, and even religious identity. Authenticity is undermined whether in national character, religion, race, or the self. The three main characters merge at various moments with "not – I," namely Zenia. Despite their hatred for her, they reflect themselves in Zenia, at times they desire to be her in a play of splitting and doubling. "Tony looks at her [Zenia], looks into her blue-black eyes, and sees her own reflection: herself, as she would like to be. *Tnomerf Ynot*. Herself turned inside out" (p. 166). "Sometimes – for a day at least, or even for an hour . . . sometimes [Roz] would like to be Zenia" (p. 389).

According to Tony the historian, populations are nothing but hybrids. For this reason she has a peculiar arrangement on her table display of war maps down in the cellar. Tony uses kitchen spices for every different tribe or ethnic group. In this way she can visualize interbreeding and hybridization; for she is convinced that populations are not homogeneous but mixtures. As for religious identity, the novel presents an assortment of blends. Roz is first a Catholic, then a Jew because of her father. In the end she proudly proclaims herself a "pastiche" (p. 343). For Roz national identity is like putting on an act, it is staged as in a play: "Even the real thing looks constructed . . . Maybe that's what people mean by a national identity. The hired help in outfits. The backdrops. The props" (p. 88). Unlike her partner, the American draft dodger Billy, terms like "country" and "nation" don't mean all that much to Charis. "For Billy his country *was* a kind of God, an idea that Charis finds idolatrous and even barbaric" (p. 211). Charis herself would very much like to be like Shanita, the only non-white character in the novel. Shanita can metamorphose into anything non-Western she wants. As Charis considers: "She can be whatever she feels like, because who can tell? Whereas Charis is stuck with being white" (p. 57). Charis finds this condition exhausting, and hopes in her next life that she will be, like Shanita, of mixed race. Shanita's capacity to be "in-between" like the "indeterminate colour" of her skin, "neither black nor brown nor yellow. A deep beige, but beige is a bland word" (p. 57), envisages the liberating effects of multiple locations "between cultures" as opposed to the restraint and constraint of origins.[17] It is not accidental that such an aspiration to a liminal condition is experienced primarily by Charis, who is represented as a "vagrant" (p. 19), a drifter, "wandering" (p. 18), and "transient" (p. 217).

It is orphaned and nationless Zenia who disrupts the other three women's illusory stability, who "reminds them of their divided, multiple conditions," and "makes them feel disoriented and unsettled" (Staels, *Margaret Atwood's Novels*, p. 196). *The Robber Bride* does not emphasize fluidity without borders but rather the awareness of the non-static, non-fixed quality of borders: "There is a continuous ebb and flow, a blending, a shift of territories" (*RB*, p. 112). Hence the desire to transgress, to trespass beyond the borders of nation and race, to extend beyond the bounds of the self. In the tension between place, cultural homogeneity, and national identity it is the migrant figure who exceeds the space of nation-state because her status remains in-between. Cultural, temporal, spatial, and political displacements complicate the space in-between, "resisting the neat containment of multiculturalism's ethnic categories as well as generalized notions of nomadism."[18] Atwood's recent short short story "Post-Colonial" foregrounds the divisions within Canadian society, the existence of a "we" and a "them."[19] That story ironically emphasizes a version of Canadian history which highlights "the narrative of Canada as a generous land open to immigrants (where the other is welcomed on *our* soil") (Manning, *Ephemeral Territories*, p. 68).

Children of the future

We children of the future, how can we be at home in this world of today![20]

Oryx and Crake partakes of a similar logic of representing processes of inclusion and exclusion, of inside and outside. The protagonist's isolation and temporal displacement makes him the ultimate outcast, compelled to "live," albeit surreptitiously, in the past, a past which is populated by reveries, dreams, memories, and nostalgia. In this, Atwood's recent novel, the notion of a geographical and historical home gives way to constructs of imagination and memory. In *Oryx and Crake* Atwood has gone back to the future with the dystopian genre, and as in *The Handmaid's Tale* the reader is aware of two dimensions of time (a before and after) through the narrative reconstructions of the protagonist Jimmy/Snowman. When the novel opens it seems that, besides Snowman, this barren world is populated only by the genetically engineered beings called Crakers, invented by Snowman's best friend, Crake, in a secret experiment intended to generate a new race not troubled by sexual needs, aggression, religious and racial impulses. They are infantile, multicolored, and consider Snowman their mentor. After all, it is he who has led them to a place called "*home*."[21]

In the dystopian future described by Snowman's narrative before the catastrophe occurs, life in the Compounds where Jimmy and Crake grew up is coerced and controlled – though in a soft and seemingly privileged manner. In the Compounds live the privileged gated communities which belong to vast international biotech corporations. The inhabitants' movements in and out of them are strictly monitored. One of the main worries of these immensely wealthy corporations is to protect their employees from the lawless "pleeblands." Thus the novel reveals that here already "home" is a "compromised site."[22] The supposed security of Jimmy's family is achieved at a high cost by means of implementing a policy of authoritarian monitoring and control. This is how Jimmy's father explains it to his son:

> Long ago, in the days of knights and dragons, the kings and the dukes had lived in castles, with high walls and drawbridges and slots on the ramparts so you could pour hot pitch on your enemies . . . and the Compounds were the same idea. Castles were for keeping you and your buddies nice and safe inside, and for keeping everybody else outside. (*O&C*, p. 28)

Atwood here returns to the medieval images of turrets and fortresses; as in *The Robber Bride*, such imagery is suggestive of strong demarcations between inside and outside. In *Oryx and Crake* to be "at home" implies living within a policed enclosure.

After the catastrophe, however, Snowman finds himself stranded and displaced in an alien environment. In this new context he is portrayed as the ultimate outsider, possibly the last survivor of the human species. Snowman is in a position where he feels excluded from other living beings but obscurely related to them, and he wishes that he could make them understand that relationship, and so recognize kinship with himself: "*I'm your past*, he might intone. *I'm your ancestor, come from the land of the dead. Now I'm lost, I can't get back, I'm stranded here, I'm all alone. Let me in!*" (p. 106). He is outside the world of the living and of the dead, but somehow still in both of them. He remains an in-between figure, a state that anthropologist Victor Turner has called "liminality," where a group or individual, having separated from an established place in the social structure, is "neither here nor there, betwixt and between all fixed points of classification."[23] Snowman's liminal status is underscored repeatedly in the text: "But those rules no longer apply, and it's given Snowman a bitter pleasure to adopt this dubious label. The Abominable Snowman – existing and not existing, flickering at the edges of blizzards, apelike man or manlike ape, stealthy, elusive, known only through rumours and its backward-pointing footprints" (pp. 7–8). Like a foreigner in a culturally and linguistically alien environment, Snowman must be always on the alert; like a foreigner he is profoundly alone in his condition, cannot share his pain with anybody, and lives haunted by his memories.

An outsider, a stranger, ultimately an exile. Like an exile he has been split into two, with two different names, Jimmy and Snowman; like an exile he is split between a "before" and an "after," a "here" and a "there" (which exists only in his mind), and an elsewhere where he would like to be: "Maybe he's merely envious. Envious yet again. He too would like to be invisible and adored. He too would like to be elsewhere. No hope for that" (p. 162). Like an exile he has to cope with loss: loss of his previous life, but more importantly, the loss of his beloved Oryx. Like an exile he is haunted by nostalgia, and by the "presence of absence" (Rubinstein, *Home Matters*, p. 5). Like an exile he is in that liminal condition between longing and belonging. Like an exile Snowman constantly desires: another place, other company, another future. He is in a state of suspension between two dimensions: a past he cannot recover and a future which is unimaginable. As a liminal figure he is in a state of suspended time; when the novel opens and when it ends, it is "zero hour." Snowman looks at his watch and its blank face "causes a jolt of terror to run though him, this absence of official time" (p. 3). He is at a crossroads, suspended in the present, "up to his neck in the here and now" (p. 162).

In such a displaced condition Snowman's relation to language soon becomes one of estrangement. Like an exile, he experiences a vertigo of meaning, as English starts to become like a foreign language to him. Snowman's peculiar relation to language comes, however, not as a surprise. In his prior life as Jimmy, the protagonist of this novel, he is defined as a "word person." The thematics of language, of different sensitivities towards it, is highlighted by the constant distinction in the text between "word persons" and "numbers persons." Jimmy/Snowman is repeatedly defined as a "word person," unlike his father and Crake, who as scientists are definitively "numbers persons." Even as a youngster, Jimmy shows a particular sensitivity towards language; for example he is very aware of clichés and for the most part avoids using them, except when he is trying to seduce women. His love for words is underscored throughout the text:

> He compiled lists of old words too – words of a precision and suggestiveness that no longer had a meaningful application in today's world, or *toady's world*, as Jimmy sometimes deliberately misspelled it on his term papers . . . He'd developed a strangely tender feeling towards such words, as if they were children abandoned in the woods and it was his duty to rescue them. (p. 195)

The reassuring effect of words returns again and again, as he whispers them quietly to himself, like a magic incantation: "*Succulent. Morphology. Purblind. Quarto. Frass*," for through such words he finds a peculiar sense of calm (p. 344). It is, perhaps, for this reason that in a time of crisis and depression Jimmy's relation with language changes dramatically. When the sense of temporariness and rootlessness overwhelms him, language looses its "solidity"; it becomes "thin, contingent, slippery" (p. 260). That condition becomes exacerbated when Jimmy turns into Snowman. For him, signifier and signified are disjointed, and as a result language loses its ability to evoke any meaning at all: "From nowhere, a word appears: *Mesozoic*. He can see the word, he can hear the word, but he can't reach the word. He can't attach anything to it. This is happening too much lately, this dissolution of meaning" (p. 39). Snowman at times is afraid of having lost control over his mind and consequently over language. In the post-catastrophe world he finds himself in a vertigo of sense which tries to suck him in and from which he is constantly trying to escape. He feels as if he is on the border of a cliff above a precipice where it would be too dangerous to look down. Yet unpredictably, words also preserve their meaning at times and allow Snowman to tell, remember, think over his story, on how he got where he is now, in the narrative present. Words are also a salvation, a way to remind him that he is still human and alive; they become like stones fastened to his body in order to prevent him from falling down into the abyss of non-sense: "'Hang on to the words,' he tells himself. The odd words, the old words, the rare ones" (p. 68).

The act of storytelling, here as in *The Handmaid's Tale*, has multiple resonances. It is a means of survival that allows Snowman to avoid sinking into a world where words lose their consistency, use, and meaning. He would like to resume his old habits as a "word man," telling and listening, reading books and studying them, immersing himself in the shifting patterns of language. Instead, he is in danger of being overwhelmed by the loss of his most valuable skill: "'I used to be erudite,' he says out loud. *Erudite*. A hopeless word. What are all those things he once thought he knew, and where have they gone?" (p. 148). In his liminal condition of stranger, the act of storytelling becomes the only place where he can feel housed. For Snowman narration becomes his itinerant, nomadic home, where his *étrangeté*, understood as strangeness, estrangement, alienation, foreignness, "take[s] up residence" (Manning, *Ephemeral Territories*, p. 73). Snowman's narration also signifies hope for the future, since it implies a "you," as in *The Handmaid's Tale*: "a story is like a letter. *Dear You*, I'll say. Just you, without a name."[24] As Atwood's protagonist, Offred, elaborates: "By telling you anything at all I'm at least believing in you, I believe you're there, I believe you into being. Because I'm telling you this story I will your existence. I tell, therefore you are" (*HT*, p. 279). Snowman's narrative is also therapeutic in that it helps him to cope with the oppressive sense of guilt for merely witnessing Crake's dangerous plan without acting; but non-acting has, of course, its consequences. Snowman does his best to forget the past and his own willful self-centered ignorance, though of course being human he cannot be like the Crakers, who have been constructed without a sense of past and future; at best, he can repress memory, but it has the uncanny habit of returning, and ironically his only relief comes through storytelling. The act of telling his tale to an unspecified listener (or any listener at all, even a rakunk) helps Snowman to understand what happened; but his story is full of gaps for himself and for the reader. Meaning constantly escapes him, till the very end of the novel with its elusive, open-ended conclusion. Does Snowman survive? Who are the people he sees? Are they going to kill him? Is he going to kill them?

As in Atwood's earlier dystopian novel, *The Handmaid's Tale*, her major concern in *Oryx and Crake* lies in the present, rather than in the future. It is perhaps useful to stress that in *Oryx and Crake* there is no single mention of Canada. Atwood's most recent novel to date is suggestive of a thinking and feeling beyond the nation. Her quest for Canada's and Canadian literature's visibility started in the 1970s, and now fully realized, has provided room for a whole set of different themes and concerns: the possibilities and risks involved in the fast-paced discoveries of new technologies, as well as the "second wave" of xenophobia and intolerance for cultural, class, and racial diversity. The persistent habit of considering "strange" whatever is different from ourselves (in skin color, habit, custom, ultimately citizenship) is hard to do away with.[25] For such reasons her recent novels put into question narratives of national attachment by refusing to adhere to the limitations of the nation-state and its related discourses of territory and identity. Those nationalist discourses sustain certain definitions of the domestic, where the capacity of home to domesticate lies in its very power to define inside and outside, not solely because of what is enclosed, but also because what remains the "outside" is still controlled by the logic of the enclosure. Despite such investments in power and control, these novels seem to warn us that "any notion of habitation is fragile" and that home is no longer "a locus of safety" (Manning, *Ephemeral Territories*, pp. 56, 52).

NOTES

1. Margaret Atwood, *The Blind Assassin* (London: Bloomsbury, 2000), p. 447.
2. For an analysis of the role of Laura vis-à-vis her sister Iris, see Hilde Staels, "Atwood's Specular Narrative: *The Blind Assassin*," *English Studies* 85.2 (April 2004): pp. 147–60.
3. Margaret Atwood and Robert Weaver, eds., *The New Oxford Book of Canadian Short Stories in English* (Oxford: Oxford University Press, 1995), p. xiii.
4. Erin Manning, *Ephemeral Territories: Representing Nation, Home, and Identity in Canada* (Minneapolis: University of Minnesota Press, 2003), p. 40.
5. Margaret Atwood, *Cat's Eye* (London: Bloomsbury, 1989), p. 21.
6. Carol Osborne, "Constructing the Self through Memory: *Cat's Eye* as a Novel of Self-Development," *Frontiers* 14.3 (1994): p. 104.
7. For a lucid analysis of Elaine's displacement see Arnold Davidson, *Seeing in the Dark: Margaret Atwood's "Cat's Eye"* (Toronto: ECW Press, 1997).
8. Margaret Atwood, *The Robber Bride* (New York: Doubleday, 1993), p. 36.
9. Trinh Minh–ha, "Writing Postcoloniality and Feminism," *Woman, Native, Other* (Bloomington: Indiana University Press, 1989), p. 90.
10. Benedict Anderson, *Imagined Communities* (London: Verso, 1991), pp. 6–7.

11. Hilde Staels, *Margaret Atwood's Novels. A Study of Narrative Discourse* (Tubingen and Basel: Francke Verlag, 1995), p. 187.
12. Margaret Atwood, *Bodily Harm* (London: Virago, 1983), p. 18.
13. Shannon Hengen, "Zenia's Foreignness," *Various Atwoods*, ed. Lorraine York (Toronto: Anansi, 1995), pp. 271–86. See also Coral Howells, "*The Robber Bride*; or, Who Is a True Canadian?" and Carol L. Beran, "Strangers within the Gates: Margaret Atwood's *Wilderness Tips*," *Margaret Atwood's Textual Assassinations*, ed. Sharon R. Wilson (Columbus: Ohio State University Press, 2003), pp. 88–101 and pp. 74–87.
14. Biddy Martin and Chandra Talpade Mohanty, "Feminist Politics: What's Home Got to Do with It?" *Feminist Studies/Cultural Studies*, ed. Teresa de Lauretis (Bloomington: Indiana University Press, 1986), pp. 196–97.
15. Roger Rouse, "Mexican Migration and the Social Space of Postmodernism," *Diaspora* 1.1 (Spring 1991), quoted in Angelika Bammer, "Editorial," *The Question of Home, New Formations* 17 (Summer 1992): p. viii.
16. Rosemary George Marangoly, *The Politics of Home: Postcolonial Relocations and Twentieth-Century Fiction* (Cambridge: Cambridge University Press, 1996), pp. 6–9.
17. Chandra Talpade Mohanty, "Feminist Encounters: Locating the Politics of Experience," *Destabilizing Theory: Contemporary Feminist Debates*, eds. Michelle Barrett and Anne Phillips (Stanford, CA: Stanford University Press, 1992), p. 89.
18. Dianne Nemiroff, "Crossing," *Crossing* (Ottawa: National Gallery of Canada, 1998), p. 28.
19. Margaret Atwood, *Bottle* (Hay: Hay Festival Press, 2004), p. 39.
20. Friederich Nietzsche, *The Gay Science*, trans. Walter Kaufmann (Vintage: New York, 1974), Book v, par. 377.
21. Margaret Atwood, *Oryx and Crake* (London: Bloomsbury, 2003), p. 354.
22. Roberta Rubenstein, *Home Matters: Longing and Belonging, Nostalgia and Mourning in Women's Fiction* (New York: Palgrave, 2001), p. 73.
23. Victor Turner, *Drama, Fields, and Metaphors: Symbolic Action in Human Society* (Ithaca, NY and London: Cornell University Press, 1974), p. 232.
24. Margaret Atwood, *The Handmaid's Tale* (London: Vintage, 1996), p. 50.
25. See Earl G. Ingersoll, ed., *Margaret Atwood: Conversations* (London: Virago, 1992), p. 139 and p. 214.

8

MARTA DVORAK

Margaret Atwood's humor

One of the greatest storytellers of modern times, Mark Twain, remarked that "there are several kinds of stories, but only one difficult kind – the humorous."[1] He differentiated the humorous story, which he claimed to be truly American, from the comic story and the witty story, which he classified as respectively English and French. Like Twain, and like certain Canadian writers who preceded or followed him, Margaret Atwood anchors her playful writing in the motifs and mindset of North America. While her novels, stories, and short fictions can be poetic, biting, or even grim, they are almost invariably suffused with the humor that Twain identified as being indissociable with the *manner* of the telling, as opposed to the comic and the witty story which rely on the *matter* (Twain, *How to Tell a Story*, p. 7). Also investigating the mechanisms of humorous writing, Atwood herself has classified it into three commonly acknowledged genres: parody, satire, and "humor" (although her writing thoroughly blurs these artificial boundaries). In the characteristic way of postcolonial writers promoting their distinctive national culture, she has set out to identify British and American humor and distinguish Canadian humor from the two metropolitan forms.[2] Yet the discrete dimension of Canadian humor in her analysis rests not on techniques of production, but on notions of reception, or the complex relations between what she terms the "laugher," the "audience," and the "laughee" (*SW*, p. 175).

These are the relations involved in Atwood's skillful use of irony, a slippery concept apprehended differently from one culture to another, and considered to be a dominant mode of self-defining discourse in the literatures of postcolonial societies in which heterogeneity and difference are the rule. Canadian literature has notably produced a profusion of parody, satire, and caricature which distance themselves from European aesthetic models, yet continue a long tradition of ambivalence unconfined to any national borders. Such texts both assert and undermine prevailing values and conventions. Atwood's general humorous manner, to revert back to Twain's term, is characteristic of the rural Nova Scotia of her childhood – a region infused with the oral tradition – and conforms to the modes of indirection recommended by Twain, which consist in apparent gravity, deferral, and underemphasis, associated with a sense of pace. It relies fundamentally on various forms of incongruity, derived from the tall tale or yarn, an outlandish mode of oral storytelling grounded in a subversive carnivalesque tradition stretching back to Aristophanes. Honed by Twain[3] but first developed by Nova Scotia writer Thomas Chandler Haliburton, the yarn is rooted in the pre-existent topographical, social, and cultural features of a North American pioneer way of life, a lost world of horse-drawn carriages, chamber-pots, homemade bread, and storytelling that Atwood reconfigures in the story "Significant Moments in the Life of My Mother." This chapter will position Atwood's techniques within the broad framework of humorous literary production involving notions such as the burlesque (both high and low, including the satirical imitation of parody or travesty), or other textual dynamics of low comedy such as the carnivalesque. I shall pay attention to how Atwood makes use of carnival's liberating laughter of the grotesque, and, more specifically, to how her tall tale strategies generate the laughter that accompanies incongruity. The passages which will be analyzed using a combination of stylistic, narratological, and rhetorical approaches will be drawn from a variety of Atwood's novels and short stories.

The yarn and the carnivalesque

The essential principle of grotesque realism is degradation,[4] a practice which generates carnivalesque laughter by undermining elevated subjects through the low or trivial, notably the life of the belly (copulation, gestation, ingestion, digestion, elimination). This exhilarating reversal of established order to which Atwood subscribes is both the prolongation of a popular tradition stretching back to antiquity and a manifestation of the indigenous in the new literatures of North America – a society which has largely constructed its identity on the leveling of hierarchies. Atwood's prevalent discourse of alimentary and sexual consumption challenges institutions and social practices from American corporate culture to patriarchy in a manner ranging from the benevolent irony of Horatian satire (as practiced by Chaucer, Rabelais, or Byron) to the corrective derision of militant Juvenalian satire (rendered notorious by Swift). The predominant culinary imagery in *Cat's Eye* alone, incongruously comparing women to uncooked chickens or flabby pork fat, creates taxonomical equivalence as commodity. In ironic statements on the unflattering dictates of the fashion industry ("I can't wear the ruffled things, I'd look like a cabbage")[5], the laughter is often directed both at the narrating self and at the extratextual society which is mimetically represented. In this sense, Atwood's humor does indeed belong to the Canadian brand which she identifies as "concealed self-deprecation" involving laugher, laughee, and audience alike (*SW*, p. 188).

In "Significant Moments," Atwood juxtaposes ingestion anecdotes with earthier ones: the underpants falling around the mother's galoshes, or the cat peeing on her skirt in a time and place when even mentioning such objects or acts was an unthinkable breach of decorum. The humor is rooted in the *pantalonnade*, the brand of low comedy favored by the *commedia dell'arte* and taken up by contemporary comic performers. Participating in the comic effect is the characteristic recourse to the low register of colloquial idiom visible in the same story collection in "Uglypuss":

> This isn't the first phone call like this he's had. Sometimes they're anti-Semites, wanting to cut his Jewish nuts off; sometimes they're Jews, wanting to cut his nuts off because they don't think he's Jewish enough. In either case the message is the same: the nuts must go. Maybe he should introduce the two sides and they could cut each other's nuts off; that seems to be their shtick. He likes his where they are.[6]

The well-articulated combination of highly contrived syntactic and antithetical parallelisms, various modes of repetition and mirroring, jars comically with the lexical choice of slang, in particular the deliberately repeated circumlocution signifying emasculation. The binary rhythm of the second sentence constructions mounts and descends, culminating in periodic understatement which amplifies by attenuating, and censures prejudice by downplaying it. The satirical overtones will be discussed further on. Suffice it here to say that the laughter ridiculing ethnic prejudice is elsewhere directed at multiple socio-political institutions or mindsets or even at literary or cultural traditions. In the story "Uncles," in which the protagonist Susanna ventures into the male world of journalism, the objects of laughter include not only the upholders of patriarchal attitudes but also the cliché-ridden formula writing which they deride, in yet another carnivalesque collision of parodically stylized high and low registers:

> "Susie-Q is sleeping her way up the ladder. We've seen those artsy-fartsy reviews of yours. By-paragraph and all, very nice."
> "Listen to this: 'Lyrical, uncluttered paragraph, and good placing of spatial mass.'"
> "What's that from, a girdle ad? Sounds like a nice bum to me."
> "She's got old Vedge by the balls."

> "If he has any."
> "If he has any *left*."
> "Bugger off," said Susanna, resorting to their own language. The newsroom hooted.[7]

These gentle early versions metamorphose into more virulent ridicule in the novel published two decades later: *Oryx and Crake*. There, tucked away in indirect discourse, Trojan-horse-style, is a frontal satirical attack on contemporary society's advances in and abuses of genetic engineering. Crake's description of the side effects of the BlyssPluss Pill (designed to augment the libido) is couched in explicit, even raunchy, idiomatic locutions grounded in the life of the belly:

> It was an elegant concept, said Crake, though it still needed some tweaking. They hadn't got it to work seamlessly yet, not on all fronts; it was still at the clinical trial stage. A couple of the test subjects had literally fucked themselves to death, several had assaulted old ladies and household pets, and there had been a few unfortunate cases of priapism and split dicks. Also, at first, the sexually transmitted disease protection mechanism had failed in a spectacular manner. One subject had grown a big genital wart all over her epidermis, distressing to observe, but they'd taken care of that with lasers and exfoliation, at least temporarily. In short, there had been errors, false directions taken, but they were getting very close to a solution.[8]

The grotesque realism generating carnivalesque laughter combines with the hyperbolic dynamics of the yarn, producing hilarity as it swells and inflates with implausible details, the whole presented in the customary laconic manner of understatement. Suicidal behaviour, assault of the innocent, painful as well as fatal diseases, disfigurement and mutilation are simultaneously exaggerated and comically attenuated in a clear illustration of one of Atwood's trademark devices – structural irony – often deployed for satirical purposes. A qualifying locution ("at least temporarily") immediately invalidates an asserted solution ("though they'd taken care of that"), which in turn challenges Crake's global stance. The use of litotes ("errors, false directions") intensifies the Swiftian distance between Crake's insensitive stance and the stance of Jimmy, whose point of view governs the vision which the reader is invited to share. The structural distance between the two stances produces Juvenalian satire, more militant and reform-oriented.

The tall tale strategies Atwood deploys essentially involve three parameters: the outrageous combination of understatement and exaggeration; the overlapping of the ordinary and the extravagant; and, finally, the collision of myth with a mimetic restitution of reality. Keenly aware of how modernists like James Joyce disrupted code systems (*SW*, p. 337), Atwood injects the fantastic into the apparently ordinary. Like William Faulkner, who used the "real" material of local legends, she mixes stories grounded in local experience with the fabulous or mythological, as in *Surfacing*, for example. These parameters are the driving force in novels such as *Oryx and Crake*. They overlap and erupt in passages such as the following: "Amanda was from Texas, originally; she claimed to be able to remember the place *before it dried up and blew away*, in which case, thought Jimmy, she was about ten years older than she made out. She'd been working for some time on a project called Vulture Sculptures" (*O&C*, p. 244, emphasis added). One can remark the false attenuation of litotes in this laconic rendering of a hyperbolic situation – an outrageous tongue-in-cheek subversion of the cultural clichés surrounding America's biggest state which postmodern writers are fond of caricaturing.[9] Atwood's reader is projected into the *muthos* of the folk tale, submitted both to a careful restitution of reality and to fabulous displacement. The extravagant statement about Texas blowing away is inserted parenthetically into a sequence ostensibly devoted to describing Jimmy's current lover. This conforms to the staple technique of humorists which Twain identified as diverting attention away from the nub, point, or snapper "by dropping it in a carefully casual and indifferent way, with the pretence that he does not know it is a nub" (Twain, *How to Tell a Story*, p. 8).

Orality and polyphony

Closely linked to the carnivalesque and the yarn, this manner of taking the audience off stride is characteristic of the dynamics of postmodern writing, consisting in opening up the conventions of print texts to the codes of orality (conflating baroque practices and Aboriginal orature). Conforming to Twain's identification of "the rambling and disjointed humorous story" which strings "incongruities and absurdities together in a wandering and sometimes purposeless way" (Twain, *How to Tell a Story*, pp. 8, 11), "Significant Moments in the Life of My Mother" deploys a similar discursive strategy grounded in blurring and deferral. It tells the story of the narrator's mother telling stories, in a comically dizzying spiral of multiple narrators, mediators, and points of view which defamiliarize experience and generate humor.[10] The anecdote of the cat which wet itself all over the young woman's skirt while she and the young man beside her pretended nothing had happened invites gentle amusement on the part of a contemporary reader through the self-conscious narrator's intrusive comments on social conventions and cultural taboos, presented as ridiculously, albeit deliciously, obsolete. "'I was ready to sink through the floorboards,' says my mother. 'But what could I do? All I could do was sit there. In those days things like that' – she means cat pee, or pee of any sort – 'were not mentioned.' She means in mixed company" (*BE*, p. 19). The structural counterpoint (she says/she means) evident in this extract shows the complexity of Atwood's technique, in which the superimposition of levels (the fictional audience listening to the mother's tale and Atwood's "real" or implied audience) shifts the dynamics of connivance and transforms the laugher into the laughee.

One cannot fail to notice the abundance of dialogue in Atwood's œuvre, as well as the orality of the narratorial voice, generated by devices such as the choice of present tense for story time, contractions, the conjunctive use of the comma, and the deliberately low style privileging colloquial idioms. The discussion that follows will continue to integrate the way in which these participate in the carnivalesque strategy of counter-expectation and bathos, deflating through the recurrent gap between registers of language and experience. The strategy is grounded in the concept that Bakhtin has identified in comic novels and termed heteroglossia or hybridity,[11] involving the layering of two or more speech manners, styles, and belief systems within the utterance of a single speaker. We have already seen at work in "Uncles" the parodic stylization of opposed generic and professional languages. This is projected against a third level of discourse, that of the authorial utterance grafted onto and calling attention to both Susanna's simplistic perspective and the intellectual dishonesty of her trade: "She learned to use a lot of adjectives. They came in pairs, good and bad. The same painting could be energetic or chaotic, static or imbued with classical values, depending on whim" (*WT*, p. 137). The double-styled utterance invites readerly distance from both the pompous language protocol Susanna learns to produce and the locker-room protocol with which the male reporters deride it. Similarly, in *Oryx and Crake* Atwood introduces Crake's speech on the BlyssPluss Pill as indirect discourse only to refract it by surrounding it with the hidden utterance of Jimmy, the focalizer (or holder of the point of view) behind which the reader can perceive the diffused authorial voice. In *The Handmaid's Tale* and *The Blind Assassin*, critics have remarked on the heavy use made of the polyphonic interweaving of the narratorial and authorial voices which crisscross with the disembodied voices of characters such as Aunt Lydia or Reenie respectively.

> I didn't enter a movie theatre until after I was married, because Reenie said the Bijou was cheapening, for young girls by themselves at any rate. Men went there on the prowl, dirty-minded men. They would take the seat next to you and stick their hands onto you like flypaper, and before you knew it they'd be

> climbing all over you. In Reenie's description the girl or woman would always be inert, but with many handholds on her, like a jungle gym. She would be magically deprived of the ability to scream or move.[12]

The polyphonic superimposition contains the multi-tiered speech of current opinion, itself a construct handed down from generation to generation. The heterogeneity of voices is amplified by recourse to linguistic cliché (flypaper), which is extended, outrageously concretized (jungle gym), and mixed to produce comical incongruity, in turn mocking cultural clichés and accepted social values. The gap between the literal and the figurative twists and trivializes. This particular sequence shows how ideological stances are manufactured and transmitted, and how often at their core we find an emphasis on gender and identity construction. The story "The Age of Lead" conceals the speech of current opinion underneath the speech of the protagonist's mother which is filtered through the young girl's understanding, while the whole is masked by the omniscient narratorial voice. The merging and masking of multiple utterances is unmasked through the extravagant escalation characteristic of the yarn:

> In her mother's account of the way things were, you were young briefly and then you fell. You plummeted downwards like an overripe apple and hit the ground with a squash; you fell, and everything about you fell too. You got fallen arches and a fallen womb, and your hair and teeth fell out. That's what having a baby did to you. It subjected you to the force of gravity.
>
> (*WT*, p. 157)

Such polyphonic devices enable Atwood to deconstruct certain historico-political developments on a broader scale. The playful indirect mode, situated outside the sphere of logical argument, renders her attacks more difficult to parry. In *The Blind Assassin*, for instance, heteroglossia allows the writer to satirize commercial empire building during the nineteenth-century colonial period. Ironic overcoding is visible in certain passages which give agency to nascent Canadian capitalism, yet are overlaid by Iris's voice, which in turn blends with the authorial voice coloring the original proposition.[13] The humor in the passages discussed is indissociable from the multiple forms of doubleness involving deviation and displacement, or disarticulation and rearticulation, which it is productive to examine more closely.

Irony and satire

The privileged mode of displacement and deferral of meaning is evidently the double voice of irony, which both asserts and undermines, and which we have already seen at work in the passages above. By inverting the usual semantic levels, privileging the connoted or latent over what is denoted or announced, Atwood subverts. To be effective, however, her doubled discourse relies on the reader's ability to decode the clues of a trope grounded in deviousness. Her ironic strategy can involve recourse to the ambiguities of polysemy, equivocation, or duplicity foregrounding what Linda Hutcheon terms "the slippery nature of language."[14] In the story "Weight," revolving around a woman murdered by her lawyer husband, one is struck by a discrepancy in the assertion "He was a lawyer, he had the proper suits" (*WT*, p. 183). The predicate does not coincide with the opening topic or the subject of the speech act. The comic cleavage in such an appositional construction draws attention to the incongruities of our culture (Hutcheon, *Splitting Images*, p. 8) – in this case an answer to the question as to why battered women don't just get a good lawyer (*WT*, p. 184). In addition to such linguistic instability, irony can also involve the instabilities of situational defamiliarization and recontextualization. In both cases, irony operates within the paradigms of distance and normativity (a discrepancy generating the ironic situation), which include the doubling dynamics of self-consciousness and detachment. The ironic distance is at times suffused with amused benevolence. In "Significant Moments," the narrator depicts in a heteroglossic manner the people that her mother as the child of a country doctor would witness arriving at her door,

> clutching parts of themselves – thumbs, fingers, toes, ears, noses – which had accidentally been cut off, pressing these severed parts to the raw stumps of their bodies as if they could be stuck there like dough, in the mostly vain hope that [her] grandfather would be able to sew them back on, heal the gashes made in them by axes, saws, knives, and fate. (*BE*, pp. 11–12)

The comic dimension of the list enumerated by a wiser narrator is further enhanced by the closing syllepsis, where "fate" is incongruously added to the number of offending instruments. For Atwood uses the full range of forms of irony, from verbal and dramatic (relying on the speaker's intention or ignorance of the ironic intent) to structural and cosmic (resting on narratorial or authorial duplicity). Through a wide variety of tropes ranging from metaphor and syllepsis to antithesis and word play, Eurocentric master narratives can be debunked. In "The Age of Lead," the Franklin Expedition which set out to find the Northwest Passage is comically diminished from the stuff of epic and legend into that of the banal through understatement reinforced by a closing sentence which emphasizes the low registers of the carnivalesque: "she knows what the Franklin Expedition was. The two ships with their bad-luck names have been on stamps – the *Terror*, the *Erebus*. Also she took it in school, along with a lot of doomed expeditions. Not many of those explorers seemed to have come out of it very well. They were always getting scurvy, or lost" (*WT*, p. 156).

In the same story collection, Atwood focuses on how a settler nation like Canada has constructed its differentiation from Great Britain through totem transfer, a process of identification with the indigenous cultures of its New World space. The cult of the noble savage allowing transference across cultures is the recurrent butt of structural irony in "Wilderness Tips," ridiculed in a heteroglossic manner which combines the techniques of enumeration and seriation, with those of parenthesis and italicization – devices signaling a multiplication of utterances:

> There was a lot [in the manual] about the Indians, about how noble they were, how brave, faithful, clean, reverent, hospitable, and honourable. (. . . When was the last time Roland heard anyone praised for being *honourable*?) They attacked only in self-defence, to keep their land from being stolen. They walked differently too. There was a diagram, on page 208, of footprints, an Indian's and a white man's: the white wore hobnailed boots, and his toes pointed outwards; the Indian wore moccasins, and his feet went straight ahead . . .
>
> That summer he ran around with a tea towel tucked into the front of his bathing suit for a loincloth. (*WT*, p. 208)

The additional amplifying dynamics of the absurdly meticulous factual details are invalidated by the antithetical parallelism – essentially reductionist – and the discordant collision of worlds through the unheroic substitution of tea towel for loincloth.

Alongside such benevolent irony containing self-derisive overtones are more militant forms of satire. Atwood's satiric targets are on the whole consistent with the concerns of her generation, social class, region, education, and gender. Successful reception thus requires certain shared frames with respect to values, cultural context, or a communal consensus. Ecological preoccupations are dominant in novels such as *Cat's Eye*, in which the narrator criticizes clear-cutting in British Columbia through a clever combination of social irony – she praises by seeming to blame and blames while seeming to praise, suggesting that Canadians are working hard at spoiling their natural habitat: "It's not real, it's not drab, not flat, not grubby enough. They're working on it though. Go a few miles here, a few miles there, out of sight of the picture windows, and you come to the land of stumps" (*CE*, pp. 43–44). In the more direct vein of invective, hunting is presented as slaughter in *Surfacing* or "Wilderness Tips," in which Roland has lost the taste for hunting and its end result: "the antlered carcasses strapped to the fronts of cars like grotesque hood ornaments, the splendid murdered heads peering dull-eyed from the tops of mini-vans. He can see the point of venison, of killing to eat, but to have a cut-off head on your wall? What does it prove, except that a deer can't pull a trigger?" (*WT*, p. 205). The parallelism of head and hood ornament belongs to Atwood's destabilizing technique of situational defamiliarization and recontextualization. The heavily value-laden qualifiers combined with the rhetorical questions and final twist produce a ferocious indictment of the sport, and target moreover a male power that feeds on such practices. Ironically, in "Weight," a story in the same collection, a conceit sets up an equivalence between men and meat: "It's the age called *prime*, like beef. They all have that beefy thing about them. A meaty firmness. They all play something: they begin with squash, progress with tennis, end with golf. It keeps them trim. Two hundred pounds of hot steak" (*WT*, p. 177). Reinforcing the carnivalesque debunking of male machismo is the effective ternary structure with its rhythm mounting only to descend. The comic reductionism of the final nominal sentence is mirrored formally in the shift from triple to duple metre, and given even more "weight" through the closing spondee.

That the ideological stances governing gender and power roles are a recurrent butt of Atwood's ridicule has been amply demonstrated over the years and no longer constitutes the original facet of Atwood's production. The above passage once more demonstrates that the author's originality resides in her rhetorical virtuosity, and the mastery with which the satiric view shifts back and forth from amused detachment to moral indignation. Metalinguistic play with both polysemy and paronomasia are notoriously recurrent devices in *The Handmaid's Tale* to critique the institutional linguistic practices serving to promote ideology. In *The Blind Assassin*, simply calling attention to gaps between the signifier and the signified can ridicule and diminish, as when Iris notes that nouveau-riche society hostess Winifred Griffen Prior "'sailed', which meant, for her, sitting on a cushion on a boat, in a hat, with a drink" (*BA*, p. 231). On a more general level, word play can generate smiles of a complicitous nature, as Atwood's trademark use of the inclusive second person pronoun suggests: "*menopause*. A pause while you reconsider men" (*WT*, p. 179). Playfully redefining the term "battered women" in a polyphonic manner and in terms of popular fast food culture foregrounds a form of commodification through the grimacing laughter of black humor: "*Battered women*. I can see it in lights, like a roadside fast-food joint. *Get some fresh*. Sort of like onion rings and deep-fried chicken" (*WT*, p. 183). A witty play with semantic pluralism mocks the stereotypes fostered by male chauvinism when the protagonists of "Weight" invent alternative definitions of the labels applied to career women: "*Strident*. A brand of medicated toothpick used in the treatment of gum disease" (*WT*, p. 175). Sympathy with the tired and aging feminist is invited in startling similes: "I think of the next man as an aging horse must think of the next jump . . . I shine away at [my career] like an antique brass . . . It props me up: a career like an underwired brassiere" (*WT*, p. 181). The conflation of laugher and laughee in such self-derision invites readerly operations of inference and recognition. Elsewhere in the same story, the narrator's reflection on choice and power(lessness) invites identification more explicitly, guiding the reader more firmly in characteristic periodic structures which mount only to descend: "We were going to take on the system, get better divorce settlements, root for equal pay. We wanted justice and fair play. We thought that was what the law was for" (*WT*, p. 176).

Alongside the Horatian and Juvenalian forms of satire generating, respectively, the laughter of recognition and identification or that of derision and distancing, the reader encounters the indirect Menippean mode favored by so many contemporary writers. Like Robertson Davies, Mordecai Richler, Mavis Gallant, or Thomas King, Atwood's satiric pose sets up complex relationships between reader, narrator, and character. It conveys the implicit affirmative values that the authorial voice defends as well as the negative values that it attacks. These seem to be grounded in the general paradigms of dominance and dogmatism rather than in specific political entities, since targets of mockery range from ultra-conservative capitalism to collective bargaining, unions, and strikes. Novels such as *The Handmaid's Tale, The Blind Assassin*, or *Oryx and Crake* are constructed around a series of often specious dialogues, frequently combined with the sophistic banquet setting identified by Northrop Frye,[15] which stage figures incarnating the sundry socio-economic communities being targeted. Their values are undermined more or less covertly: either through a smug but seemingly uncontested exposition designed to manufacture readerly resistance, or by being pitted more overtly against authorial mouthpieces such as Offred and Iris (blurring direct first-person and indirect third-person forms), or Jimmy/Snowman. The characters embodying the mocked ideas or values are stylized to the verge of caricature, from Aunt Lydia's long, yellowish rodent-like teeth and Winifred Griffen Prior's cultivated artifices to Crake's pedantic mad scientist erudition.

Parody and metatextuality

We have seen that when discussing the mechanisms of humorous writing, Atwood herself classified it into three generally acknowledged genres which, rather arbitrarily, distinguish satire from parody. While Atwood undeniably directs derisive laughter at what she deems to be the abuses of power in the multiple fields of human experience, there is also a strong self-reflexive quality to her writing, which often engages with the conventions of the creation process itself, as well as with the mechanisms of reception. The different subgenres of journalistic writing are mocked in novels such as *Alias Grace* or *The Blind Assassin*: the latter caricatures not only a certain haziness with respect to veracity but also certain aesthetic codes, such as that of gushingly formulaic fashion columns, piling up outrageous alliterations and circumlocutions. The weapons of exaggeration and distortion are frequently aimed at the visual arts as well, for the art world tends to stand for the larger community of intellectuals comprising those who produce, those who evaluate, and those who buy. While the story "Uncles" targets fraudulently pretentious art reviews, *Surfacing* and *Cat's Eye* mock artistic conventions themselves in order to foreground the relationships between art and power or profit. The narrator of *Surfacing* is a commercial artist proficient in churning out the visual clichés codified by market demand, who has learned to compromise even before being asked.[16] In the provocatively reductionist manner of the travesty, the narrator of *Cat's Eye* notes the "rich people pretending to be gods and goddesses," and observes that "fruit and slaughters are not usually combined, nor are gods and peasants. The naked women are presented in the same manner as the plates of meat and dead lobsters" (*CE*, p. 346). Yet Atwood's favorite object of parody is literature itself.

Lady Oracle, one of the earliest metafictional novels to expose the trite conventions of formula writing, has attracted a great deal of scholarly attention. Atwood's turn-of-the-century novels, *The Blind Assassin* and *Oryx and Crake*, also conform to and transgress popular, highly coded genres in a parodic manner and for satirical purposes. *Oryx and Crake*, like *The Handmaid's Tale*, belonging to the subgenre of speculative fiction, is anchored in the (anti)utopian tradition which, by shifting the angle of scrutiny, has always blended with the genre of the satire. In an address titled "*The Handmaid's Tale*: A Feminist Dystopia?" Atwood has irreverently identified two of these anti-utopian conventions as "the tour of the sewage system" – the speech or narrative sequence which explains how the society functions – and the "just-so story," giving a "historical overview of how things got that way, usually involving a breakdown, some social catastrophe."[17] While the writer positioned the "just-so story" right at the end of *The Handmaid's Tale* so as not to – in her own words – "disrupt the body of the text" (Dvorak, *Lire Margaret Atwood*, p. 20), in *Oryx and Crake* she integrated it directly into the narrative comprised of systematic flashbacks, along with the "sewage system tour" through the aftermath of apocalyptic social breakdown. The macro "tour" is mocked in miniature by the delayed micro tour of "Paradice." This term itself is merely one of the profuse neologistic compounds serving as markers of the dynamics of bathos in the novel, which the writer turns not only in the direction of social satire, but also towards metatextual generic parody, in countless passages such as the one playfully echoing Mary Shelley's *Frankenstein*, and satirizing the programmed (self)healing commonly found in (anti)utopias:

> Crake had worked for years on the purring. Once he'd discovered that the cat family purred at the same frequency as the ultrasound used on bone fractures and skin lesions and were thus equipped with their own self-healing mechanism, he'd turned himself inside out in the attempt to install that feature. The trick was to get the hyoid apparatus modified and the voluntary nerve pathways connected and the neocortex systems adapted without hampering the speech abilities. There'd been quite a few botched experiments, as Snowman recalled. One of the trial batch of kids had manifested a tendency to sprout long whiskers and scramble up the curtains . . . one of them had been limited to nouns, verbs, and roaring. (*O&C*, p. 156)

To be remarked once more are the trademark mechanisms of the yarn consisting essentially in the collision of the extravagant and the ordinary. Fabulous invention (manufacturing a new, self-healing human race) and a mimetic restitution of reality (the verifiable lexicon of anatomy and high technology, or phrases calling up the familiar world of manufacturing and car options) coexist and collide through the opposing dynamics of understatement and hyperbole. Like humorists from Thomas Haliburton and Mark Twain to Robert Kroetsch and Thomas King, Atwood builds a mode of exaggeration moving from the domain of the plausible to the domain of the wildly exaggerated and hilariously incredible. The humorous cocktail's main ingredient is bathos, reinforced through the intrusion of a familiar register, homely objects, and unheroic actions, which culminate in a list which jars with its final odd man out.

In contrast with Stephen Leacock's choice of high burlesque, which involves applying a grand style to trivial events, Atwood favors the alternative approach of low burlesque. She takes an elevated subject – humankind usurping the divine powers of creation and generating destruction and self-extinction – to which she applies a deliberately low style. The burlesque contains a strong carnivalesque dimension notably in the recurrent gap between the event and the register of language used to depict it. When Crake unveils to Jimmy the new breed of human being he and his genetic scientists have created, he boasts of having done away with the evils of racism, territoriality, greed, lust, superstition, and hunger. But the sequence, which is in perfect conformity with the utopian tradition, shifts to travesty when among the qualities of the new breed being vaunted Crake lists its ability to recycle its own excrement. The dialogue that follows obeys a pattern of carnivalesque reversal produced through double irony: verbal (involving the speaker's ironic intention) and structural (not intended by the persona but by the implied author):

> "Excuse me," said Jimmy. "But a lot of this stuff isn't what the average parent is looking for in a baby. Didn't you get a bit carried away?"
> "I told you," said Crake patiently. "These are the floor models. They represent the art of the possible. We can list the individual features for prospective buyers, then we can customize. Not everyone will want all the bells and whistles, we know that. Though you'd be surprised how many people would like a beautiful, smart baby that eats nothing but grass. The vegans are highly interested in that little item. We've done our market research."
> Oh good, thought Jimmy. Your baby can double as a lawn mower.
>
> (*O&C*, pp. 305–06)

Jimmy's ironic intention is signaled through multiple devices: the low idiomatic register reducing Crake's grand exploits to "stuff," the double understatement of verb and quantifier (getting carried away/a bit), and the homely metaphor positing an incongruous interchangeability (baby/lawn mower) that generates hilarity. The rather Swiftian structural irony is more oblique and requires the reader's alert connivance in order to be decoded. Crake's "sewage-system tour" is devoid of deliberate irony but suffused with the authorial intention to deride and distance. His heavy use of the language of marketing, combined with reiterated understatement and circumlocution, is designed to produce disapproval of the processes of commodification he has set in motion and incredulity at the folly and callousness of a "whiz kid" standing for a society gone mad. Through its parodic espousal of the literary genre of the (anti)utopia, *Oryx and Crake* undeniably satirizes contemporary social patterns. Rather remarkably, the novel's hypertextual structure comprised of intratextual and intertextual echoes complements and arguably even outrivals the social critique.

The Blind Assassin is a more hybridized literary parody. The main narrative merely contains a fragmented science fiction story-within-a-story. In the framing narrative, the young Iris's encounter with cheap magazines and comic books is an ironic metanarrative which analyzes the way in which popular sites of representation construct our perception, desires, and values. The naive angle of vision allows the author to ridicule the formulas of such mass-produced literature. Multi-tiered descriptions are infused with the voice of an older narrator who perceives the patterns and decodes the rules of the generic game: "The criminals and white slavers were in the detective magazines, with their pistol-strewn, blood-drenched covers. In these, the wide-eyed heiresses to great fortunes were always being conked out with ether and tied up with clothesline – much more than was needed – and locked into yacht cabins or abandoned church crypts, or the dank cellars of castles" (*BA*, p. 153). Through her own accumulatory devices, Atwood mockingly mimics pulp fiction's mechanical aesthetics of sensation and excess. The framed narrative as well comically foregrounds generic codes by drawing an analogy between writing and cooking: both assemble ingredients which even with certain substitutions always result in the same identifiable dish. The target of Atwood's irony is undeniably the cultural clichés from which these fictional formulas emerge. But the clever commingling of the different levels of narrative also serves to emphasize the manipulative mechanisms of her own novel. The disruptive metafiction superimposing an identifiable "real" world onto an outlandish, invented world unveils the writer's skill in setting "poetic booby traps"[18] for the unsuspecting reader/laughee.

While this chapter has investigated convergent strategies and practices in Atwood's texts, notably in the aims, means, and structuring principles of her humorous representations, it is a delicate matter to discuss the mechanisms of humor, rooted by its very essence in indirection and duplicity, and dependent not only on production but on reception. For laughter is a social phenomenon belonging to the spheres of communication and community, and the rhetorical techniques which Atwood so masterfully deploys rely in the end on the reader's perception and interpretive strategies which in turn require certain shared belief systems. She manipulates these cultural frames with as much virtuosity as she manipulates language, playing with the formal features which underlie the spheres of social action and of ideas. In the manner of humorists since antiquity, Atwood is a moralist who expertly reconciles the double function of literature: to entertain and to teach.

NOTES

1. Mark Twain, *How to Tell a Story and Other Essays*, vol. XXII (New York/London: Harper & Brothers, 1906), p. 7.
2. Margaret Atwood, "What's So Funny? Notes on Canadian Humour," *Second Words* (Toronto: Anansi, 1982), pp. 175–89.
3. See "The Notorious Jumping Frog of Calaveras County," in "What's So Funny?"
4. See Mikhail Bakhtin's introduction to *Rabelais and His World* (Bloomington: Indiana University Press, 1984), p. 19.
5. Margaret Atwood, *Cat's Eye* (Toronto: Seal Books, McClelland-Bantam, 1989), p. 46.
6. Margaret Atwood, *Bluebeard's Egg* (London: Virago, 1988), p. 87.
7. Margaret Atwood, *Wilderness Tips* (Toronto: Seal Books, McClelland-Bantam, 1992), p. 137.
8. Margaret Atwood, *Oryx and Crake* (London: Bloomsbury, 2003), p. 295.

9. See Steven Millhauser, *The Knife Thrower and Other Stories* (New York: Vintage, 1999), pp. 134 and 140.
10. See M. Dvorak, "Writing Beyond the Beginning: or, Margaret Atwood's Art of Storytelling," *Commonwealth Essays and Studies* 22.1 (Autumn 1999): pp. 29–36.
11. Mikhail Bakhtin, *The Dialogic Imagination* (Austin: University of Texas Press), 1996.
12. Margaret Atwood, *The Blind Assassin* (New York: Doubleday, 2000), p 201.
13. M. Dvorak, "The Right Hand Writing and the Left Hand Erasing in Margaret Atwood's *The Blind Assassin*," *Commonwealth Essays and Studies* 25.1 (Autumn 2002): pp. 59–68.
14. Linda Hutcheon, *Splitting Images: Contemporary Canadian Ironies* (Toronto: Oxford University Press, 1991), p. 28.
15. Northrop Frye, *Anatomy of Criticism* (London: Penguin, 1990), p. 312.
16. Margaret Atwood, *Surfacing* (London: Virago, 1979), p. 53.
17. M. Dvorak, ed., *Lire Margaret Atwood*: "*The Handmaid's Tale*" (Rennes: Presses Universitaires de Rennes, 1999), p. 20.
18. George Woodcock, "Margaret Atwood: Poet as Novelist," *Critical Essays on Margaret Atwood*, ed. Judith McCombs (Boston: GK Hall, 1988), p. 90.

9

BRANKO GORJUP

Margaret Atwood's poetry and poetics

A poetics of metamorphosis

In his book *The Protean Self*, the renowned American psychologist Robert Jay Lifton describes the contemporary individual as possessing an identity that is "fluid and many-sided . . . [and therefore] appropriate to the restlessness and flux of our time."[1] Like Proteus, the shape-shifting sea-god of Greek mythology, the contemporary individual is understood by Lifton to be engaged in an ongoing process of re-creating the self. While this process "is by no means without confusion and danger," Lifton believes that "it allows for an opening out of individual life, for a self of many possibilities" (*The Protean Self*, p. 5). Margaret Atwood's poetry and poetics make clear that she shares this belief.

Most critics have approached Atwood's work in terms of what Sherrill Grace has described as the aesthetics of "violent duality."[2] They point to a long line of oppositional forces that are laid out in startling contrast throughout Atwood's poetry and her prose. In the discussion of Atwood's poetry that follows here, I suggest that Atwood's poetics of metamorphosis contains this "violent duality" of oppositional forces (civilization and nature, male and female, etc.) but also offers a way of transcending it. I will argue here that Atwood's interest in the transformative power of the imagination, in evidence throughout her poetry, overrides the rigid boundaries of a dualistic universe and allows for the emergence of the protean self described by Lifton.

Space, both physical and psychological, the mapping of the world and of the psyche, is of central importance in Atwood's poetry. Her poems are commonly located in a territory that is *both* the phenomenal world of ordinary experience *and* a mythologized landscape of the imagination. The ordinary, phenomenal world frequently overlaps with an artificial, urban enclosure dominated by a rational, narcissistic, language-driven civilization, and the mythologized, imaginative world overlaps with the primordial Canadian wilderness. These are indeed polar opposites, expressing a "violent duality," but the line of demarcation between the two is also – very importantly for Atwood – a point of contact, an interactive space of engagement where the two may come together, and from which new possibilities for the recreation of the self may emerge.

In this borderline setting, the landscape itself shifts as layers of past and present human history form a moving, multi-layered palimpsest. Images from one zone disappear into the other only to re-emerge as new mutations, new possibilities for the future. In such an imaginative space, self and other, human beings and objects, are events that occupy a location only for a certain period of time; both can change. The poet's role is to write and help us read the possibilities inherent in the palimpsest. She is a determined navigator whose task it is to negotiate the perilous split between subject and object, to reveal the possibility of change, to bridge the gap that was opened in the Western mind by the dualism of Christianity and Platonism.

Atwood's writing, like her landscape, is susceptible to disruptions and dislocations in time. This quality, which disorients the reader, is strongly apparent in the early, frequently anthologized poem "This is a Photograph of Me." Here, instead of using the past tense – or what Susan Strehle calls the "preterite," which has been "the operative mode" for most writing about the past "because it affirms finality, centrality and causality"[3] – Atwood employs the present continuous tense. The poem becomes a space in which multiple traces of the past appear as so many scattered instants rather than as a continuum; the effect is not only to disorient the reader, but also to challenge the idea of necessity or fixedness. Atwood's men and women are frequently portrayed as suspicious of, or confused by, the absence in the world around them of solid references and permanent markers – maps, signs, labels, and so on. But they are just as often skeptical of their own presence, of their usefulness and trustworthiness. Thus, both subject and object, self and other, become provisional; both are open to new interpretations and to change.

It is to this ambiguous, unfolding, and forever evolving inter-zone that Atwood's characters belong. And these characters can be anything from cold-blooded torturers of bodies and souls to the determined healers of wounded and dying cultures and environments. The "characters" most often overlap with the speaker of the poem or are superimposed onto the poem's "you" (who can also be the reader); often they are disembodied. Some remain paralyzed or corrupt, and some attempt themselves to become agents of positive transformation. A new level of awareness strengthens the resolve of these changed characters to make change in the world. They may or may not succeed. Oppositional forces continue their pitched battle; and possibilities for transformation, for the evolution of the protean self and the improvement of the world, also continue.

Atwood's people live in a fluid reality which the ancients knew as metamorphic. Troy falls, Rome rises. Nothing is permanent. This is the gist of Ovid's *Metamorphoses*: characters assume new shapes, and so does the world, as characters and world interact. Like Ovid, Atwood animates her protean world with the imagery of ingestion, transmogrification, and mythological and phantasmagoric shape-shifting. Like Ovid, she gives us a world of mutation that is governed by principles of uncertainty and accident as well as cause and effect. (All is not chance, not everything is a matter of perspective, and our actions have consequences.) Mythology, both Native American and Greco-Roman, is central to Atwood's poetic vision, because myth both recounts and facilitates the process of metamorphosis, turning whatever is local in the imagination into what is universal. Historically, the space-mapping impulse has been at the heart of Canadian writing. Northrop Frye has observed how, in Canadian writing, we frequently see that "man, meaning European man, cannot endure the thought of an environment that was not made primarily for his benefit, or, at any rate, made without reference to his own need to see order in it."[4] Frye shows how this bias for order translates into a cultural fetishism that sees space – the North American wilderness – as void of any meaning prior to the white man's inscription of himself upon its face. "Progressive Insanities of a Pioneer," published in Atwood's second collection, *The Animals in That Country* (1968), dramatizes the primal encounter between the white pioneer and the Canadian wilderness.[5] The representation of nature in this poem – fluid, unconfined, pre-linguistic – is characteristic of a great many other Atwood poems in which the individual attempts either to close or to keep open the gap between subject and object, between the self and the natural world. This poem can be read both as a failed attempt at maintaining that separation and as an unwittingly successful closing of the gap. In being "swallowed" by the green whale of nature, the white settler has metaphorically passed from an "outside" to an "inside" position in relation to his environment. When this spatial metaphor is assigned a cultural/political value, it signifies the de-colonization of the Canadian imaginative space. The either/or condition imposed by the rigid duality of an oppositional mind has been dissolved.

Atwood's pioneer fits perfectly the trope described by Frye: the sense of nature as devouring, the "civilized" man's fear of being swallowed by an unknown space, even as that space is being systematically colonized by the imperial authority under the guidance of the rational mind. While the process of the "discovery" of the unknown – the attempt of the colonizing, rational mind to impose order continues and is being celebrated, ultimately that order breaks down and is disavowed. The wilderness talks back within the psyche of the pioneer through ghostly apparitions, and fear overcomes him. Even as he attempts to impose order, he is disconcerted and threatened by the absence of order. When the unknown presences overwhelm the newcomer's consciousness, the result is catastrophic: "in the end / . . . / the green / vision, the unnamed / whale invaded" (*SP*, p. 63). The rational mind then breaks down into madness. The would-be invader is himself invaded.

The Circle Game

Excluding *Double Persephone*, which appeared as a pamphlet, Atwood has published eleven collections of poetry, including the *Selected Poems*, which appeared in two separate volumes (1976 and 1986). Her first full collection, *The Circle Game* (1966), won the Governor-General's Award. Indeed, her work signaled the emergence of a new vitality in Canadian writing – a change of heart, demanding, as the title poem of this first collection clearly states, that the old colonial mental maps be "erased" (*SP*, p. 24). The speaker of this poem challenges every form of the psyche's insularity, as symbolized by closure and by the repetitive character of a circle game that children play: "We might mistake this / tranced moving for joy / but there is no joy in it" (*SP*, p. 18). The game suggests to the speaker a mechanical activity that allows for no external contact:

> . . . (the grass
> underfoot ignored, the trees
> circling the lawn
> ignored, the lake ignored)
> that the whole point
> for them
> of going round and round
> is (faster / slower)
> going round and round.
> (*SP*, p. 18)

The speaker is issuing a wake-up call to the somnambulist inhabitants of the poem, who are walled in by their own mirrored distortions. She urges them to stumble out into an unprotected, open world, and without fear or paranoia to search for ways of coexisting with the shadows that walk along "these night beaches" (*SP*, p. 18). They should "want the circle / broken" (*SP*, p. 24). Commenting on "The Circle Game," Rosemary Sullivan identifies the poem's fundamental concern: "The rational mind must be integrated with the dark side of the psyche that has been repressed by humanistic ideas of order." To achieve this integration, Sullivan says, Atwood believes the psyche must "enter the wilderness of the self."[6]

The Circle Game introduced into Canadian poetry a new idiom that would be recognized as quintessentially Atwoodian: ironic, direct, unadorned, accessible, emotionally detached, and as precise and pointed as a stiletto. It also introduced Atwood's preoccupation with perception. Is our perception of reality necessarily a gross distortion? How do we see ourselves, others, and the world we inhabit? Do we need clear eyes to see truly? As Atwood suggests in a later poem, "Notes Toward a Poem That Can Never Be Written," it may rather be the case that "The facts of this world seen clearly / are seen through tears"[7] – that is, blurred or seen aslant or seen with the heart.

"This is a Photograph of Me" may serve as a conceptual entrance to the world of *The Circle Game*. The photograph of "me" is the photograph of a landscape: "At first it seems to be / a smeared / print." The photograph itself (like a poem) is an art object, an act of observation that is imaginatively aslant, and the blurring of the landscape on this print makes it possible for "me" to be revealed as its subject, "if you look long enough." The photograph offers a scaled down, partial version of reality – "a small frame house," "a small branch," "a lake," and "some low hills" (*SP*, p. 8) – and at first appears one-dimensional, flat. But the perceiving eye can detect in it other hidden features left by the accumulation of time. The landscape of this poem is not merely a surface beneath which the speaker's image may be discovered; it is an intersection of place and time, subject and object, a palimpsest that includes, among other traces, the memory of the speaker's drowned body. The poem is a portrait of the artist as landscape, of the artist who *enters* landscape.

In many other poems from *The Circle Game* – "A Place: Fragments," "Pre-Amphibian," "The City Planners," "The Explorers," and "The Settlers" – space is constructed as possessing binary attributes. It is at once phenomenal and imaginary, primordial and contemporary, firm and fluid, one-dimensional and cross-sectional, depending on the point of view of the speaker. Each of these poems explores some aspect of a rift between a reality that is structured, orderly, and fixed and a reality that is forever in a state of flux. "The cities are only outposts" (*SP*, p. 41), proclaims the speaker in "A Place: Fragments"; they are only temporary apparitions of permanence. In "The City Planners," she admits, "the houses in pedantic rows, the planted / sanitary trees" offend us with their "transitory lines rigid as wooden borders" (*SP*, p. 11). Yet metamorphosis is present everywhere, visible, alarming, inexorable: "land flows like a / sluggish current, / the mountains eddy slowly towards the sea" (*SP*, p. 41). Borderlines are erased, and edges dissolve before our eyes. In "Pre-Amphibian" time is measured not in years or centuries or millennia but in eons. In "The Explorers" and "The Settlers," Atwood returns to more recent history, but moves with giddy ease back and forth in time: "The explorers will come / in several minutes / and find this island / . . . / but they will be surprised / . . . / at the two skeletons" (*SP*, pp. 44–5). As in so many poems in *The Circle Game*, Atwood challenges the myth of empty lands. Anne McClintock, in her useful examination of the colonial appropriation of so-called "new" lands, says that "'Discovery' is always late. The inaugural scene is never in fact inaugural or originary: something has always gone before."[8] Atwood knows this. She insists upon the precedence of Native people in Canada, challenging our distorting perceptions of reality in this way too. By telescoping geological, evolutionary, and historical time in her visual representations of landscape, the poet takes us into a space that is larger and longer still.

The representation of the landscape as an imaginary space has characterized a good deal of Canadian writing, but no one before Atwood had infused it with such paradigmatic significance. At this early stage of her career, Atwood already employs phenomenal reality as an extended metaphor for the protean self. If our landscape helps to define us, as Canadians have imagined in their search for a sometimes elusive Canadian "identity," it is also we who, for our own psychic purposes, "determine" the landscape and its poetic function.

The Animals in That Country

In *The Animals in That Country* (1968), Atwood continues to explore these aesthetic and thematic concerns. But now she embraces a more contemporary reality and it becomes clear that the poetics of metamorphosis is useful to Atwood when applied to cultural as well as to natural environments. In this volume, as in *The Circle Game*, we find a great deal of shape-shifting and also of voyeurism. Eyes are everywhere in the landscape, sometimes *of* the landscape, hiding behind "a cliff or a cardboard storefront" (*SP*, p. 70), or "watching you from under the water" (*SP*, p. 55). There are also voices, voices of the land, coming from remote places and distant times to inhabit the speaker's landscape. The land is still teeming with presences, unseen by us but active, claiming the same space we occupy, and sending out alarming signals. In "Backdrop Addresses Cowboy," the presence is "what surrounds you: / my brain / scattered with your / tincans, bones, empty shells, / the litter of your invasions. / I am the space you desecrate / as you pass through" (*SP*, p. 71). In *The Animals in That Country*, however, more than in *The Circle Game*, Atwood ventures into spaces created by human beings. These include a tourist office, a subway station, a rooming house, a hospital, a futuristic module, and a pioneer's cabin – and all are governed by the same principle of animation. Each setting is a microcosm of some momentous shift taking place simultaneously in the environment and in the speaker's consciousness. In "Elegy for the Giant Tortoises," a subway station (presumably in Toronto) becomes a stage upon which the speaker projects a vision of a "straggling line" of tortoises marching towards extinction, straight into "the square glass altars / where the brittle gods are kept, / the relics of what we have destroyed" (*SP*, p. 56).

One of the more vivid applications of the poetics of metamorphosis in *The Animals in that Country* involves another photograph, this time of a brain that is "read" in terms of natural imagery. In scanning the photograph, the speaker of "I Was Reading a Scientific Article" sees an entire cosmos. The brain is "an earth," "a seascape / with corals and shining tentacles," "a new planet," "a lost civilization" – and, above all, everything that is still unknown. "My hands trace the contours of a total / universe, its different / colours, flowers, its undiscovered / animals, violent or serene / its other air / its claws / its paradise rivers" (*SP*, p. 72). We find here not simply the old oppositions – "violent or serene" – but metamorphosis, as the photograph of the brain (itself a human artifact) becomes the cosmos when "read" by the imagination. The world disappears into the brain and the brain into the world – and still nothing is over; the process is continuing.

The Journals of Susanna Moodie

The decidedly ironic and detached voice that prevails through *The Circle Game* and *The Animals in That Country* becomes more intimate and immediate in Atwood's third collection, *The Journals of Susanna Moodie* (1970). Here Atwood introduces a fully fleshed-out historical character, one who is familiar as Canada's first significant female immigrant writer. The poetics of metamorphosis, the depiction of the protean self in relativistic space, and questions of perception and duality assume new implications as they are carried over into a recognizably historical Canadian environment. In Susanna Moodie's *Roughing It in the Bush* Atwood sees her own poetic themes at play – as the heroine internalizes the tension between an orderly universe, represented by the civilization she had left, and the chaotic, unpredictable Canadian wilderness she had entered.

"Moodie's personality," Atwood writes in an "Afterword" to the *Journals*, reflects Canada's "paranoid schizophrenia." She is "divided down the middle: she praises the Canadian landscape but accuses it of destroying her . . . She claims to be an ardent Canadian patriot while all the time she is standing back from the country and criticizing it as though she were a detached observer, a stranger." Back in the 1970s, Atwood described this dual response to Canada as typical not only of Moodie's generation but of all subsequent generations, including Atwood's own. "We are all immigrants to this place," Atwood proclaimed, "even if we were born here." Canada is too big and for the most part unknown to its citizens; the result is a feeling of exile and fear. Yet Atwood goes on to say that "this country is something that must be chosen – it is so easy to leave – and if we do choose it we are still choosing a violent duality."[9]

"Two voices / took turns using my eyes," confesses Atwood's Moodie. "One saw through my / bleared and gradually / bleaching eyes, red leaves, / the rituals of seasons and rivers / The other found a dead dog / jubilant with maggots / half-buried among the sweet peas" (*JSM*, p. 104). But Moodie also becomes, precisely because of her double vision, the symbol of a metamorphosed self. Atwood does not suggest that we must opt for the "either/or" condition; we can, as Moodie does – or as Atwood makes her do – struggle to recognize the divided world and make a workable arrangement between the two extremes within ourselves. Only then will we be able to move on to another level of perception, as the unnamed heroine of *Surfacing* succeeds in doing.

The representation of Moodie's life in Canada is structured around a double journey. The first moves forward in time, relying on historical facts, and commenting on what Atwood imagined would have been Moodie's responses to her immigrant experience. The second moves backward in time, into the primordial wilderness, a world yet to be articulated or named. The backward journey enacts a process of metamorphosis, which gradually but inexorably transforms Moodie into the very landscape that she tries, in her forward journey, to dominate or escape. Going deeper into the bush to start a new life as a pioneer is synonymous with entering a "large darkness" (p. 81). Step by step, Moodie is turned into a "green ark" inhabited by the entire natural world. By turning "herself inside out," Moodie assumes, according to Atwood, the status of "the spirit of the land she once hated" (p. 64).

Procedures for Underground

In *Procedures for Underground* (1970), most of the poems revisit familiar ground, with a strong emphasis on the power of the landscape to shape the human psyche. In some poems, there is a darkening of the experience as various characters are literally absorbed by the landscape into its mysterious compendium of presences. In "Cyclops," emblematic of these transactions, the presences are again unseen; but this does not mean that they or the heart's terror are any less real. The speaker's advice to "you" is also familiar: "let your eyes go bare, / swim in their darkness as in a river / do not disguise / yourself in armour" (*SP*, p. 125). Only the inner eye will comprehend the multiple traces in the landscape, in which nothing is ever lost. There are always afterimages, similar to those of the dead young man in "Projected Slide of the Unknown Soldier." The slide itself may be an illusion, but the earth that claims the decomposing body will remain a testimony to his life.

In the title poem of *Procedures for Underground*, Atwood makes extensive use of Native mythology, which is itself predicated on the idea of transformation. The speaker makes a descent into a space inhabited by ancestral voices, but this is a transactional space (both imaginary and phenomenal) in which the living are also present. The poem's underworld is depicted as an inverted ordinary reality – "the earth has a green sun / and the rivers flow backwards" – and the backward journey retraces an evolutionary path through the "tunnels" and "burrows" to "the caves in the sea / guarded by the stone man." As in Greek mythology, this is a dangerous place, yet it is a place of "wisdom and great power" once we know how to "descend and return safely" (*SP*, pp. 22–23).

If there is a deity presiding over such a world, it is not a Christian sky-god hovering over his creation and promising an apocalyptic separation of white and black sheep. Instead we have the Native shape-changer god who is an agent of transformation, a presence within the world that he endlessly destroys and re-creates. In this world the imagination erases temporal boundaries, time is collapsed, and everyone is forever present. This is not a "virgin" land conjured up in the brain of a European colonizer, not an empty place void of memory; rather it overflows with it. This poem evokes the famous lines of Atwood's fellow Canadian poet Al Purdy, in which we are warned not to forget those who "had their being once / and left a place to stand on."[10] If we do forget, Atwood suggests, the dead could get angry – and, as in "Progressive Insanities of a Pioneer," destroy our sanity. At the very least, our capacity for vision will be sorely damaged.

Power Politics and *You Are Happy*

Atwood's writing – especially her fiction – has addressed a remarkable range of urgent social issues, and many of these issues are also addressed in her poetry, particularly in the period starting with the publication of *Power Politics* (1971) and *You Are Happy* (1974). These two collections explore sexual politics in contemporary relationships between men and women and the language through which such relationships are constructed. This exploration, in a well-established Atwoodian manner, draws on the natural imagery of transformation laid out in her earlier poems as well as on popular and classical archetypes. Its field of action is the internalized landscape of a female speaker, one who lives in a reality defined and deformed by the patriarchal mind that sees the world as a battleground for oppositional forces. We enter her psyche's hall of mirrors, and witness her journey through a refracted landscape of distortion, menace, and terror. The synthetic landscape here belongs to the genre of Gothic fiction, in which the soul fears disintegration because of humanity's ability to invent its own terrible monsters.

The violent imagery of *Power Politics* is predicated on the oppression of women by men, as well as on the entrapment of the female within social, cultural, and linguistic constructions. At the heart of this extraordinary sequence is the word "love," which Atwood turns into a frightening mask, hiding predatory intentions. Love is a cover for egotistical self-fulfillment and dominance of the other – in fact, it *creates* and *destroys* the other. On the cover of the first edition there is a harrowing image that is also echoed in the poem "My beautiful wooden leader": the speaker, the entrapped female psyche, the historical woman, is bound upside down, and suspended from the arm of the historical man, a faceless warrior in chain mail. But in her dreams, fantasies, and nightmares, the female speaker creates her *own* victim. Now the victim is the man, locked inside a series of cultural representations that he created, from Superman to Frankenstein to Christ. But this inversion of roles is not straightforward, not a simple, therapeutic revenge. It is rather a profound study of how the female victim ends up internalizing her status as victim, and assuming in recompense the role of victimizer, only to discover its sickening effect and the guilt it produces. The only possible solution to this entrapment is through personal transformation, relying on an inner, imaginative strength. The speaker must deconstruct herself, as the heroine of *Surfacing* does, undertaking a metaphorical journey back in time and into the primordial landscape. This is the same journey that abounds in Atwood's earlier collections, where at journey's end the speaker can begin to "correct" the future *de novo*.

In "Yes at First," the speaker initiates her journey by dismantling the language: "the adjectives / fall away from me." This is followed by a more general disintegration, which creates the condition for her essential self to break free: "I flake apart / layer by / layer down / quietly to the bone, my skull / unfolds to an astounded flower." Again, she is metamorphosed into landscape. The speaker's disavowal of speech is important because it identifies social discourse as a deliberately constructed artifice that is open to re-evaluation and transformation. This will not be an easy task to accomplish, but it is one that must be undertaken: "regrowing the body, learning / speech again," she admits, may take "days and longer" (*SP*, p. 151).

The "Circe/Mud Poems" sequence from *You Are Happy* shifts attention from a psychological to a mythological spatial paradigm. Here Atwood explores the theme of the male fixated on quests, as represented by Odysseus. The reader enters the mythical dimension from the perspective of Circe, the archetypal seductress of Western culture and a notorious agent of metamorphosis, the one who turns men into pigs. Circe finds the whole business of being Circe rather tiring, a monstrous invention of male fantasy. She asks Odysseus: "Don't you ever get tired of saying Onward?" (*SP*, p. 206). She is unimpressed by Odysseus and those like him, "with the heads of eagles." Instead, she looks "for the others, / . . . the ones who escaped from these / mythologies" (*SP*, p. 202). Again, in "Siren Song," from the same collection, Atwood presents a female locked inside the body of a mythological creature, wanting out. Like Circe, this siren is tired of playing the role of lethal enchantress, fed up with "squatting on this island / looking picturesque and mythical." She wants the "boring song" ended; she wants it transformed into a "cry for help" (*SP*, p. 195). The witty parody of metamorphosis that we find in these two volumes does not subvert the crying need for seismic change, or metamorphic upheaval, in the relationships of men and women; indeed, it signals it.

Two-Headed Poems to *Interlunar*

In the next three collections – *The Two-Headed Poems* (1978), *True Stories* (1981), and *Interlunar* (1984) – Atwood continues to explore familiar themes, approaching them from different angles and in new contexts. The question of Canadian identity, for example – previously discussed in terms of geography, archeology, anthropology, history, and so on – is given a sharp political focus in *Two-Headed Poems*. Once again, she directs our attention to what is essential in the Canadian psyche: a doubleness that is represented here in the figure of Siamese twins. Two speaking heads that share the same body reinforce the image of Canada as an imaginative space in which similarities and differences must coexist.

The two voices, representing Canada's French and English founding cultures, speak at times in unison and at times in contradictory terms. Like all Siamese twins, they "dream of separation." The problem of identity in *Two-Headed Poems*, however, is also the problem of communication more generally. "Your language hangs around your neck," the speaker tells the politician, "a noose, a heavy necklace; / each word is empire, / each word is vampire and mother." This is the wrong kind of language, a language of bigotry and betrayal that is sterile, empty, and demeaning: each word "wrinkled / with age, swollen / with other words, with blood, smoothed by the numberless / flesh tongues that have passed across it" (*SP*II, p. 31). What we require instead is language capable of metamorphosis, of fostering social change and growth.

In the next collection, *True Stories* – as in the grim, futuristic novel *The Handmaid's Tale* – the salutary quality of the metamorphic impulse is again transposed into its own parody as Atwood turns her attention to political tyranny. In one of her darkest poems, "Notes Towards a Poem That Can Never Be Written," she targets the complacency of Canadian political culture by dramatizing the horrors of political abuse elsewhere, practiced *now* – literally as we read the poem. While elsewhere individual liberties are suspended, in Canada the individual can do and say what he likes because "it's safe enough" here and because no one "will listen to you anyway." In that other place, people are tortured and murdered, and a woman lies "on the wet cement floor / under the unending light," "dying for the sake of the word" which in a country like Canada has lost its meaning and power.

This poem is partly about writing, about the role of the poet and the power of poetry, and also about the difficulty and necessity of taking useful political action. Her mood is dark: it seems that all we can do for the victims is "to make wreaths of adjectives" and "turn them into statistics & litanies / and into poems like this one." In safe countries, those who care may nevertheless feel paralyzed: "this poem must be written / as if you are already dead, / as if nothing more can be done / or said to save you" (*SP*II, pp. 79–81). But "Notes Towards a Poem That Can Never Be Written" is, of course, paradoxically, a poem of extraordinary power that *has* been written; and this speaks also to the possibility of corrective action. The dark metamorphosis of cultures overtaken by tyranny or complacency can and must be changed again, by word and by deed.

Entering the penultimate collection, *Interlunar*, is like entering a landscape in which the laws of gravity have been abolished, and legend, fable, myth, and pagan rituals prevail. Mystical transformations, extrasensory revelations, and powerful visions are everywhere – and a great struggle is afoot. Madness and death threaten, but the possibility of positive transformation is also present. In the remarkable "Snake Poems" sequence, the human psyche struggles to comprehend this mysterious and feared creature of the earth, whose many representations speak to binary thinking – especially the pernicious disavowal of the body by the mind – and to our vexed relationship to a world that is both good and evil.

In "Psalm to Snake," the snake is both movement and time, a "prophet under a stone," "a voice from the dead," and a "long word, cold-blooded and perfect" (*SP*II, p. 115). Those who can explain snakes, we're told, "can explain anything" (*SP*II, pp. 100–11), including the riddle of the universe, which the snake seems to embody. It slithers throughout our collective unconscious, symbolizing nature, or those parts of it we have not been able to pin down or control. The speaker of "Lesson on Snakes" warns that the snake is not "the devil in [our] garden" – but still we would "batter it / with that hoe or crowbar / to a twist of slack rope" (*SP*II, p, 109). We attempt to kill our fear, but in vain.

In "Quattrocento," the snake holds out the possibility of freedom and love, the fullness of a life that rejects alienation from the body and accepts the inevitability of death. Choosing to eat the apple (also a "heart") offered by the snake, the Eve figure of this poem ceases to be the "idea of a body" and slides down into *her* "body as into hot mud." "Love is choosing, the snake said. / The kingdom of god is within you / because you ate it" (*SP*II, p. 116). Eve is metamorphosed into a true protean self as the whole of a diverse creation disappears into her and she is a free agent now, alive with possibility.

The poem "After Heraclitus," another in the snake series, draws on that Greek philosopher's view of the universe as a place of ceaseless change, where opposites are harmonized through the creative energy symbolized by fire. Here the snake, "one name of God," stands for endless metamorphosis: "All nature is a fire / we burn in and are / renewed, one skin / shed and then another." Again, the snake puts us in contact with the body, and we have two choices: to pray to the snake "for the answers" to our "sickness" or to go "for the shovel" with "old blood on the blade" (*SP*II, pp. 117–18).

Morning in the Burned House

Atwood's most recent collection, *Morning in the Burned House* (1995), is poignantly elegiac and deeply humane. It is also centrally concerned with metamorphosis and with the consolations of the protean self as it confronts mortality. In "Waiting," for example, a poem of great autumnal beauty and comforting wisdom, the reader is invited to enter a twilight zone in which the great duplicitous divide between life and death is no longer alien and terrifying, but familiar – more like "your home, fifty years ago."[11] As we travel through life towards death, we leave behind us emanations, imprints in places to which we may return, catching a glimpse of former selves. And so it will be when we are gone. In the poem "You Come Back," the speaker asks, "What's been going on / while I was away? Who got / those sheets dirty, and why / are there no more grapefruit?" (*MBH*, p. 3) Time and space are a palimpsest on which traces of us remain – and the speaker is a ghost already absorbed into the past and the landscape.

This collection is lit by recurrent fire imagery, most often associated with cleansing and renewal. In "A Fire Place," the speaker muses on scars left by a forest fire: "Earth does such things / to itself : furrowing, cracking apart, bursting / into flame. It rips openings in itself . . ." But "Only we can regret / the perishing of the burned place. / Only we would call it a wound" (pp. 116–17). In the penultimate poem, "Shapechangers in Winter," the metamorphic journey nears its apparent end, as we see "footprints / becoming limestone" (p. 123). But with the title poem, the last of the collection, there is a beautiful assertion of life's renewal by fire, for the speaker is a ghost, "alone and happy" in the "burned house" of the body's death, and it is morning again. Atwood is not reaching here for anything like the Christian consolation of an afterlife that defies the reality of death. Rather, she is placing human life within the larger context of nature and ceaseless change. "Morning in the Burned House" is a great metamorphic gesture through which Atwood dissolves barriers, synthesizes contradictions, resolves paradoxes, and collapses time and space.

The circle in Atwood's poetry is not closed or static. Metamorphosis is ongoing: the snake of life continues to move and shed its skins. And if our own metamorphosis, as individuals and in society, is to be positive, the critical issue for Atwood is that we must learn to reject domination: the devastation of our natural world, the oppression of women, and political tyranny. In Atwood's most recent, profoundly tender volume of poetry, the voice of the poet has metamorphosed into something more personal, less detached, and marvellously brave as she considers the question of mortality. The protean self here meets its final and most intimate challenge. As protean selves alive in an ever-changing world, in which complexities and the speed of change have increased so dramatically, we have nevertheless a responsibility to be fully aware and to act in ways that contribute to positive metamorphosis. Resisting the lure of fundamentalist, rigidly binary thinking, remaining strong moral actors, we must also finally apply our complex understanding of the place of human beings on this planet to the prospect of our own death.

NOTES

1. Robert Jay Lifton, *The Protean Self* (New York: Basic Books, HarperCollins, 1993), p. 9.
2. Sherrill Grace, *Violent Duality: A Study of Margaret Atwood* (Montreal: Véhicule Press, 1980). Throughout her pioneering work in the field of Atwoodian critical scholarship, Grace discusses the aesthetics of oppositional doubleness as it applies to Atwood's prose, poetry, and criticism.

3. Susan Strehle, *Fiction in the Quantum Universe* (Chapel Hill: University of North Carolina Press, 1992), p. 229.
4. Northrop Frye, "Haunted by Lack of Ghosts," *Mythologizing Canada: Essays on the Canadian Literary Imagination*, ed. Branko Gorjup (Ottawa: Legas, 1997), p. 121.
5. Margaret Atwood, *Selected Poems* (Toronto: Oxford University Press, 1976), p. 63.
6. Rosemary Sullivan, *The Oxford Companion to Canadian Literature*, eds. Eugene Benson and William Toy (Toronto: Oxford University Press, 1997), p. 64.
7. Margaret Atwood, *Selected Poems* II: *Poems Selected and New, 1976–1986* (Toronto: Oxford University Press, 1986), p. 81.
8. Anne McClintock, *Imperial Leather* (New York: Routlege, 1995), p. 28.
9. Margaret Atwood, *The Journals of Susanna Moodie* (Toronto: Oxford University Press, 1970), p. 62.
10. Al Purdy, *The Collected Poems of Al Purdy*, ed. Russell Brown (Toronto: McClelland and Stewart, 1989), p. 133.
11. Margaret Atwood, *Morning in the Burned House* (Toronto: McClelland and Stewart, 1995), p. 8.

10

REINGARD M. NISCHIK

Margaret Atwood's short stories and shorter fictions

A repertoire / of untold stories, / a fresh beginning.[1]

Surveying earlier criticism of Margaret Atwood's short fiction, one becomes aware of a seeming critical paradox: Atwood is a major figure on the contemporary literary scene, and is the figurehead of Canadian literature; the short story, in turn, has been hailed by the German critic Helmut Bonheim in 1981 as "the most active ambassador of Canadian literature abroad."[2] Atwood's short stories, nevertheless, have long been passed over in survey works on her writing, have been treated as preparatory exercises, or simply as less important than her major novels and poetry collections.[3] There is indeed always the danger that one branch of a multitalented author's work should languish in relative critical neglect. And there is the additional barrier of an implied genre hierarchy, which, at least in the mind of the general reading public, gives precedence to the novel over other forms of literary expression. Seen from this perspective, the critical fate of Atwood's short fiction for some two decades reflects that of the reception of the genre as a whole. The decade leading to the turn of the century, however, also saw a turn in the reception of Atwood's short fictional prose, with several contributions which either exclusively or in combination with other generic texts by Atwood finally devoted their attention to Atwood's short fiction. From the perspective of teaching, Atwood's short stories have always been a favorite which could perhaps even rival her novels, and rightly so: Atwood's short stories alone would suffice to place her in the forefront of twentieth- (and twenty-first-) century writers. She has thus far published six short fiction collections (between 1977 and 2004), alongside twelve volumes of poetry and eleven novels. Although there are discernible currents and even cross-references linking Atwood's short stories to her poetry and novels,[4] her work in the genre is as free of derivativeness as it is varied. This chapter traces some of its main themes, techniques, and lines of development, taking the prominent theme of gender relations in Atwood's short fiction as its cue.

Short stories

Atwood's exceptional thematic and technical variety is already evident in her debut short story collection, *Dancing Girls* (1977), the individual stories of which were first published between 1964 and 1977. In looking for a common denominator to link these stories, a statement from Atwood's poetry springs to mind: "This is not a debate / but a duet / with two deaf singers" (*Eating Fire*, p. 227) – for these early stories often portray individuals in unfulfilling, dysfunctional, or disintegrating relationships:

> This is an interval, a truce; it can't last, we both know it, there have been too many differences, of opinion we called it but it was more than that, the things that mean safety for him mean danger for me. We've talked too much or not enough: for what we have to say to each other there's no language, we've tried them all . . . We love each other, that's true whatever it means, but we aren't good at it.[5]

In *Dancing Girls*, the characters often confuse their dependence on their partners with love. The stories make clear that dependence is often the result of a character's personality defects or poor self-image – ideal prerequisites for becoming embroiled with an unfulfilling, harmful, and often loveless partner (see e.g. "The Man from Mars," "Polarities," "Under Glass," "Hair Jewellery," "A Travel Piece," "Training," or "Lives of the Poets"). "Ontological insecurity," as Ronald D. Laing puts it in *The Divided Self*, a lack of self-confidence, the feeling of being trapped within the wrong body – such feelings of inadequacy lead many characters in *Dancing Girls* into relationships which only serve to confirm and reconfirm their negative opinions of themselves, whether through their partner's open lack of interest, attitudes of dominance, or sexual betrayal. The stories demonstrate how the failure to come to terms with oneself is inextricably linked to an inability to form meaningful relationships: the protagonists are, ultimately, defeated not by their partners but by themselves.

A number of stories in *Dancing Girls* seem to be ingenious literary reworkings of Ronald D. Laing's *The Divided Self*, a popular psychiatric work of the 1960s. This study presents a theory of the schizoid or schizophrenic personality which Atwood, up to date as always, took up in her writings of the 1960s and 1970s. "Schizo-id" means "almost split"; (neurotic) schizoid behavior therefore constitutes a pre-form of (psychotic) schizophrenia: "The term schizoid refers to an individual the totality of whose experience is split in two main ways: in the first place, there is a rent in his relationship with his world and, in the second, there is a disruption of his relation with himself."[6] Atwood's works examine the grey area between (still "normal") neurosis and (abnormal) psychotic behavior, repeatedly portraying the incursion of the irrational into everyday life or even the descent into a world of madness (cf. "Polarities" 1971, "The War in the Bathroom" 1964, "Under Glass" 1972, and "A Travel Piece" 1975, all in *Dancing Girls*, as well as the novels *The Edible Woman* 1969, *Surfacing* 1972, and *Lady Oracle* 1976). Following the unorthodox, "unpsychiatric" approaches of R. D. Laing, Gregory Bateson, and others, Atwood questions the very concepts of "normality" and "abnormality." Her open-ended stories repeatedly imply that it is the social context which is "sick," and which in its rigorously anti-emotional conformism prevents the normal development of the "wilderness" of the individual psyche, pushing sensitive individuals, most frequently women, over the brink into what is – for these characters – a more acceptable world of madness.

An excellent example of this can be found in Atwood's short story "Polarities," first published in 1971. Morrison, the protagonist, is a classic representation of the schizoid personality. Although he initially seems to fit well enough into his social environment, Atwood's use of a combined authorial and figural narrative allows the reader an insight into his mental world. It becomes obvious that there is a conflict between Morrison's behavior on the one hand and his thoughts and opinions on the other. He often asks Louise questions, ostensibly signaling some kind of interest in her – a tactic which takes her in for large stretches of the narrative. The narrator's comments, however, expose Morrison's emotionally dysfunctional personality: he must confuse Louise with his combination of apparent interest in her on the one hand and distance and coldness on the other, e.g. "'What's finished?' he asked. He hadn't been paying attention" (*DG*, p. 40); "'What aspect?' Morrison asked, not interested" (p. 46). Morrison thus distorts the purpose of questions, using them as a defensive tactic; he wants to prevent any meaningful communication with Louise which might force him to commit himself, paradoxically using questions as a means of maintaining emotional distance. Louise, desperate for certainty and dependent on Morrison in her state of mental crisis, is thus pushed over the brink into a world of madness which she can, after all, control.

Louise's communicative strategies are diametrically opposed to Morrison's. Her statements carry the dialogue forward rather than slowing it down. She expresses emotions and even fear, and her questions communicate a genuine interest in Morrison and a desire for information. The title of the story is thus an accurate reflection of the characters' relationship: activity and passivity, action and reaction, directness and indirectness, openness and dissimulation, initiative and blockage, interest and indifference – these polar opposites constantly clash in the dialogues and narrative, inevitably leading to tragedy. Morrison is able to open himself to Louise, and to come to terms with his feelings, only after she has mentally divorced herself from reality and is no longer in a position to place any demands upon him. Only then does Morrison, in a crisis of his own, become aware of his own psychological inadequacy: "He saw that it was only the hopeless, mad Louise he wanted, the one devoid of any purpose or defence. A sane one, one that could judge him, he would never be able to handle" (p. 62).[7]

As is often the case in Atwood's works, "Polarities" presents the problems of individuals against a national backdrop. It is no coincidence that Louise, who is obsessed by the idea of wholeness, is a bilingual Canadian ("her mother was a French Protestant . . . her father an English Catholic" [p. 60]), now living in Anglo-Canada. Interestingly, during one of Morrison's visits to her sickbed, she falls back into French, cutting him off from her completely. It is, moreover, a typically Atwoodian conceit that Morrison, who thinks in terms of dominance and power, should be an American teaching at a Canadian university (probably the University of Alberta in Edmonton). Atwood is an ardent Canadian nationalist who has often spoken out against the political, economic, and cultural dominance of the USA.[8] The polarity between Canada and the USA can be traced throughout the course of "Polarities," e.g. in Leota's claim that Americans are stealing Canadians' jobs (the question of Americans being employed at Canadian universities was hotly debated in political circles during the 1960s). Atwood also makes use of the USA/Canada dichotomy in stories such as "Hair Jewellery," "Dancing Girls," and "The Resplendent Quetzal" from *Dancing Girls*, or in "Death by Landscape" from *Wilderness Tips*. Finally, "Polarities" also serves to demonstrate the centrality of the (often Canadian) setting of Atwood's texts, which frequently has huge importance for the characters involved (cf. "Death by Landscape"). In "Polarities," external (e.g. climatic) conditions often parallel the characters' mental states, functioning almost as an "objective correlative": external and internal paralysis go hand in hand.

Atwood's second short story collection, *Bluebeard's Egg* (1983), is no longer concerned with schizoid and schizophrenic mental states (although rudimentary traces might still be detectable in Joel in "Uglypuss"; the protagonists of "The Salt Garden" and "The Sunrise" have other pathological problems to contend with, e.g. epileptic fits). In these stories, written in the 1970s and early 1980s, there is a move away from individual psychological problems towards socio-psychological themes. Individuals are seen as a part of their social surroundings, and operating as members of specific groups. It is noteworthy that in Atwood's first collection, characters are often presented in exceptional circumstances, separated from their accustomed social surroundings (for example on journeys, or abroad), reinforcing the rootlessness of these "tourist" characters.[9] In *Bluebeard's Egg*, on the other hand, characters are usually portrayed at home or within their family circle. The collection contains a number of "family stories," such as "Significant Moments in the Life of My Mother," "Unearthing Suite," and "Loulou; or, The Domestic Life of Language," which exude a warmth completely alien to the desperate characters and the dark tone of the earlier stories.[10] Nevertheless, Atwood in this second collection keeps faith with one of her favorite themes: relationships in their terminal stages, partnerships in crisis. In contrast to *Dancing Girls*, however, where stories on these themes are suffused with desperation and hopelessness, the stories of *Bluebeard's Egg* hold out a glimmer of hope, alternative realities, which provide a source of comfort for the (usually female) protagonists in their times of crisis – not solving their problems, but at least rendering them more tolerable.

The contrasts outlined between Atwood's first and second short story collections could be clearly illustrated by a comparison of "The Resplendent Quetzal" (1977) from *Dancing Girls* and "Scarlet Ibis" from the later collection, a comparison which would be particularly appropriate given the strong thematic similarities between the two stories. For reasons of space, only "Scarlet Ibis" can be dealt with here.

"Scarlet Ibis," first published in 1983, presents a marital relationship which is drained of life and of any hint of joy. The spouses, Christine and Don, travel on holiday to Trinidad with their youngest, four-year-old daughter, Lilian, in the hope of finding new impulses for their bleak existence. The trip ostensibly fails in its purpose: Don and Lilian complain about everything, even about the activities Christine proposes for them. Christine, the focus of the story, is repeatedly rejected by her exhausted, overworked husband. The two seem unable to communicate on a level of any profundity, even during the climax of the holiday, a boat-trip to a bird reserve. Conflicts are not aired, but are transplanted into imaginary worlds. Christine's internal monologues replace dialogues between her and her husband. She constantly withdraws from the threat of reality by fleeing into a world of the imagination, for example when she imagines her (not very rosy) future with Don. Correspondingly, the story contains a high number of modal verbs and adverbs, conditional forms, and *if* and *as if* clauses: "*Maybe* he *would, maybe* he *wouldn't*. *Maybe* he *would* say he was coming on with a headache. *Maybe* she *would* find herself walking on nothing, because *maybe* there was nothing there" (*BE*, p. 186; my italics). The imaginary alternative world thus exists parallel to the real world of experience, and appears at times to have a greater reality for Christine, as it is mentally more present and holds out more hope. The alternate reality provides relief from the drudgery of married life, but can offer no real hope of escape from the misery of the real world. This comes to a head during the climactic sighting of the rare tropical birds:

> She felt she was looking at a picture, of exotic flowers or of red fruit growing on trees, evenly spaced, like the fruit in the gardens of mediaeval paintings . . . On the other side of the fence was another world, not real but at the same time more real than the one on this side, the men and women in their flimsy clothes and aging bodies. (p. 199)

This short, epiphanic experience of remarkable beauty and freedom, which for a short time even leads to a rapprochement between Don and Christine, and briefly awakens in her a feeling of existential security ("Don took hold of Christine's hand, a thing he had not done for some time . . . Christine felt the two hands holding her own, mooring her, one on either side" [pp. 199–200]), is retrospectively trivialized by Christine, reduced to a "form of entertainment, like the Grand Canyon: something that really ought to be seen" (p. 201). Brought back down to earth in this way, even the alternative realities can provide no relief for Christine, serving only to increase her existential insecurity and immobility. By conforming to expectations and ignoring her own emotional needs, she prevents change: "She tried to think of some other distraction, mostly for the sake of Don" (p. 182). Untold stories, no fresh beginnings.

When Margaret Atwood's third short story collection, *Wilderness Tips*, was published in 1991, it was given the kind of reception – not only in Canada, but also abroad – usually reserved for the author's novels.[11] In these stories, written in the 1980s, the "untold stories" in the protagonists' lives come to the surface more often. The characters admit their existential needs more readily, both to themselves and to others, and have a greater ability to transcend catastrophes in their lives, achieving at least the suggestion of a "fresh beginning." The collection moves away from the family-oriented stories of *Bluebeard's Egg*, often presenting characters at the workplace. In "Hairball" and "Uncles," we see talented women who have worked their way up the career ladder in the face of the resentment and envy of male colleagues who cannot accept a woman in high places.

In "Hairball," the opposition of money- and power-mad colleagues to Kat, a calculating, career-oriented fashion designer, leads her lover – in a way her pupil and her "creation" – to dethrone his mentor in a coup d'état while she is undergoing an operation. Nonetheless, this betrayal, so bitter because it is both personal and professional, does not lead, as it might well have done in *Dancing Girls*, to the victim's retreat into denial (or an escape into severe illness), but rather to a symbolic act of revenge. This retaliation cannot make good the harm that she has already suffered, but by accepting her pain, by realizing how unhappy her work-oriented life is, and by meeting an outrageous act with an outrageous act of her own, Kat is preparing herself psychologically for a fresh beginning; the story ends like this: "She has done an outrageous thing, but she doesn't feel guilty. She feels light and peaceful and filled with charity, and temporarily without a name" (*WT*, p. 56). In *Wilderness Tips*, women at times appear as victims of very subtle gender discrimination. They now refuse, however, to participate in their subjugation and domination, rising up and transforming previously "untold stories" into (symbolically encoded) spoken texts.

A number of stories in *Wilderness Tips* are narrated retrospectively, demonstrating on the one hand how experiences from the past are reinterpreted in retrospect, and on the other how formative they can be. "Death by Landscape" contains also an innovation within Atwood's short prose (cf. also her novel *Cat's Eye*, 1988), placing gender problems for the first time in a same-sex context which goes beyond the mother–daughter and father–son relationships the author had hitherto examined. In this story, the tentative friendship which for several years links the Canadian schoolgirl Lois with the American girl Lucy, turns out in retrospect to carry more emotional power than any of her subsequent relationships, including that with her husband, Rob. The lasting bond which links Lucy to Lois is strengthened by Lucy's mysterious, unsolved disappearance into the Canadian wilderness. After the death of her husband, Lois reviews her life up to that point, recognizing that it has taken two paths: as is often the case in Atwood's writing, an "official" life which Lois has lived physically, and an "unofficial" inner life of the mind. In this story, however, the "untold story" develops into the conscious, dominant path:

> She can hardly remember getting married, or what Rob looked like. Even at the time she never felt she was paying full attention. She was tired a lot, as if she was living not one life but two: her own, and another, shadowy life that hovered around her and would not let itself be realized – the life of what would have happened if Lucy had not stepped sideways, and disappeared from time.
> (*WT*, pp. 127–28)

Here (as in "Weight" in the same collection), the gender conflicts found in many early stories are reduced in their importance by the fact that for the female protagonists, their emotional and (in "Weight") intellectual friendships with other women turn out to be the deepest, most personal, and most formative. Man–woman relationships, on the other hand, are marked too strongly by conventional gender patterns (not to say rituals) of behavior, and seem rather to get in the way of the women's development.

It becomes clear in examining the configuration of relationships in *Wilderness Tips* that Atwood has come full circle in comparison with her earliest collection: in the later stories, in contrast to her first ones, Atwood presents profound partnerships between kindred spirits who are so closely linked they do not even need physical closeness, and yet are far away from the claustrophobic relationships of dependency portrayed in earlier volumes. In *Wilderness Tips*, these profound relationships overcome not only physical distance, but also marriages to another partner, even outliving the death of one of the partners in the mind of the other (e.g. in "Isis in Darkness" or "The Age of Lead"). These relationships are, however, rarely enjoyed in a conventional sense. The characters always recognize their importance too late, and do so only tacitly; the death of one of the partners, or their idiosyncratic fears, always represent insuperable hindrances.

"Death by Landscape" and "Hairball" from *Wilderness Tips* are good examples of Atwood's often firmly Canadian perspective: the huge expanses of the Canadian landscape, its unexplored wildernesses, which, particularly in "Death by Landscape," make nature into a "protagonist" with a profound effect on the plot; the importance in the story of landscape painting, particularly that of the Canadian Group of Seven; the contrasting of Canada and the USA; the canoe trips and summer camps in "Death by Landscape" (and in "True Trash"); the contrasting of Canada and Britain in "Hairball"; the historical examination of a curious piece of Canadian exploration lore (the failed Franklin expedition to the Arctic in the nineteenth century) in "The Age of Lead," combined with the contemporary ecological problems which affect Canada so profoundly, not least due to its geographical proximity to the USA; the theme of immigration in "Wilderness Tips"; contemporary Canadian political problems in "Hack Wednesday" – these and other motifs in *Wilderness Tips* (whose stories are nearly all set in Canada) demonstrate how "Canadian" a writer Margaret Atwood is, in spite of her cosmopolitanism. As well as dealing with supranational themes, such as gender relations, she also conveys specifically Canadian characteristics to an international audience.

Shorter fictions

Since the 1980s, Atwood has employed a new text format for her challenging explorations and rewritings, a type of short text which is hard to classify and has few genuine ancestors in Canadian literature. Works in these hybrid genres appeared in *Murder in the Dark: Short Fictions and Prose Poems* (1983), *Good Bones* (1992), and *Bottle* (2004).[12] Due to the challenging originality of their form and modes of representation these pieces of short prose and prose poetry were neglected by critics for a long time. It has now been recognized, however, that with these collections Atwood introduced a hitherto unfamiliar genre into Anglo-Canadian literature, the Baudelairean prose poem, and that, additionally, the short texts in these collections constitute a radical, "postmodern" contribution to the development of genre hybridization.[13] A closer evaluation of many of the texts in these volumes reveals Atwood's literary art at work in the smallest of spaces. The highly intertextual nature of these works creates networks of meaning and significance despite their limited scope, going frequently hand in hand with what I have described as

> Atwood's "poetics of inversion": her technique of undermining conventional thought patterns, attitudes, values, or textual norms by turning them on their heads. The result is a multifaceted interplay between explicit and implicit meaning or, to put it another way, a prismatic multiplication of sense. Since this technique is used in a very restricted space, it almost inevitably results in strongly delineated, suggestive, and highly intensified representations, thus providing a possible explanation for the satirical and parodic tendencies discernible in many of the texts. (Nischik, "Murder in the Dark," p. 6)

The tremendous structural and technical variety of Atwood's short fiction can particularly be seen in these three collections in which Atwood explodes the boundaries of the (short) short story genre. Although these volumes contain pieces which clearly operate within the parameters of the genre, it would be inaccurate to describe them simply as short short story (or, see above, prose poetry) collections: mini essays, "essay-fictions," short dialogues, dramatic monologues, and reflections are among the various "genres" they contain. Atwood's commentators have yet to discover an appropriate collective critical term for these highly varied short texts.

Atwood's prose poem "Men at Sea"[14] is a striking example of Atwood's often gender-oriented intertextual dialogue with pieces of world literature, here Charles Baudelaire's poem "L'Homme et la mer," from *Les Fleurs du mal* (*The Flowers of Evil*, pp. 21–22). In Baudelaire's text, the relationship between man(kind) and the sea is raised to a mythological level, with the sea portrayed as a mirror of the soul or of the subconscious, "its eternal billows surging without end" (p. 21). Just as the wild, untamable depths of the sea remain unfathomable, so the soul of self-obsessed man remains darkly brooding: "You plunge with joy into this image of your own . . . no one has mapped your chasm's hidden floor" (p. 22). In Baudelaire's poem, the unfathomableness of the "inner sanctum" is metaphorically intentionalized: "no one knows your inmost riches, for / Your jealousy hides secrets none can repeat" (p. 21). The poem also suggests a typically Baudelairean treatment of gender relations, provoked by the double meaning in French of *l'homme* (meaning both "man" and "mankind") and by the homonyms *la mer*/sea and *la mère*/mother. The female, then, is presented as a passive and expressionless, yet mysteriously fascinating object in which man is reflected, and into which he projects his desires. In the closing part of the poem, the meaning of *l'homme* is indeed narrowed down to the sense of "man" ("oh, relentless brothers!", p. 22), and the relationship between man and the sea becomes, in a stylized way, the ultimate expression of danger and adventure: "You two have fought without pity or remorse, both / From sheer love of the slaughter and of death" (p. 22).

In the prose poem "Men at Sea," a rewriting of Baudelaire's "L'Homme et la mer," Atwood magisterially deconstructs the self-centered heroic machismo of her Baudelairean intertext, and her revision ruthlessly exposes the gender stereotyping which had, in the pre-text, merely been hinted at subtextually. Her inverse portrayal of the fundamental relationships presented by "L'Homme et la mer" is crystallized in her minimalist, yet radical modification of the poem's title, "Men at Sea," in the closing line. Through the enervatingly simple addition of a comma – "Men, at sea" – the title takes on completely new connotations: heroic, virile seafarers are reduced, by means of this compressed linguistic manipulation, to a state of insecurity and helplessness. This male insecurity is a result of the female perspective from which "Men at Sea" is written, and which promotes woman, who had been completely neutralized in "L'Homme et la mer," to the same level as Baudelaire's brooding, self-centered, introverted male heroes. In doing so, Atwood employs clichés just as Baudelaire does – yet intentionally and ironically.

Atwood's text, then, begins with a subject which Baudelaire had ignored: "You can come to the end of talking, about women, talking" suggests, ambivalently, that women talk about all sorts of things with various degrees of definiteness, but especially "about what they feel" (*GB*, p. 71). Darkly brooding male profundity, on the other hand, is initially supplanted in Atwood's text by an energetic male desire for action for its own sake. Nevertheless, neither man's need for emotional compensation ("to drain the inner swamp") nor the unpredictability of gender relations ("and above all no women. Women are replaced by water, by wind, by the ocean, shifting and treacherous; a man has to know what to do") are lost from sight. In this hyperbolically caricatured world of adventure, where men assert themselves only through their physicality ("a narrowing of the eyes, sizing the bastard up before the pounce, the knife to the gut . . . all teeth grit, all muscles bulge together"), there is no place for women, not even in their supposedly favorite occupation: "out here it's what he said to him, or didn't say" (p. 72).

The ending, with its more realistic restaurant setting, reverts to the start of the text. The one-sidedness of the male narration, with its concentration on action and its rejection of emotion, is countered by: "She says: But what did you feel?" The reaction to the question at first mirrors Baudelaire ("Your jealousy hides secrets none can repeat," *The Flowers of Evil*, p. 22, versus "never give yourself away" [*GB*, p. 73]). Atwood's inverse intertextual counter-representation, however, not only highlights the weaknesses of the myth of male virility, with its suppression of emotion – it also makes clear how fundamentally false the myth is: "They're all around her . . . one per woman per table. Men, at sea" (p. 73).

Whereas "Men at Sea" is mainly concerned with the (self-)conception and representation of men, "The Little Red Hen Tells All" (1992; from *Good Bones*) is an outstanding example of Atwood's gender revisionism concerning the representation of women. It again demonstrates her ability to weld two versions of a story together in the smallest of spaces, creating a new complexity which opens up significant new vistas of meaning in the individual versions. In the case of this wonderful short short story, we once again have before us an "official," conventional version, and an "unofficial" version of a story. In this parable-like tale, however, the differences between the two versions are openly explored and, so to speak, made public. This short text is also an example of Atwood's recurring revisionist use of received stories, i.e. folkloristic popular culture texts such as fairy tales or myths. Atwood rewrites these stories, turning them inside out and upside down, placing them in new contexts, and undermining conventional thought patterns and textual norms, especially the gender portrayals perpetuated by such formative popular tales. The result is a typically Atwoodian mixture of themes and motifs taken from popular literature imaginatively juxtaposed with their intellectual significance in an often witty and humorous way. The resulting combination of approachable textual structures, funny impact, and impressive intellectual strength is an important reason for Atwood's appeal to a broad readership.

"The Little Red Hen Tells All" is based on a popular tale familiar to many children (and adults) in the English-speaking world. The basic structures of this fable are reproduced in Atwood's rewriting, supplemented by the author's imaginative amplifications and ambivalent word play (e.g. "A grain of wheat saved is a grain of wheat earned," *GB*, p. 12), as well as her precisely integrated comments on the plot, which with apparent casualness expose the popular tale's intellectual implications – for example the ideology which supports a capitalist economic system concerned only with production and the maximization of profits: "Sobriety and elbow-grease. Do it yourself. Then invest your capital. Then collect" (p. 11).

Atwood's most important reinterpretation in this story concerns, however, gender difference. By highlighting the gender of the female "narrator," Atwood brings to light the ideological impact of the tale, both in its original and its new version. The gender roles in the original folk tale (which is often passed on orally from mothers to their children) are on closer inspection somewhat strangely conceived. The egocentric, hoarding, greedy behavior (*"I'll eat it myself, so kiss off"* [p. 13]) does not comply with the typical female image, which tends to revolve around nourishment and generosity; it resembles rather the typical behavior of a "rooster." Atwood further develops the conventional story by sarcastically and parodically reconciling this behavior with that traditionally associated with "feminine" qualities. The conflict is thus transferred from the external to the internal: because of her gender-specific socialization, the "hen" acts contrary to her own interests and needs, in a way that is very much in favor of the "common good," but verges on self-denial for the hard-working hen. The capitalist ideology of the folk tale is modified in Atwood's retelling through a foregrounding of gender difference. Atwood makes clear the pitfalls of gender differentiation, to which the "hens" fall victim far more often than the "roosters." The fact that women's self image, propagated by gender-specific socialization and social context, is one of the main causes of this, is also demonstrated by this apparently humorous story: "The Little Red Hen," in fact, "is horrible fun."[15]

Something similar might be said about Atwood's short text "Gertrude Talks Back" (*GB*, pp. 15–18), in which she applies her technique of gender-oriented revisioning irreverently to one of the greatest works of world literature, Shakespeare's *Hamlet*. More than any of Shakespeare's other plays, this drama concentrates on the figure of its protagonist: Hamlet *fils* speaks more than half the text – in dialogues as well as in numerous monologues and asides. The figure of Hamlet, therefore, provides the perspective through which we view the action, as well as being the focus of our sympathies. This takes place at the expense of the drama's female characters: Ophelia, Hamlet's platonic lover, and even more Gertrude, his mother. She rarely speaks, and when she does so, says little, even in the famous "closet scene" with Hamlet (III. 4).

In her revisionist short dramatic monologue "Gertrude Talks Back," Atwood rewrites Shakespeare's plot, promoting Gertrude to a position of prominence, making her the title figure, and giving her freedom of speech – to such an extent that she now indeed embarks on a monologue, reducing her son and supposed dialogue partner Hamlet to passive silence: we can only infer his reactions from what Gertrude says in her monologue. Apart from this drastic reversal in the basic speech situation, Atwood also takes various other aspects of the Shakespearean pre-text and parodically inverts them in the smallest of spaces. Whereas Gertrude in the original Shakespeare text is submissive, addressing her royal husband (appropriately for the period) as "my lord," in Atwood's revised version she speaks with considerable self-confidence about her two husbands, Hamlet *père* and Claudius. She brands the fact that Hamlet should have been named after his father as selfish ("I wanted to call you George" [p. 15]). Hamlet's long, resentful lecturing of Gertrude in the original, in which he compares Claudius unfavorably to his father (III. 4. 182), is rejected by Atwood in favor of Gertrude's version of the story. In doing so, Atwood modernizes Shakespeare's play, revising the representation of Gertrude and Ophelia as passive sexual adjuncts to the male figures, representations which complied with the sexual morality of the time. Hamlet's use of sexual innuendo when speaking to Ophelia – which he uses simultaneously to attract and reject her (cf. her madness and suicide) – similarly, yet conflictingly, demonstrates male control and definition of female gender roles in the original intertext.

Atwood's modernized Gertrude strongly rejects such gender inconsistencies, openly acknowledging that Hamlet *père* was a failure in bed who could not fulfill her sexual desires (cf. I. 5. 42, 45–50). She also rejects the male restriction of female sexuality to youthful women; indeed, the older Gertrude seems much more sexually at ease than her son: "I must say you're an awful prig sometimes. Just like your Dad. *The Flesh*, he'd say. You'd think it was dog dirt. You can excuse that in a young person, they are always so intolerant, but in someone his age it was getting, well, very hard to live with, and that's the understatement of the year" (p. 17). The manner in which Atwood's Gertrude dismisses Hamlet *père* on account of such sexual deficiencies, while upgrading the "energetic" Claudius for equally sexual reasons, not only serves as justification for Gertrude's remarriage (an act which is not so clearly motivated in Shakespeare's *Hamlet*), but also upgrades female sexuality, which had previously been reduced to passivity, and places it in the center of attention. Atwood gives this inversion a final twist when the sexually oriented Gertrude at the end of the text openly acknowledges, in the ultimate daring inversion: "It [the murderer of Hamlet *père*] wasn't Claudius, darling. It was me" (p. 18). Atwood's Gertrude, then, openly proclaims her guilt, whereas Shakespeare's character relies on displacement strategies, repressing her emotions; she contradicts, defends, and justifies herself, whereas the original Gertrude, even when under fire from Hamlet's patriarchally declaimed accusations in the "closet scene," remains silent; Atwood's Gertrude has a zest for living and robust self-confidence; she is concerned mainly (but not only, if we consider her remarks about the difficulties Hamlet's name bring him) with her own needs, and without beating about the bush accepts responsibility for her own actions. She represents, then, the modernized polar opposite of Shakespeare's Gertrude. Atwood's Gertrude, whose conception has many similarities to the protagonists of Atwood's novels *The Robber Bride* (1993) and *Alias Grace* (1996), is, cleverly so, not the "better" Gertrude. She is, however, the freer, more self-determined Gertrude, who fits better into a century in which a woman's self-image no longer depends on how she sees herself mirrored by men, but where she can look in the mirror herself – and can be satisfied with what she sees. To that extent, this "talking back" by an inversely conceived Gertrude almost four hundred years after the fact is an appropriate and necessary riposte to Hamlet's "frailty, thy name is woman!" (I. 2. 146).

It could be argued that in the course of decades Atwood's treatment of gender issues in her short fiction has by and large developed according to the various stages of "victim positions" she differentiated early on in *Surfacing* (1972). Especially in *Murder in the Dark* and in *Good Bones* her often inverse views on gender conceptions have become even more incisive, perceptive, challenging, and demanding, not losing sight, though, of an apparently lighthearted, humorous treatment of a complex issue. She exposes with penetrating insight the often gender-linked conventions and psychological, linguistic, and mythological substructures which are embedded in daily reality. If, as Atwood sees it, human beings tend to transform threatening and irrational elements of their environment into rationally comprehensible ones, then it is the task of the writer to counter this move towards the conventional. Seen *in toto*, her treatment of gender relations in her short stories and shorter fictions may in the final analysis be read as "Instructions for the Third Eye," to take up the title of the resonant rounding-off text of *Murder in the Dark*. Atwood admonishes us, female and male readers, to transcend the dualistic thought pattern of either/or, which chains us into fixed identity positions and gender roles, and to be open towards liberating, non-essentialist views of gender relations.

Her short stories and short fictions are remarkable both in their thematic variety, their tremendous intellectual astuteness, and in their almost uniformly high literary quality. Although this treatment of Atwood's short fiction has hinged on gender issues, it might also have examined, for example, environmental or multicultural aspects of Atwood's short fiction, or studied the importance of language in these works for the perception and construction of reality. What should be emphasized, however, is the outstanding quality and significance of Atwood's work in this critically still somewhat neglected genre. In her short fiction in particular, she acts as a chronicler of our times, exposing and warning, disturbing and comforting, opening up chasms of meaning as soon as she closes them, and challenging us to question conventions and face up to hitherto unarticulated truths.

NOTES

1. Margaret Atwood, "The Paper Bag" (from *Two-Headed Poems*) in *Eating Fire: Selected Poetry 1965–1995* (London: Virago, 1998), p. 199.
2. Helmut Bonheim, "Topoi of the Canadian Short Story," *Dalhousie Review* 60 (1980–81): p. 659.
3. See e.g. B. H. Rigney, *Margaret Atwood* (London: Macmillan, 1987), pp. 108–09, where "A Travel Piece" (1975) from *Dancing Girls* is interpreted as a thematic pre-form of *Bodily Harm* (1981). The little attention given to Atwood's short fiction in P. Cuder, *Margaret Atwood* (London: Hodder and Stoughton, 2003) in what claims to be an overview of Atwood's œuvre is symptomatic.
4. See Lee Briscoe Thompson, "Minuets and Madness: Margaret Atwood's *Dancing Girls*," *The Art of Margaret Atwood: Essays in Criticism*, eds. Arnold E. and Cathy N. Davidson (Toronto: Anansi, 1981), pp. 107–22; Charlotte Sturgess, "Margaret Atwood's Short Fiction,' *Margaret Atwood: Works and Impact*, ed. Reingard M. Nischik (Rochester, NY: Camden House, 2000), pp. 87–96; Sharon R. Wilson, "Fiction Flashes: Genre and Intertexts in *Good Bones*," and Reingard M. Nischik, "Murder in the Dark: Margaret Atwood's Inverse Poetics of Intertextual Minuteness," *Margaret Atwood's Textual Assassinations: Recent Poetry and Fiction*, ed. Sharon R. Wilson (Columbus: Ohio State University Press, 2003), pp. 18–41, 1–17 respectively.
5. Margaret Atwood, "The Grave of the Famous Poet" (1972), in *Dancing Girls and Other Stories* (Toronto: McClelland & Stewart/Bantam-Seal, 1977), p. 84.
6. R. D. Laing, *The Divided Self: An Existential Study in Sanity and Madness* (Harmondsworth: Penguin, 1965), p. 17.
7. For a more detailed analysis of the polarities in the communication structure and of Morrison's frequent indirect speech acts, see R. M. Nischik, "Speech Act Theory, Speech Acts, and the Analysis of Fiction," *Modern Language Review* 88.2 (April 1993): pp. 297–306.
8. Paul Goetsch, "Margaret Atwood: A Canadian Nationalist, *Margaret Atwood*, ed. Nischik, pp. 166–79.
9. Cf. the classic statement on this in Atwood's short story "A Travel Piece": "for those who are not responsible, for those who make the lives of others their transient spectacle and pleasure. She is a professional tourist, she works at being pleased and not participating; at sitting and watching" (*DG*, p. 152).
10. Margaret Atwood, *Bluebeard's Egg* (Toronto: McClelland and Stewart, 1983).
11. Margaret Atwood, *Wilderness Tips* (Toronto: McClelland and Stewart, 1991).
12. The nine (very) short texts published in *Bottle* (Hay: Hay Festival Press) in 2004 will not be considered here in any detail since, according to a correspondence with Atwood of June 11 and 14 2004, it appeared in a limited edition of 1,000 copies as a fundraiser for the Hay Festival in Wales. "The short fictions in it will be incorporated into a longer book of them . . . which will probably . . . appear in Fall 2005."
13. For a more elaborate treatment of these issues, several analyses of texts from *Murder in the Dark*, and further bibliographical references, see Nischik, "Murder

in the Dark," *Margaret Atwood's Textual Assassinations*, ed. Wilson, where the argument of this paragraph was first presented.

14. Margaret Atwood, *Good Bones* (Toronto: Coach House Press, 1992), pp. 71–73, previously published in "New Poems" in *Selected Poems* II*: Poems Selected and New, 1976–1986* (Toronto: Oxford University Press, 1986). The following quotations from Baudelaire in English are from *The Flowers of Evil*, selected and translated by Marthiel and Jackson Mathews (New York: New Directions, 1963).
15. Atwood speaking about her dystopian novel *The Handmaid's Tale* in an interview with Katherine Govier, "Margaret Atwood: There is Nothing in the Book that Hasn't Already Happened," *Quill & Quire* 51.9 (September 1985): pp. 66–67.

11

CORAL ANN HOWELLS

Margaret Atwood's dystopian visions: *The Handmaid's Tale* and *Oryx and Crake*

All fictions begin with the question *What if*. The *what if* varies from book to book . . . but there is always a *what if*, to which the novel is the answer.[1]

Atwood's hypothesis about narrative beginnings assumes a particular urgency in relation to her two near-future novels, *The Handmaid's Tale* (1985) and *Oryx and Crake* (2003), for both of them are an imaginative writer's response to contemporary situations of cultural crisis as they suppose what *may* happen at what Atwood has called "definitive moments" after which "things were never the same again."[2] Already the shifts between past, present, and future in my opening remarks will have illustrated the distinctive qualities of the genre to which these two novels belong, namely the dystopia. Perhaps the primary function of a dystopia is to send out danger signals to its readers: "Many dystopias are self-consciously warnings. A warning implies that choice, and therefore hope, are still possible."[3] This chapter will focus on Atwood's two dystopian novels, their narrators and narrative techniques, arguing that together they represent a synthesis of her political, social, and environmental concerns transformed into speculative fiction. They are embedded in very different historical contexts: *The Handmaid's Tale* is a product of the 1980s, focusing on the possible consequences of neo-conservative religious and political trends in the United States, while *Oryx and Crake* written at the beginning of the twenty-first century projects not a national disaster but a global catastrophe "in a world that has become one vast uncontrolled experiment."[4] Yet in many ways *Oryx and Crake* might be seen as a sequel to *The Handmaid's Tale*. The pollution and environmental destruction which threatened one region of North America in the earlier novel have escalated into worldwide climate change through global warming in the latter, and the late twentieth-century Western trend towards mass consumerism which Gilead tried to reverse by its fundamentalist doctrines and its liturgy of "moral values" has resulted in an American lifestyle of consumerist decadence in a high-tech world which is ultimately death-doomed by one man's megalomaniac project of bioterrorism. While Atwood was writing about a fictional catastrophe on the east coast of the United

States in 2001, a real one occurred with the September 11 attack on the World Trade Center in New York, enhancing the eerily predictive quality of her dystopian visions.[5]

I shall position these two novels within broader concepts of the dystopian genre though noting that Atwood has resisted the ghetto of science fiction, insisting that she writes "speculative fiction" which rehearses possible futures on the basis of historical and contemporary evidence. Though these two texts share common generic features (failed utopian visions, counter-narratives of resistance to a new prevailing order, survivors' stories and open endings) it will be the differences between them on which I shall focus my analyses. The major differences are in the situations and genders of the two main protagonists, and I shall draw out the implications of this. The Handmaid Offred is imprisoned in a domestic disaster situation where she is always aware of a world beyond Gilead and hopes for a different future as she addresses her putative audience, whereas *Oryx and Crake* shifts the emphasis to a world ruined by global warming and pollution in a Last Man narrative told by a character called Snowman where no alternative frame of reference is available, until the shock ending. The strange title of the novel signals this change, for both Oryx and Crake are dead when the story begins. These are the names (or rather the pseudonymns) of Snowman's lover and his best friend who is the hero-villain of the book. Disturbingly, they are the names of extinct species taken from a video game, Extinctathon, so that death hangs over the novel from the start. Snowman's storytelling role is divided between his public mythmaking for the Crakers and his private monologue – addressed to whom? "Any reader he can possibly imagine is in the past" (*O&C*, p. 46). An early manuscript version includes the sentence, "Dear Oryx, this is for you," and though this is omitted in the published version, Snowman's narrative compulsion remains.[6]

Returning to the generative principle of dystopias (and of utopias too, for as Atwood has frequently pointed out, they are two sides of the same fictional coin), the hypothetical situations are very different in these two novels. Of *The Handmaid's Tale* Atwood asked: "Or *what if* you wanted to take over the US and set up a totalitarian government, the lust for power being what it is? How would you go about it?" ("Writing Utopia," p. 91). Here the explosive conjunction of elements include widespread environmental catastrophe, high incidences of infertility, the rise of right-wing Christian fundamentalism as a political force, and deep hostility to the post 1960s feminist movement. Nearly twenty years later, Atwood registers a different aspect of popular anxieties with her concerns about the biosphere and advances in the biological sciences: "The *what if* of *Oryx and Crake* is simply, *What if we continue down the road we're already on? How slippery is the slope? What are our saving graces? Who's got the will to stop us?"* ("Writing *Oryx and Crake*," p. 323).

Both novels are set in the near future in the United States, with *The Handmaid's Tale* scenario occurring around 2005 and that of *Oryx and Crake* around 2025. (The protagonists' birth dates and ages offer clues to the reader: Offred is 33 when she becomes a Handmaid and she must have been born some time in the 1970s; Snowman is 28 and was born around 1996, though Atwood is deliberately unspecific about precise dates for her dystopias.)[7] On reasons for her choice of the United States, her answer to this question after writing *The Handmaid's Tale* might also serve for *Oryx and Crake*: "The States are more extreme in everything . . . It's also true that everyone watches the States to see what the country is doing and might be doing ten or fifteen years from now."[8] For *Oryx and Crake* there is a more sinister suggestion made by Bill McKibben: "The fight [for and against germline genetic engineering] is already underway, around the world and especially in the United States."[9] Clearly, they are very different kinds of dystopian vision, and either one precludes the other. *The Handmaid's Tale*, centered on human rights abuses and particularly the oppression of women under a fundamentalist regime, is entirely social and political in its agenda, whereas *Oryx and Crake* projects a world defamiliarized not through military or state power but through the abuse of scientific knowledge, where genetic engineering has created transgenic monsters and humanoid creatures in a post-apocalyptic scenario much closer to conventional science fiction. McKibben's comment on the relation between science and science fiction is relevant here: "Those people committed to imagining the future [science fiction writers] have taken all the possibilities raised by the new technologies, and thinking them through, have dreamed up a galaxy of dystopias, each more unpleasant than the one before" (McKibben, *Enough*, p. 108). *Oryx and Crake*, published on the fiftieth anniversary of Crick and Watson's discovery of the structure of DNA and in the same year that the entire human genome was sequenced, thinks through these stages of scientific enlightenment to their possible negative consequences, which, given human nature (as we know it) need to be taken into account. As McKibben points out, genetic engineering of human beings is "an issue" to be debated right now, but "not a fact" (p.183), and it is in the pause before any "definitive moment" of choice that *Oryx and Crake* delivers its urgent warnings.[10]

These two novels belong to distinct dystopian traditions, as Atwood acknowledged when citing her main literary models: George Orwell's political satire *Nineteen Eighty-Four* for *The Handmaid's Tale*[11] and for *Oryx and Crake* John Wyndham's science fantasy *The Day of the Triffids*.[12] Other models for *Oryx and Crake* would include Swift's *Gulliver's Travels*, H. G.Wells's *The Island of Dr Moreau*, and most hauntingly Mary Shelley's *Frankenstein*. (She also wrote a novel, *The Last Man*, where humanity was wiped out by a deadly plague, though it was not man-made.) Atwood shares the dystopian impulse to shock readers into an awareness of dangerous trends in our present world, though she always includes "something which isn't supposed to be there" in order "to surprise the reader" (Ingersoll, *Conversations*, p. 193). It is her innovative use of dystopian paradigms and the ideological significance of her generic revisions that I wish briefly to highlight. With *The Handmaid's Tale* her choice of a female narrator turns the traditionally masculine dystopian genre upside down, so that instead of Orwell's analysis of the public policies and institutions of state oppression, Atwood gives us a dissident account by a Handmaid who has been relegated to the margins of political power. This narrative strategy reverses the structural relations between public and private worlds of the dystopia, allowing Atwood to reclaim a feminine space of personal emotions and individual identity, which is highlighted by her first-person narrative. Though *Oryx and Crake*, told in the third person and focalized through a male narrator, is closer to dystopian masculine discourse (and to the discourse of science), Atwood does manage to surprise the reader, not least by telling her story for the first time from a male perspective and by switching the plot at the end. Both novels offer not one but two futuristic scenarios, though *The Handmaid's Tale* with its shift from Gilead to the historical conference at Nunavit two hundred years later is relatively optimistic, whereas *Oryx and Crake* projects a darker vision altogether. Both its virtual-reality scenarios represent modern nightmares, where the post-catastrophe world of Snowman and the Crakers is preceded by Atwood's ferocious satire on late modern American capitalist society.

Several critics have commented that *Oryx and Crake* contains strong elements of a *Boys' Own* adventure story, though arguably the surprise comes (as it did in *The Handmaid's Tale*) with its gendered reversals of traditional assumptions. As Helen Merrick remarks (and as Mary Shelley long ago demonstrated), "The master narrative of science has always been told in sexual terms,"[13] and so it is here with the focus on human reproduction, though Atwood insists on the emotional and imaginative contexts within which human sexuality is embedded. From this perspective, the novel might be read within a wider context of feminist debate over scientific issues related to birth technologies.[14] Of course, all these surprises within the dystopian genre come down to the fact that Atwood's primary focus is on human particularity: "So the real problems in the writing of *The Handmaid's Tale* [and also *Oryx and Crake*] were the same as the problems involved in the writing of any novel: how to make the story real at a human and individual level" ("Writing Utopia," pp. 93–94).

The Handmaid's Tale

Hélène Cixous begins her polemical feminist essay "The Laugh of the Medusa" with the sentence: "I shall speak about women's writing: about *what it will do*."[15] A critical reading of *The Handmaid's Tale* might usefully begin with this statement, for Offred's fictive autobiography comes to us as a written text, and only at the end do we discover that what we have been reading was actually a spoken narrative which has been transcribed from old cassette tapes and reconstructed for publication long after the narrator is dead. This complicated transmission process from private speech act to written text illustrates the historical problem of women's silencing which Cixous has highlighted, and also the potentially disruptive effects of women's writing. Moreover, the issue of language and power has always been crucial in the construction of dystopias: "Throughout the history of dystopian fiction the conflict of the text has often turned on the control of language" (Moylan, *Scraps of the Untainted Sky*, p. 148), and it is Offred's attempt to "seize it [the language], to make it hers" (Cixous, "Medusa," p. 343) which gives her narrative its appeal as one woman's story of resistance against patriarchal tyranny. By an irony of history, it is Offred the silenced Handmaid who becomes Gilead's principal historian when that oral "herstory" is published two hundred years later.

However, during her lifetime Offred finds herself in the familiar dystopian predicament of being trapped inside a space and a narrative where she is denied any possibility of agency. As a Handmaid deprived of her own name and identity, she has no rights as an individual but instead has been conscripted into sexual service to the state, reduced by its doctrine of biological essentialism to her female role as a child breeder, a "two-legged womb"[16] and to the ghost of a person, "a wraith of red smoke" (*HT*, p. 219). Under such threats of erasure Offred fights for her psychological and emotional survival as she tells her story. Her storytelling has a double purpose, for not only is it her counter-narrative to the social gospel of Gilead, but it is also her way to self rehabilitation against the "deadly brainwashing" (Cixous's phrase) of the totalitarian state. Offred insists on remembering who she was and hopes to be again, treasuring her former name as her "secret talisman" or a kind of guarantee of her future life after Gilead. But "meantime" as she says, "there is so much else getting in the way" (p. 281). Offred is a virtual prisoner in her Commander's house, and even when she goes outside on her regular shopping trips or on the rare Handmaids' group excursions, she is under constant surveillance. Within such constraints she needs to tell stories if only to herself, as a way of escape from the time trap of the present, "Otherwise you lie with your face squashed up against a wall . . . Otherwise you live in the moment. Which is not where I want to be" (p. 153).

The novel opens as a memory narrative (or is it a prison narrative?), with its rows of women in single beds patrolled by Aunts armed with cattle prods. "We slept in what had once been the gymnasium" (p. 13). Who is "we" and where is here? This scene induces a sense of dislocation, where the room is described as a haunted space full of "afterimages" – the markings on the floor for vanished games, the smells of sweat and chewing gum, and the faint imagined echoes of dance music. That faded lyricism contrasts sharply with the present, but at the same time it signals connections with the narrator's remembered past. As yet we do not know who the narrator is, for she does not identify herself in that first list of names whispered in the dormitory: "Alma. Janine. Dolores. Moira. June" (p. 14).[17] Only when the narrative switches to the present tense do we discover that she is a Handmaid and this is her story. Much later we are told that her official name is not her real name, though by then we have been initiated into this woman's secret life and her condition of double consciousness which is her strategy for survival.

Offred survives in the present by continually slipping back into the past – and for her this is not difficult as the heartland of Gilead where she now lives is her own home town, formerly Cambridge, Massachusetts. Every day as she walks the streets "doubled" by her red-robed companion, she is retracing the old city map in her head: "I'm remembering my feet on these sidewalks, in the time before, and what I used to wear on them" (p. 34), and with her double vision she sees through the new shop signs to their former names as she makes implicit comparisons between "now" and "then." "Lilies of the Field," the shop where the Handmaids order their "habits" (and the pun is not lost on Offred) used to be a cinema showing films starring actresses like Lauren Bacall or Katharine Hepburn who wore blouses which could be "*undone*": "They seemed to be able to choose. We seemed to be able to choose, then" (p. 35). It soon becomes evident that Offred's doubled narrative is more than a device for her private reorientation; it is one of the ways by which she defies Gileadean ideology. Her memories are continually in conflict with the official version of late twentieth-century America and her story exposes the lies of official history, just as on her illicit visit to Jezebel's club with the Commander she registers the hypocrisy and inauthenticity of the regime: "I try to remember if the past was exactly like this . . . A movie about the past is not the same as the past" (p. 247). Such memories remind her of the gap between her present life and the life she once led, paradoxically giving her a stronger sense of her own identity as separate from its present Gileadean frame.

Offred also uses memory narrative as a deliberate escape strategy which she repeatedly indulges in the "Night" sections as she lies alone in her room at the Commander's house:

> The night is mine, my own time, to do with as I will, as long as I am quiet . . . The night is my time out. Where should I go?
> Somewhere good. (p. 47)

She escapes out of time back into memories of student days with her friend Moira, the separatist feminist, or further back to childhood memories of her mother, the old-fashioned Women's Libber, both of them condemned as dissidents by the new regime. Offred resurrects these vanished women as she tells their stories of female heroism, imitating their own irreverent idioms as she simultaneously celebrates and mourns for them: "I've tried to make it sound as much like her as I can. It's a way of keeping her alive" (p. 256).

However, there is for Offred one central traumatic memory, which is the loss of her husband Luke and their small daughter. The jagged edges of that trauma show through in fragmented flashbacks of a time of "roaring and confusion" (p. 49), and only gradually does she allow herself to remember the full story of her family's failed escape attempt across the border into Canada, when Luke was shot and her child snatched from her. Although she heard the gunshots, she still cannot accept that Luke was killed, and such is the power of her longing that she continues to believe that one day she will receive a message from him and that their family life will be restored: "It's this message, which may never arrive, that keeps me alive." Where is hope located in this nightmarish culture of fear? Only, it would appear, in Offred's mind and in the cemetery: "*In Hope*, as they say on the gravestones" (p. 205).

Ironically, Offred's only real hope centers on her own body, whose femaleness has been resinscribed by Gilead's biological discourse and its oppressively Old Testament sexual practices. Though she has no power to reject her Handmaid's role and stay alive, she does have the power to defy patriarchal prescriptions by aligning herself differently through her private narrative about her body. Reversing Gilead's authority, she claims her body as her own territory which baffles male invasion: "I sink down into my body as into a swamp, fenland, where only I know the footing" (p. 83). In Offred's inner-space meditations Atwood writes her version of Cixous's *écriture féminine:* "Write yourself. Your body must be heard," as Cixous advises ("Medusa," p. 338). Offred explores her own dark continent, "though black-red rather than black" (p. 84), where her womb expands into an image of cosmic wilderness which is regularly traversed by the moon. However, the end result is not triumph as Cixous promised, but the sad recognition that in Gilead her female body is a failure: "I have failed once again to fulfil the expectations of others, which have become my own" (p. 83). However, Offred's definition of femininity insists on those very qualities of excess that Gilead condemns. She allies female desire with natural processes of growth and fertility, like the flowers in Serena Joy's summer garden which insist on "bursting upwards, wordlessly, into the light, as if to point, to say: Whatever is silenced will clamour to be heard, though silently" (p. 161).[18]

There are at least two occasions where her body refuses to be silenced. In her outburst of hysterical laughter after her first game of Scrabble with the Commander, the laughter boils up in her throat "like larva": "I'll burst. Red all over the cupboard . . . oh to die of laughter" (p. 156), and in her account of her forbidden lovemaking with Nick, the Commander's chauffeur, she confesses that she has invented the sound effects around their sexual encounter : "To cover up the sounds, which I am ashamed of making" (p. 275). Falling in love with Nick releases Offred into what Cixous calls "the marvellous text of herself" ("Medusa," p. 338): "I'm alive in my skin, again, arms around him, falling and water softly everywhere, neverending" (p. 273). Though Offred disconcerts the reader by adding "I made that up," nevertheless she leaves it there as one version of their love story. She adds: "The way love feels is always only approximate" (p. 275), for she knows that words never represent the complexity of lived emotional experience.

If Offred is intensely conscious of her body, she also shares the postmodern narrator's self awareness of the dimensions of fabrication in her memoir. Many times she reminds us that this is only a "reconstruction," but one that she needs to tell ("tell, rather than write," p. 49) in order to invent listeners and readers who inhabit a world elsewhere, and she also likens her story to a letter, "*Dear You*, I'll say. Just *you*, without a name . . . *You* can mean thousands" (p. 50). Always aware of the dialogical nature of narrative, Offred addresses that same *you* when she engages the reader in a sympathetic act of communication, as she imagines exchanging stories at some future time: "I will hear yours too if I ever get the chance . . . Because I'm telling you this story I will your existence. I tell, therefore you are" (p. 279). Although she is surrounded by people, Offred has nobody to whom she can talk, so she resorts to telling other women's stories within her own, creating the impression of a multi-voiced narrative which undermines Gilead's myth of women's silence and submissiveness. She succeeds in incorporating not only her own ironic view of the new neo-conservative women's culture but also presents a critical analysis of North American feminism since the 1960s, from the Women's Liberation Movement of her mother's generation to the rise of the New Right and Christian fundamentalism of the late 1970s and 1980s, represented here by the Commanders' Wives and the terrible Aunts. Her account dispels any singular definition of "Woman" as it emphasizes Atwood's resistance to reifying slogans, whether patriarchal or feminist: "Eternal Woman. But really, "Woman" is the sum total of women" (Ingersoll, *Conversations*, p. 201).

Offred's storytelling helps her to survive the psychological oppression of Gilead and she even manages to twist the masculine genre of dystopia into a feminine romance plot by falling in love, but her narrative ends poised on the edge of the unknown as she steps up into the Black Van. However, her gendered body has been so written into the body of the text that her typically feminine gesture of giving herself "into the hands of strangers, because it can't helped" (p. 307) might easily be read as her story offering itself to be interpreted by unknown future readers. That story is lost for two hundred years and when it is rediscovered and published by the male professor from Cambridge, his version threatens to erase its significance as thoroughly as Gilead had tried to erase her identity. The professor is not interested in her personal memoir except as evidence for his grand impersonal narrative of a fallen nation's history, and readers are left with the challenge of Offred's unfinished story. Do we understand more about the past (or is it the future?) from her story or from official history? I suspect that it is the female author's voice at the beginning of the Historical Notes which offers readers two coded words of advice on how to read Offred's dystopian narrative: "*Denay, Nunavit*" (p. 311).

Oryx and Crake

Atwood has used epigraphs from Swift's satires in both *The Handmaid's Tale* and *Oryx and Crake*, and I would argue that in the period between them her own dystopian vision has darkened in a way similar to Swift's. She has moved through political and social satire to a satire against mankind, as Swift did in *Gulliver's Travels*. Snowman, like Gulliver, is both mouthpiece and butt of Atwood's satire, but unlike Gulliver he does not become alienated from human beings. On the contrary, he emerges as a morally responsible man and the novel's unlikely hero, who regards the prospect of entering again into human relationships with a kind of fearful excitement. "What do you want me to do?" (*O&C*, p. 432) are his last words, which leaves a "tiny peephole" (*HT*, p. 31) for optimism in an open-ended situation unlike the ending of *Gulliver's Travels*.

As a sequel to *The Handmaid's Tale, Oryx and Crake* is a survival narrative on a different scale: Snowman has survived the end of the world and has to confront the scandal of apocalypse alone. Different situations demand different inflections of the dystopian genre, and his story is closer to a wilderness or castaway narrative than to Offred's prison narrative, where for him the question of survival is primarily a physical imperative. (He is in danger of starving to death.) Whereas Offred felt isolated in the Commander's household, Snowman is the only one of his species remaining and is solely responsible for the gentle tribe of humanoid creatures called Crakers, so unlike himself that it is he who becomes the monster: "The Abominable Snowman – existing and not existing" (p. 8).[19] His anomalous position raises a more radical question than any in *The Handmaid's Tale* and closer to Swift's: what does it mean to be human? Not only different questions but different quests dominate these narratives, for Offred's aim was to survive Gilead through the powers of memory and hope but Snowman has no hope and his quest leads him back into Crake's ruined Paradice dome, the center of the catastrophe and the site of his own traumatic memories. It might be likened to a journey to the Underworld where Snowman has to confront his ghosts in order to become aware of the complex dimensions of his own humanity. Unlike Offred, he returns to the ruined world and to the Crakers, only to discover that the plot has changed. He is not the Last Man after all, and the novel ends with Snowman being forced to choose a course of action as he cautiously approaches three other battered human survivors on the beach. Offred had no choice but to go with the armed guards into the Black Van. Although neither of them knows what will happen next, that shift in balance from passivity to action codes in the gender differences between the two protagonists which are reflected in these very different dystopian forms.

Returning to the epigraphs (one from *Gulliver's Travels* and one from Virginia Woolf's *To the Lighthouse*), we find that gender difference is also highlighted in the counterpoint between Gulliver's emphasis on "plain matter of fact" and a female artist's more speculative view of the world. These two different ways of apprehending reality hint at the oncoming tensions in the novel between the values of science and reason versus the values of art, emotion, and imagination. Atwood's narrative sets out to erode that binary opposition in two ways: she makes both her protagonists male (Crake is the "numbers man" and Jimmy is the "word man") and she also suggests that creative imagination is not confined to artists but is shared by scientists, for it is one of the qualities that distinguish human beings. Speaking of the potential advances of genetic engineering, Atwood aligns science with fantasy: "It contains so much that human dreams are made of . . . eternal youth, godlike beauty, hyperintelligence, Charles Atlas strength."[20] Science and fantasy are fused as Atwood's creative imagination transforms the facts of her well-documented research into speculative fiction. The contents of her famous Brown Box, now catalogued in the Fisher Library in Toronto, contain a list of Alphabetical Research files on such topics as Animals-Extinction, Biotechnology, Climate Change, Nanotechnology, Stem Cell Research, as well as files on Slavery, Video Games, and warnings about bioterror and bioerror; there is also a webpage address in her Acknowledgments, citing references consulted. These are her raw materials, but as a novelist she is as much engaged with psychological and emotional complexities as she is with science, and it is the interaction between those forces which provides the dynamics of the plot.

A Last Man narrative poses special problems: how to tell that story, who to tell it, and to whom? Snowman does not tell the story himself in the first person; he is the focalizer, but his story is refracted through an omniscient narrative voice. The novel takes the form of a third-person indirect interior monologue as it shifts between the fictive present (always in the present tense) and Snowman's memories of his own and other people's stories (always in the past tense), contextualized and written down by the other shadowy presence. The difficulty of getting the story told is illustrated in the manuscript versions, where Atwood changed the voice from an early first person version which included "Snowman's Address to the Absent Reader," through a later version told in the third person, before finally settling on the present structure.[21] Significantly, in the published text Snowman writes nothing down, for "he'll have no future reader" (*O&C*, p. 46). Much later he finds his own last written words in his abandoned office, but now "It's the fate of these words to be eaten by beetles" (p. 405). Instead, he talks to himself or to the dead, imploring Oryx to speak to him or shouting accusations at Crake. Snowman had done quite a lot of writing in early manuscript versions when writing may have seemed like a guarantee of his existence, though Atwood abandons the convention of the found manuscript in favor of a more stringent realism. Writing would be as pointless as "whittling" (p. 44) in Snowman's present situation.

Yet the psychological need to talk and to tell, to remember and to imagine (all the things associated with the narrative impulse) remains in Snowman. He talks to the Crakers, though in his public capacity as Crake's prophet, improvising a version of the Genesis myth with Crake as God creator and Oryx as Earth Mother, while secretly wishing to endow Crake with "horns and wings of fire" (p. 121). Through storytelling he teaches the Crakers the rudiments of symbolic thinking. And the Crakers love his stories, which makes us wonder if the primitive human brain is hard-wired not just for dreaming and singing as Crake had discovered, but for narrative as well.

Snowman's "conversations" are with aspects of his old self (when he was Jimmy) and with the people who belong to the past. He, like Offred, exists in a state of double consciousness, working by associative leaps between "now" and "then" in an effort to escape from a devastated world littered with the wreckage of late twentieth-century civilization reminding him daily of what he has lost. So great is his need to hear a human voice that he hallucinates voices in his head: Oryx's "storytelling voice" (p. 371) and the voices of Crake, his mother, and his former lovers. Even old books "speak" to him, but it is only when he thinks he hears a slug answering that he begins to fear for his sanity. As his narrative slips strangely between reality, memory, and fantasy, we come to realize that Snowman like Offred is telling stories in a desperate bid to reclaim his own identity, ironizing his present situation, and delighting in language and word play. However, there is now a new urgency for it is Snowman's unique task to rescue words from oblivion: "'Hang on to the words,' he tells himself. The odd words, the old words, the rare ones. *Valance. Norn. Serendipity. Pibroch. Lubricious.* When they're gone out of his head, these words, they'll be gone, everywhere, forever. As if they had never been" (p. 78). Snowman, champion of the values of art and literature, degraded to "wordserf" in his former life as writer of advertising copy, takes up his word warrior role again when there is nobody to listen. The Crakers would hear him, but with brains from which passion and imagination have been erased, they would not understand him. It is the lack of these distinctively human qualities in Crake's Houyhnhnmlike creatures which reminds Snowman of his radical isolation.

There are times when Snowman needs to do more than recount his memories to himself, most crucially as he approaches the Paradice dome, tracking his way through the trashed evidence of what really happened. He feels the urgent need to suppose that there is someone who would understand, and for the only time in the novel he invents listeners in the future. Like Offred, he "wills them into being" (p. 260), as he imagines their questions which only he can answer: "*How did this happen?* Their descendants will ask, stumbling upon the evidence, the ruins" (p. 260). His wasteland journey leads him back to the heart of darkness where he has to confront his own skeletons in the closet, the bodies of Oryx and Crake, "or what's left of them" (p. 391), scattered like pieces of a giant jigsaw puzzle left for Snowman to fit together into a narrative. In his crisis of moral realization he is forced to confront his own complicity in Crake's genocidal project: "Some of that darkness is Snowman's. He helped with it" (p. 389). He confesses that he locked himself away to watch the extinction of the human race on computers and television screens, deliberately blurring the boundaries between Crake's game of Extinctathon and reality: "The whole thing seemed like a movie" (p. 399). When we recall that Atwood wrote this section after 9/11, her fictional scenario resonates against that real-life catastrophe.

Unlike everyone else, Snowman is not dead and his story continues into the new dystopian space of the post-apocalyptic world. It is he, "the neurotypical" (as Crake described him) who becomes the Crakers' rescuer, leading them out of Paradice into their new "home" in the wilderness. In this version of Milton's *Paradise Lost* for a postmodern secular world, Crake's ruined Paradice (with the pun encoded into the spelling of the name) is briefly regained by Snowman, and then rejected when he decides to return to the Crakers. That pattern of mythic repetition with variations suggests that nothing is inevitable and that surprises are always possible. The change in plot at this point surprises the reader, though nobody is more surprised than Snowman to discover other human beings still alive. However, the biggest surprise is his emergence from the position of "dunderhead, frivol, and dupe" (p. 391) into morally responsible human agent. His story might be mapped through the changing associations around his adopted name, from "Abominable" ("his own secret hairshirt" [p. 8]) to "grinning dope set up as a joke" (p. 263), and finally transformed into "Ohhh-mun" as the Crakers chant his name, calling him back to them (p. 419).

Snowman tells his last stories to himself as he sneaks up on the three unknown human survivors, rehearsing old plots from narratives of European colonialism and the Wild West, only to discover that none of them fits his present situation. Is his role that of peacemaker, negotiator, or killer? He cannot finish the story though he knows it is "Time to go" (p. 433), as Atwood sets up (once again) an open-ended situation for readers to complete. What we think Snowman will do and what the others might do depends on how we read the complexities of human nature, where "Passions spin the plot," as Atwood has always acknowledged ("Writing *Oryx and Crake*," p. 323).

Both these novels explore "a common writerly dilemma: who's going to read what you write, now or ever? Who do you want to read it?".[22] Like the urgent question, *What if?* with which I began, Atwood answers this one about narratees, though indirectly. Discussing the solitary diary writer Doctor Glas in a novel by Hjalmar Söderberg, she comments: "But the truth . . . is that the writing is not by Doctor Glas, and it's not addressed to no one. It's by Hjalmar Söderberg, and it's addressed to us" (*Negotiating with the Dead*, p. 115). Through her fictive narrators it is Atwood who is addressing her readers in these dystopian novels. "*Not real can tell us about real*" (*O&C*, p. 118), as Snowman teaches the Crakers, and on that principle Atwood constructs her speculative fictions as fables for our time.

NOTES

1. Margaret Atwood, "Writing Utopia," *Curious Pursuits: Occasional Writing, 1970–2005* (London: Virago, 2005), pp. 85–94.
2. Margaret Atwood, *The Robber Bride* (London: Virago, 1994), p. 4.
3. Tom Moylan, *Scraps of the Untainted Sky: Science Fiction, Utopia, Dystopia* (Boulder, CO: Westview Press, 2000), p. 136.
4. Margaret Atwood, *Oryx and Crake* (London: Virago, 2004), p. 267.
5. Atwood began *Oryx and Crake* in March 2001, and continued writing it after 9/11. See "Writing *Oryx and Crake*" in *Curious Pursuits*, pp. 321–23.
6. Margaret Atwood Papers, Thomas Fisher Rare Book Library, University of Toronto. 2003 Accession. Box 1: Folder 5.
7. See Lee Briscoe Thompson, *Scarlet Letters: "The Handmaid's Tale"* (Toronto: ECW Press, 1997), p. 36.
8. Earl G. Ingersoll, ed., *Margaret Atwood: Conversations* (London: Virago, 1992), p. 223.
9. Bill McKibben, *Enough: Genetic Engineering and the End of Human Nature* (London: Bloomsbury, 2004), pp. 43–44.
10. A Canadian geneticist has criticized Atwood's invented creatures like the pigoons and the Crakers as literally impossible because scientists do not have the technology to create them. To this Atwood's reply would surely be "Not yet." See Anthony Griffiths, "Genetics according to *Oryx and Crake*," *Canadian Literature* 181 (Summer 2004): pp. 192–95.
11. Margaret Reynolds, "Interview with Margaret Atwood," *Margaret Atwood: The Essential Guide*, eds. M. Reynolds and J. Noakes (London: Vintage, 2002), pp. 11–25.
12. Noah Richler, "Atwood's Ground Zero," *Saturday Post*, 26 April 2003: p. BK4.
13. Helen Merrick, "Gender in Science Fiction," *The Cambridge Companion to Science Fiction*, eds. Edward James and Farah Mendlesohn (Cambridge: Cambridge University Press, 2003), pp. 241–52.
14. Rosi Braidotti, "Monsters, Mothers and Machines," *Nomadic Subjects: Embodiment and Sexual Difference in Contemporary Feminist Theory* (New York: Columbia University Press, 1994), pp. 75–94.
15. Hélène Cixous, "The Laugh of the Medusa," *Feminisms: An Anthology of Literary Theory and Criticism*, eds. Robyn R. Warhol and Diana Price Herndl (New Brunswick, NJ: Rutgers University Press, 1991), pp. 334–49.
16. Margaret Atwood, *The Handmaid's Tale* (London: Vintage, 1996), p. 146.
17. Marta Dvorak, "'What's in a Name?' Readers as Both Pawns and Partners, or Margaret Atwood's Strategy of Control," *Margaret Atwood: "The Handmaid's Tale"/"Le Conte de la servante": The Power Game*, eds. J-M. Lacroix and J. Leclaire (Paris: Presses de la Sorbonne Nouvelle, 1998), pp. 79–97.
18. See C. A. Howells, *Margaret Atwood* (Basingstoke: Macmillan, 1996), pp. 137–41, where I discuss more extensively this question of *écriture féminine* in Offred's narrative.
19. See J. Brooks Bouson, "'It's Game Over Forever': Atwood's Satiric Vision of a Bioengineered Posthuman Future," *Journal of Commonwealth Literature* 39.3 (2004): pp. 139–56.

20. Margaret Atwood, "Arguing Against Ice Cream: *Enough: Staying Human in an Engineered Age*, by Bill McKibben," *Moving Targets: Writing with Intent, 1982–2004* (Toronto: Anansi, 2004), pp. 33–50.
21. Atwood Papers, 2003 Accession. Box 1: Folders 1–7.
22. Margaret Atwood, *Negotiating with the Dead* (London: Virago, 2003), p. 115.

12

SHARON R. WILSON

Blindness and survival in Margaret Atwood's major novels

As Reingard Nischik notes, Atwood is "one of the most important literary chroniclers of our time" and an international bestseller; thus, the Atwood industry is "booming."[1] According to Coral Ann Howells, "From *The Edible Woman* onwards, her novels have focused on contemporary social and political issues," challenging contemporary social myths and fashionable ideologies and "endlessly surprising her readers with her ongoing experimentalism."[2] Critics have viewed Atwood's novels using formalist, biographical, psychoanalytic, feminist, Jungian, dialogic, intertextual, phenomenological, narratological, cultural, postmodern, postcolonial, generic, and deconstructionist approaches. Atwood's novels are variously described as realism, romance, ghost story, thriller, memoir, *Bildungsroman*, *Kunstlerroman*, science fiction, metafiction, anti-novel, fairy tale, satire, parody, Gothic, dystopian, nationalist, feminist, revisionist, modernist, intramodern,[3] postmodern, and postcolonial.[4]

As I suggest in *Margaret Atwood's Textual Assassinations*, "The issues of power and sexual politics that mark Atwood's earliest work have evolved."[5] In addition to the self-divided, alienated, and oppositional characters and character pairs Sherrill Grace helped us recognize with *Violent Duality* (1980),[6] by the eighties and nineties

> Atwood's characters and readers are more aware of the multicultural, colonized, racist, and classist as well as patriarchal, sexist, and hypocritical nature of the worlds they occupy. If anything, their alienation is more complex, with multiple causes. Not only is the Canadian experience itself still perceived as "strange" and sometimes estranging . . . victim positions still apply . . . Increasingly, Atwood's survivors are trickster creators, using their verbal "magic" to transform their worlds. (Wilson, *Textual Assassinations*, p. xii)

Although Atwood's fiction, poetry, short and flash fiction, prose poems, and essays all continue to illustrate paths towards survival, with *Oryx and Crake* (2003) we can no longer ignore the fact that Atwood's novels, generally varieties of Gothic and dystopian romance, also dramatize the real possibility that humanity may *not* survive. The society of this book turns the struggle to survive into a game and even has one game show called Extinctathon and another, called Blood and Roses, which balances human achievements against atrocities throughout history, raising the question whether survival is even merited. Snowman is one of few human survivors after the BlyssPluss Pill, advertised as boosting the libido and prolonging youth, ironically eradicates most of humanity. Even the created humanoid species, the Crakers, seems likely to become extinct.

True, Atwood's novels, including *Surfacing* (1972), *Lady Oracle* (1976), and *Bodily Harm* (1982), characteristically have unresolved and possibly unhappy endings, but many Atwood texts suggest at least the end of the world the character knows. Looking back, we remember early short stories, "When It Happens," "A Travel Piece" (1977), and "The Salt Garden" (1983) (*DG*, *BE*), that do suggest the end of the world or something close to it. The "It" in "When It Happens" is less specified than the event Alma in "The Salt Garden" awaits, but both stories feature characters who see more than others around them. As Mrs. Burridge puts up her green tomato pickles, looks at her kitchen clock, and writes her shopping list, she recognizes that "They are all waiting, just as Mrs. Burridge is, for whatever it is to happen,"[7] whether war, invasion, or societal chaos. She realizes she has seen her husband drive off for the last time, and she imagines electricity going off, her jars of vegetables shattered on the floor like blood, and, she who "has never killed anything in her life" (*DG*, 136), shooting two men on her journey from home. By contrast, "A Travel Piece" in the same volume prefigures *Bodily Harm* with one of Atwood's many "professional tourists" seeking "an unspoiled Eden" by using her camera to avoid looking. Annette tries to "filter out" such realities as the probability that a fellow passenger will not only be slaughtered like the pig she edited out of an earlier beach scene but that his blood will be drunk by stranded passengers dying of thirst. She may or may not be rescued (*DG*, pp. 152, 139–40), but the world as she has known it, including her concept of civilization and individual responsibility, does end. In "The Salt Garden," Alma repeatedly visualizes variations of thermonuclear explosion she is convinced will end the world: "the flash and the sound, and being blown through the air, and the moment when she hits and falls into darkness." As she makes a salt garden for her daughter, however, she is comforted knowing that "After everything is over . . . there will still be salt."[8]

Early in Atwood texts, if an individual or society was in danger, self-deception or symbolic blindness was the usual major cause. While Atwood's early texts often focus on protagonists' distortions of vision, especially through mirrors and cameras,[9] this image has received little comment in recent criticism. Vision imagery has been important in *The Edible Woman, Surfacing, Lady Oracle, Life Before Man, The Handmaid's Tale, Cat's Eye, Bodily Harm, Alias Grace*, and *The Robber Bride*, and it continues to be significant in virtually every other Atwood text, especially in the two recent novels, *The Blind Assassin* and *Oryx and Crake*. Vision images include being blind or having partial or obscured vision; projecting problems or defects onto others; using a "transforming eye" to mold a hero in Gothic romance;[10] confusing a mirror with reality; seeing through a camera, binoculars, television, or another distancing, framing agent; using "magical vision";[11] reversing the patriarchal Gaze; developing an aesthetic or artist's gaze;[12] and seeing with a magnifying lens, which may involve seeing light in the dark,[13] developing a third eye, being an "eye witness" and an "I-witness,"[14] and developing "empathetic vision."[15] The "unseeing eye"[16] is opposed to the third eye of "Instructions for the Third Eye" and other Atwood texts, in which "what you see depends partly on what you want to look at and partly on how."[17] Partial or complete blindness is, however, a necessary beginning for the partly parodied quest each narrator pursues, and regaining some vision and moving as far as possible out of the objectifying Gaze seem necessary for survival. Often this is only possible by becoming a "trickster creator" able to manipulate the Gaze and to create possibilities, as I suggest in *Textual Assassinations* (p. xv). Making allusions to other Atwood texts, I will focus on *Surfacing, Cat's Eye, The Blind Assassin*, and *Oryx and Crake*. Because the typically self-conscious narrator (aware of telling a story and discussing her procedures) is usually the one who is blind, the narrative is not only about the narrator's personal growth in the novel we are reading, and personal, national, and artistic vision, but multiple levels of survival.

Surfacing

As I pointed out in 1987, *Surfacing* (1972), Atwood's second novel, is actually an anti-novel or anti-romance like Samuel Beckett's *Molloy*: "Both Beckett and Atwood write prose which may be hard to distinguish from poetry or may have affinities to visual art, and both excel at parody. Significantly, *both* subvert conventions of genre, plot, structure, usage, and punctuation in shaping texts which question their own existence" (Wilson, "Deconstructing Text and Self," p. 54). *Surfacing* features one of Atwood's most unreliable narrators, a nameless commercial artist who illustrates Quebec fairy tales and lies about being married, having a child, seeing her brother drown, and many other aspects of her life. Because she creates false memories and projects her actions onto "the Americans," the story she tells unravels as she tells it, preceding the similar effect of the left hand undoing the action of the right hand in *The Blind Assassin*. She is on a quest for her father, mother, and past, but if this quest is heroic,[18] it is self-parodying at the same time, already illustrating the postmodern genre-bending usually associated with Atwood's fiction of the late eighties and after. Similarly, the novel's use of the Gothic, ghost story, and metafiction traditions of postmodernism and postcolonialism is also somewhat parodic. Unlike Gilgamesh, Mwindo, and most traditional heroes, the narrator does not earn a celebrated name, a choral group (or griot) chanting her story does not accompany her on her journey, and her quest is not resolved. The werewolves, ghosts, and robotic "Americans" are in the narrator's head, and much of her story erases itself. As Atwood has remarked, she knows the narrator is bonkers and does not advocate rolling around in the leaves as a means of finding identity.[19] Earlier seen as modernist and appearing before postcolonial writing was recognized, the overlapping feminism, postmodernism, and postcolonialism of *Surfacing* are apparent when viewed through the lens of her later works. The novel's use of parody, irony, metafiction, and intertextuality and the deconstruction of national and social myths and concepts like reality and identity are characteristically postmodern.[20] Atwood's intertexts (texts embedded within other texts) include fairy tales, myths, the Bible, literary works, radio and television programs, film, ballet, opera, and nursery rhymes. When compared to the toaster and marble in *Cat's Eye* and the photographs and trunk in *The Blind Assassin*,[21] scenes in *Surfacing* such as the mother feeding jays and the narrator seeing her father as a werewolf may now also be recognized as magical realism, a fusion of magic and reality that is a characteristic technique in both postmodernism and postcolonialism. Postcolonialism, the condition of throwing off colonization and beginning the process of proceeding beyond a colonized consciousness, is evident in the narrator's evolving vision and ability to survive.

As I have previously discussed in "Camera Images" (p. 30), symbolically "unseeing eyes" generally belong to Atwood narrators and personae who have fragmented or split identities typical of people who grow up in colonized countries. Despite some critics' fury over them, the victim positions of Atwood's *Survival*, published the same year as *Surfacing*, are still relevant. In addition, however, most Atwood narrators also use cameras, binoculars, telescopes, and movie cameras to gaze at – and possibly fragment – others. In *Surfacing*, fairy tale and mythic intertexts, including the Grimms' "The Juniper Tree," "The White Snake," and "The Robber Bridegroom," *loup-garou* and Wendigo stories, "The Fountain of Life," "The Golden Phoenix," and Great Goddess myth, characterize both the fragmentation and the healing (Wilson, *Margaret Atwood's Fairy-Tale*, pp. 34, 97–119). Atwood's self-conscious narrators may also seem to lack mouths, hands, legs, feet, hearts, heads, or bodies; and they frequently feel like food at the same time as they may cannibalize others.

Although many critics discuss the unreliable narrator's growth in the novel, they have largely ignored *Surfacing's* vision images. In addition to the narrator's perspective in particular scenes, the actual eye references are significant in her ritualistic anti-quest towards survival, which is actually anti-survival in the sense that she reacts against the consumerism and disrespect for the natural world that seem to define urban survival, erase the cultural myth of survival in the wilderness,[22] and leave us in open, undefined space at the end. Thus, the path is the kind of spiral we encounter in *The Circle Game* and *Oryx and Crake*.

In *Surfacing*, eyes reference not only those of the narrator but describe the people who accompany her on her journey, people in the past, village people, "the Americans," the gods, food, and unborn babies. Eyes in *Surfacing* are initially oppositional, those of gazers and the objects of the commodifying patriarchal and colonial Gaze; then this binary division is, along with other binaries (male–female, civilization–nature, American–Canadian, robot–human), deconstructed. Eyes may be open or closed, blind, vulnerable, summarizing, searching, surveying, aggressive, gloating, accusing and judging, pouncing, murderous, colonizing, scanning as in X-ray vision, guided, indoctrinated, passive, squinting, afraid, destroyed, cyclopean, blank, sad, baffled, filtering, gleaming, crying, and powerful. Their vision may be segmented and/or segmenting, cloudy, double, or "true." By the end of the novel, the "third eye," describing the uselessness of the narrator's love for Joe, appears. The novel's tone seems to signify true vision, but, like the endings of most Atwood novels, that of *Surfacing* is ambiguous and open.

Having read numerous survival manuals, the self-conscious narrator of *Surfacing* begins her quest for father, mother, self, and past – and ultimately human survival – on a twisting road where "disease is spreading up from the south." Traveling in David and Anna's car with Joe, the man she lives with, she underlines the novel's emphasis on vision by noting that, for the first time, she is bypassing the café that serves watery canned peas, "pallid as fisheyes."[23] She describes Joe as having small clinched eyes, and she knows she is not supposed to observe him. Looking out the side window like a TV screen, she remembers that her father said he could drive the old road, now closed, blindfolded, and feels deprived not to see the lake through tears and vomit, as she once did. As they approach the dock close to her family's cabin, she remembers her brother's open-eyed "drowning" (*S*, p. 92) before she was born, suggesting that an unborn baby can look out the walls of the mother's womb. As she approaches her family's cabin, she feels her missing father's "watching eyes" (p. 97), earlier seen as "summarizing" (p. 100). Joe, too, seems to scan with X-ray vision, prying under her skin, Anna complains that David watches her for mistakes, and David's eyes even gleam like test tubes. In this opposition of male and female, "the Americans" (p. 140) also have "eye rays" (p. 144), "sniper eyes" (p. 145), and "blank eggshells behind the dark glasses" (p. 153), and they gaze and survey. They are aligned with "male" (p. 178), suggesting physical, gender, and national colonization. The narrator sees even the campfire of "the Americans" as a red cyclop's eye. Conversely, the eyes of the narrator's mother are frightened as she looks straight into the "camera-gun" (Wilson, "Camera Images," p. 31), and, after contact with "the Americans," the heron, symbolizing nature, has a mashed eye.

As for most Atwood personas, societal conditioning has interfered in many ways with the narrator's seeing clearly. She remembers that the pill had made her vision blurry, as if Vaseline was in her eyes, and that "they" don't let you see when you are having a baby. In school she stared fixedly at the teacher, as she was supposed to, but put her eyes close enough to pictures that they disintegrated into grey dots. Like Elaine of *Cat's Eye*, she learned how to see without feeling. The narrator finally seeks her father's "true vision" and faces the tribunal of eyes, including the eyes of her friends, the bristling ones of the painted ladies in her scrapbook, the jay eyes of the birds her mother's ghost is feeding, and the wolf eyes of her father's ghost. She realizes that "it is better to see than to be blind" and that perhaps ones who can love have a vestigial eye (*S*, p. 161). Her vision is cloudy, double, gone, and then power flows into her eyes. She washes her eyes in the lake, sees that everything is alive, recognizes that seeing the gods in their true shape is fatal, sees in the dark as she apparently conceives a child, realizes that her reflection has intruded between her eyes and vision, re-enters her own time, and watches Joe with love "as useless as a third eye" (p. 224).

Because she realizes that she has created a "faked album" of created memories and because she resolves not to be a victim, she appears to be not only a trickster but a seer and a survivor. The narrator's sudden declaration of love for Joe is not entirely convincing, however, and, as Marge Piercy asked when *Surfacing* first appeared, "Can a victim cease being one except through some victory? . . . She can choose a man who opts to be a loser rather than a winner at her expense, but how does *she* stop being a loser after deciding to?" Piercy finds the ending of *The Edible Woman* "no great leap forward," either, and sees Marian as masochistic and Duncan as a user. In both novels, she finds no real indication of

> where the real work that presumably will replace the alienated labor is going to come from . . . Atwood seems to me still to rest in an untenable coyness about what it will mean in the daily world to attempt to take charge of one's life – as a Canadian, as a working person ([at this point] none of her protagonists have money), and as a woman.[24]

Piercy seems to miss the narrators' earlier complicity in consumerism and Americanness, and the same questions could be asked about her own fiction. In *Surfacing*, the lyrical style and almost religious tone are the best support for seeing the narrator's growth of vision.

Still, however, to a greater extent than I previously realized, we must face the real possibility that, as in *The Edible Woman* and *Oryx and Crake*, the narrator and her world may *not* survive unless they do act. Although Atwood's other novels of the seventies, *Lady Oracle* (1976) and *Life Before Man* (1979), are also open-ended, with perhaps even more critics doubting the narrators' growth of vision,[25] both do suggest growth towards being for oneself rather than for others (Wilson, *Margaret Atwood's Fairy-Tale*, pp. 120–35, 165–97), necessary elements in individual survival. If *Lady Oracle* does sometimes parody *Surfacing* as well as Gothic romance and demonstrates a necessary multiplicity of identities, *Life Before Man* dramatically suggests that human beings either may not yet exist or, like dinosaurs, are becoming extinct.

The Gaze in *Cat's Eye*

Atwood's novels of the eighties, *Bodily Harm* (1981), *The Handmaid's Tale* (1985), and *Cat's Eye* (1988), introduce new genres: the parodic thriller, a dystopian novel of ideas, and, in *Cat's Eye*, autobiographical fiction, life-writing, and coming of age fiction. *Cat's Eye* is, like *Surfacing* and *Lady Oracle*, a *Kunstlerroman*, *Bildungsroman*, and metafiction. Because Elaine Risley is a visual artist, "the development of her identity or 'I' is even more dependent upon the development of her vision, her 'eye,' than in Atwood's earlier works" (Wilson, "Eyes and I's," p. 226). *Cat's Eye* demonstrates at least eight kinds of vision: "backseat" vision, microscope vision, (the narrator's perception of) others' vision, forgotten vision of "the bad time," cat's eye vision, Virgin Mary vision, "tourist vision," and fairy tale restored vision (Wilson, "Eyes and I's," pp. 226, 230). Contrary to some views,[26] as a human being seeking to recover lost time and aspects of the self, Elaine must evolve beyond the distancing cat's eye vision of the artist to a later, integrative artist's vision.

In *Cat's Eye*, the main Gaze is that of female bullies rather than "American" robots. Its origin, though, is still patriarchal, hierarchical, and conformist: the insecure need to victimize, enforce subordination, and experience power vicariously. Despite Elaine's greater comfort in the world of boys, some of the adult male characters, such as Josef and her friends' fathers, are again dominating, patronizing, and misogynist, or at least the narrator sees them that way. Like the landlady in *The Edible Woman*, Elizabeth and Auntie Muriel in *Life Before Man*, the other two "friends" and Mrs. Smeath in *Cat's Eye*, Serena Joy in *The Handmaid's Tale*, and Zenia in *The Robber Bride*, Cordelia, the primary gazer, is partly a spotty-handed villainess on the Lady MacBeth model.[27] Although some readers remain fooled, characteristically Atwood's villains are ultimately unveiled as vulnerable human beings who double rather than foil the narrator. In the case of *Alias Grace*, Grace is the only one of Atwood's villainesses to prosper, primarily because she learns how to manipulate the Gaze. In *Cat's Eye*, Elaine gradually learns how to exist under the Gaze and then to manipulate it, whether sent by Cordelia, Grace, and Carol, by Josef or Jon, or by a conformist society resembling her mother's pressure cooker or wringer washer: one is judged according to adherence to rules. Girls must wear different clothing than boys – such as twin sweater sets – and houses must be fully furnished. Elaine notes that the eyes of engaged young women blur like those of blind baby kittens, and love alone blurs vision. Snowballs, evil eyes, and Jon's art all threaten to put the "eyeball into [the] highball."[28] Even the heavens and Elaine's doll seem to watch her. Finally, Elaine acts as trickster by ignoring Cordelia and the "friends'" attempts to control her. However, reversing the Gaze with revenge – "an eye for an eye" of terrorists, Elaine's refusal to help Cordelia, or Elaine's paintings of Mrs. Smeath – still means blindness. Much as other Atwood narrators are both attracted to and repelled by Bluebeard's locked doors, she avoids looking back to her near burial and freezing at the same time as she revisits the places and objects that will lead her to "open the door." She finally "see[s her] life entire" (*CE*, p. 398) when she finds the cat's eye marble in her red plastic purse.

Again, Elaine's individual struggle is fought against a background of more general struggle for survival. While human beings are likely to blow themselves sky-high, the future belongs to insects, who have more experience of surviving (p. 66). Readers who became aware of Atwood's concern about genetic engineering and extinct species only with *Oryx and Crake* will be surprised that, like fifties' science fiction films, *Cat's Eye* warns us not to fool with nature. Elaine's father cautions that a species a day is becoming extinct. It is obvious that the human race is doomed because diabetes is growing, fertilizers destroy fish, methane pollutes the atmosphere, water will flood coastlines after polar seas melt, and the earth will end up as a desert or a cinder. Gas masks are advised. Colonization still threatens Canada and other countries, and terrorism threatens the world. Because he is ethnically different, Mr. Banerji cannot survive the university tenure system. Ironically, Elaine's brilliant brother Stephen, who might act to benefit humanity, is arrested as a spy and killed by terrorists partly because he is different from others. Probably Cordelia also does not survive. Although Elaine is still somewhat other-directed near the end of the book, parodically still worrying about clothing and make-up and what people in the art gallery think of her, she is healing her blindness. She has learned to see in the dark like a persona of *Interlunar* and does survive.

Alias Grace and *The Blind Assassin*

Atwood's novels of the nineties, *The Robber Bride* (1993) and *Alias Grace* (1996), and of the turn-of-the-century, *The Blind Assassin* (2000), continue the increasingly meticulous research, begun in *Lady Oracle* and *Life Before Man*, that demonstrates a significant change in Atwood's writing continuing through *Oryx and Crake*. For *Lady Oracle*, Atwood asked assistants to research Diana of Ephesus. For *Life Before Man*, set in a one-mile radius of the Royal Ontario Natural History Museum, Atwood consulted paleontology, taxidermy, and media experts and asked her research assistants, Donya Peroff and Peter Boehm, to locate telephone booths, describe church services, and check other details of setting for the period in which the novel takes place (Wilson, *Margaret Atwood's Fairy-Tale*, pp. 165–66). She collected a file of clippings as background for *The Handmaid's Tale*; referenced numerous historic battles for *The Robber Bride*; researched quilt designs, prison records, cook books, and double personalities for *Alias Grace*, based on a real nineteenth-century murder; and consulted comic books, menus, and ship records for *The Blind Assassin*. As Atwood has frequently said, she likes to get the furniture, clothing, and food right.[29]

From my research into the Atwood papers, I have discerned a distinctive methodology:

> Arising from what Atwood calls the same "UR-Manuscript," *The Angel of Bad Judgment* (Margaret Atwood Papers), *Alias Grace* and *The Blind Assassin* seem to indicate a paradoxical but not uncommon direction for a postmodern writer: increasing historical documentation that compounds textual gaps and coexists with growing magical realism, in the case of the former, blood-red flowers that appear on the ground and in the cell of Grace's prison. *The Blind Assassin* (2000) parodies itself and popular taste by layering science fiction, fiction about fiction, and a romance of hidden passions and perversions underneath polished surfaces of repression to depict the war-torn thirties and forties.
>
> (Wilson, "Magic Photographs," forthcoming)

Grace, along with other women in *Alias Grace*, is always an object of a dehumanizing Gaze. As a child, she is subjected to that of her alcoholic, possibly abusive father. Then she attracts the attention of Kinnear, James, Jamie, Simon, prison and mental ward personnel, and other dignitaries, including Susanna Moodie, Canada's most important early writer. This postmodern novel again leaves interpretation to the reader, who must quilt plot pieces into a whole. If Grace does split into Grace and Mary personalities, she does so in order to survive, much as Karen copes with Uncle Vern's incestuous rapes by becoming Charis in *The Robber Bride*. On the other hand, if Grace and Jeremiah collude to set up a fake hypnosis and lie about the murder for which she has been sentenced, she still does so in order to survive. In nineteenth-century Canada, a Mary personality definitely offers freedom. In this case, unlike some of Atwood's other narrators, Grace uses her narrative to manipulate the Gaze by deceiving or "blinding" those who try to use her.

Iris, the actual narrator of the triple-tiered *The Blind Assassin*, is, along with time, the blind gods Eros and Justice,[30] and war, one of the novel's many Blind Assassins. Ironically, because she is so blind, lacking insight into history, current events, mythology, her father, husband, sister Laura, and her own motivations, she threatens the survival of others as well as of herself. The novel's photographs, of both the frame and inner narratives, reveal this blindness. In the frame narrative's portrait of the two sisters in their velvet dresses, Laura tints Iris light blue, which she thinks is the color of Iris's soul, because she is asleep. Their somewhat passive mother also wears blue. In Laura's photograph of Richard and Iris, Iris's face is bleached out, "so that the eyes and the nose and mouth looked fogged over,"[31] signifying her erasure from their marriage and Iris's life as an unaware Sleeping Beauty,[32] a condition that Iris overlooks for much of her life. Even the tricky picture of Laura, Alex, and Iris at the Button Factory Picnic, appearing with unexpected variations in both the inner and frame narratives, shows the sisters' class, ethnic, and feminine conditioning, which contributes to blindness. It appears first in the local newspaper and then in two prints Laura makes in the frame narrative: each is partly tinted and cuts off one sister, leaving only her hand. In Iris's hand-tinted print, Laura's hand is pale yellow, bringing to mind the Golden Lock of the Dido story she values. Laura's copy of the photo, pasted into her history notebook, has herself and Alex tinted yellow and Iris's detached hand blue. In the Prologue and Epilogue of the novel-within-the novel there is another apparently all black-and-white photo that the narrator finds stuck in *Perennials for the Rock Garden*. All three photographs are cut so that, significantly, even though both sisters were there, only the hand of one sister shows. This photograph is the lens that both the narrator and reader examine in order to read the assassinations, the reasons two of the three main characters do not survive, the need to explore fiction's relationship to reality, the desire to know reality,[33] and the ways we all construct stories around what we see. Although one of the "assassinated," Laura is also blind, about Iris and Alex's relationship, the meaninglessness of sacrifice, and perhaps the nature of the universe. She does not intentionally hurt others but fruitlessly sacrifices herself to save Alex.

Like the narrators of *The Edible Woman, Surfacing, Bodily Harm*, and *The Robber Bride*, Iris does see better when she accepts responsibility for her actions. Herself a trickster creator in this trickster narrative, Atwood parodies readers' need to find a reality by assuming that the main "he's" and "she's" of the inner novel are Alex and Iris; that all the photos of Alex and Iris are the same; and that all the levels of fiction, including the science fiction comics, are grounded in one "reality." Nevertheless, war is the background of all three fictions, and characters in all three levels do experience parallel growth. The "she" in the inner novel, "The Blind Assassin," which generates the science fiction stories, converses with her dead lover, realizes the futility of war, and wakes up when Sakiel-Norn is destroyed. Iris in the frame novel, whose lover has also died in a different war, earlier resembled the white foxes on her neckpiece that have glass eyes and "only bite their own tails" (p. 445). When she shows Rennie Aimee's photograph in Betty's Luncheonette, she realizes that she has been heartless and handless as well as eyeless (pp. 445–46).

Oryx and Crake

In *Oryx and Crake*, most readers overlook the extent to which the quality of these Frankensteins' unethical vision contributes to the struggle for survival depicted in this book. As in previous novels, blindness and distorted vision put male as well as female bodies, and even the newly gendered bodies of Crake's created species, in jeopardy.

In their childhood and adolescence, Jimmy and Crake, monstrous in their ways of seeing, spend much of their time on pornographic websites, including Hot Totts, Tart of the Day, Superswallowers, and Noodie News, that commodify women's and sometimes men's bodies. Significantly, we first see Oryx, the beautiful woman Jimmy loves, in the same voyeuristic way that Jimmy and Crake do, as the object of a scopophiliac gaze on a kiddie porn show, and she continues to function as an object in this book filled with images of walled, one-eyed, fish-eyed, ruptured, blind, and ultimately empty-socket vision. Always part of a Sedgwick triangle in which the central erotic figures are the two men vying for power,[34] Oryx blindly spreads the virus that may make the human species extinct. Jimmy watches Oryx through the peep-holes into the Crakers' secret space and the hallway outside Crake's private quarters.[35] After her death, when she is reduced to a voice in his head, Jimmy is the one-eyed Snowman/quester, sunburned and dressed in a bed sheet, who self-consciously tells the story.

Both Crake and Jimmy are monsters in their contrasting ways of seeing without seeing. It is no accident that Crake's Paradice dome complex is described as a "blind eyeball" with only slits for windows. Although his pseudo love intensifies Crake's blindness, Oryx ironically admires Crake's "vision."[36] Like other scientific geniuses rewarded by society, Crake is a demi-autistic "brainiac" who ironically functions as a mutant on another planet as he proceeds towards exterminating humanity on this one (*O&C*, pp. 174, 193). He reduces art to a desire to get laid, dismisses female artists as misguided, and seems to feel little human emotion except for competition with Jimmy to possess Oryx and the single-minded effort to eradicate a society obsessed with sex and war games.

Jimmy has built a life in which he turns a "blind eye" (p. 260) to whatever he doesn't want to see. As a child, he cultivates a fish-eye stare (p. 277). Later, he feels that he is "sliding around like an eyeball on a plate" (p. 260) and that looking at the present will destroy him. Part of what he doesn't want to see is that current society is "like a giant slug eating its way relentlessly through all the other bioforms on the planet, grinding up life on earth and shitting it out the backside in the form of pieces of manufactured and soon-to-be-obsolete plastic junk" (p. 243). Although his quest is again partly parodied, especially in the expected Wild West shoot-out to protect the Crakers near the end of the novel, Snowman acts as trickster creator: his attempt to keep words from becoming extinct succeeds in that he manages to tell the story we read. As in *The Handmaid's Tale*, a story implies a listener or reader and thus verifies that we aren't dead yet.

Symbolic blindness seems to be a necessary beginning for the partly parodied quest the narrator of each Atwood novel pursues, and regaining some vision and moving as far as possible out of the objectifying Gaze seem necessary for survival. Typified by Grace in *Alias Grace*, sometimes survival is only possible by becoming a trickster creator. But there seems to be a huge difference between Marian's fantasies of being eaten in *The Edible Woman* and the real, global death narrators and readers of *Bodily Harm, The Handmaid's Tale*, and *Oryx and Crake* face. Atwood used to say that she had never killed off one of her characters yet. Could it be that her work, while as filled with puns, word play, parody, and comic irony as ever, is growing more pessimistic?

NOTES

1. Reingard Nischik, ed., *Margaret Atwood: Works and Impact* (Rochester, NY: Camden House, 2000), p. 1.
2. Coral Ann Howells, *Margaret Atwood* (Basingstoke and New York: Macmillan and St. Martin's Press, 1996), pp. 6, 161.
3. "*Bildungsroman*" refers to a novel of education, "*Kunstlerroman*" to a novel dealing with an artist's life, "metafiction" to fiction about fiction, and "intramodern" to fiction in Canada existing between modernism and postmodernism and demonstrating characteristics of each.
4. See Sonia Mycak, *In Search of the Split Subject: Psychoanalysis, Phenomenology, and the Novels of Margaret Atwood* (Toronto: ECW Press, 1996); Hilda Staels, *Margaret Atwood's Novels: A Study of Narrative Discourse* (Tubingen and Basel: Francke Verlag, 1995); Eleonora Rao, *Strategies for Identity: The Fiction of Margaret Atwood* (New York: Peter Lang, 1993); J. Brooks Bouson, *Brutal Choreographies: Oppositional Strategies and Narrative Design in the Novels of Margaret Atwood* (Amherst: University of Massachusetts Press, 1993); Mary Kirtz, "'The Past Belongs to Us Because We are the Ones Who Need It': *(Alias) Grace* Notes," 1997 ACSUS (Association for Canadian Studies in the United States) Paper, Minneapolis; Karen F. Stein, *Margaret Atwood Revisited* (New York: Twayne, 1999); Sharon Wilson, "Deconstructing Text and Self: Mirroring in Atwood's *Surfacing* and Beckett's *Molloy*," *Journal of Popular Literature* 3 (Spring/Summer 1987): pp. 54, 60.
5. Sharon Rose Wilson, ed. *Margaret Atwood's Textual Assassinations: Recent Poetry and Fiction* (Columbus: Ohio State University Press, 2003), p. xii.
6. Sherrill Grace, *Violent Duality: A Study of Margaret Atwood* (Montreal: Véhicule Press, 1980).
7. Margaret Atwood, "When It Happens," *Dancing Girls and Other Stories* (Toronto: McClelland and Stewart, Bantam-Seal Books, 1977), p. 129.
8. Margaret Atwood, "The Salt Garden," *Bluebeard's Egg* (Toronto: McClelland and Stewart, 1983), pp. 207, 229.
9. See Sharon R. Wilson, "Eyes and I's," *International Literature in English: the Major Writers*, ed. Robert Ross (New York: Garland, 1991), pp. 226–27; "Camera Images in Margaret Atwood's Novels," *Margaret Atwood : Reflection and Reality*, ed. Beatrice Mendez-Egle (Edinburg, TX: Pan American University Press), pp. 29–32.
10. Ann McMillan, "The Transforming Eye: *Lady Oracle* and Gothic Tradition," *Margaret Atwood: Vision and Forms*, eds. Kathryn Van Spanckeren and Jan Garden Castro (Carbondale: Southern Illinois University Press, 1988), p. 49.
11. Margaret Atwood, *Interlunar* (Toronto: Oxford University Press, 1984), p. 103.
12. Kathryn Van Spanckeren, "Shamanism in the Works of Margaret Atwood," *Visions and Forms*, eds. Van Spanckeren and Castro, p. 189.
13. Coral Ann Howells, "*Cat's Eye*: Elaine Risley's Retrospective Art," *Margaret Atwood: Writing and Subjectivity: New Critical Essays*, ed. Colin Nicholson (New York: St. Martin's Press, 1994), pp. 210–12.
14. Margaret Atwood, "An End to Audience," *Second Words: Selected Critical Prose* (Toronto: Anansi, 1982), p. 348.

15. Sharon Rose Wilson, *Margaret Atwood's Fairy-Tale Sexual Politics* (Jackson, MS and Toronto: University Press of Mississippi and ECW Press, 1993), p. 299.
16. Lorraine Weir, "Meridians of Perception: A Reading of *The Journals of Susanna Moodie*," *The Art of Margaret Atwood: Essays in Criticism*, eds. Arnold E. Davidson and Cathy N. Davidson (Toronto: Anansi, 1981), p. 78.
17. Margaret Atwood, *Murder in the Dark: Short Fictions and Prose Poems* (Toronto: Coach House, 1983), p. 61.
18. Josie Campbell, "The Woman as Hero in Margaret Atwood's *Surfacing*," *Mosaic* 2.3 (1978): p. 18.
19. Michael Rubbo, dir., *Once in August* (1984), 57 min. 25S.
20. See Wilson, *Margaret Atwood's Fairy-Tale*, pp. 26–28; Linda Hutcheon, *The Canadian Postmodern: A Study of Contemporary English–Canadian Fiction* (Toronto: Oxford University Press, 1988), pp. 1–25.
21. Sharon R. Wilson, "Magic Photographs in Atwood's *The Blind Assassin*," *Recent Work on Recent Atwood*, eds. Theodore F. Sheckels and Paul Martin (Edmonton: Spotted Cow Press). Forthcoming.
22. See Howells, *Margaret Atwood*, p. 21.
23. Margaret Atwood, *Surfacing* (New York: Popular Library, 1976), p. 9.
24. Marge Piercy, "Margaret Atwood: Beyond Victimhood [*Survival, The Edible Woman, Surfacing*, and five books of poetry]," *Critical Essays on Margaret Atwood*, ed. Judith McCombs (Boston: G. K. Hall, 1988), pp. 55, 65–66.
25. For example, Robert Lecker says of *Lady Oracle* that the novel returns us to the beginning, in "Janus Through the Looking Glass: Atwood's First Three Novels," *The Art of Margaret Atwood,* eds. Davidson and Davidson, pp. 177–203; and Barbara Hill Rigney, *Margaret Atwood* (Totowa, NJ: Barnes and Noble, 1987), p. 66, that Joan is destroyed by her fairy-tale conditioning.
26. Howells, "*Cat's Eye*," *Margaret Atwood*, ed. Nicholson, p. 206, and Nicole de Jong, "Mirror Images in Atwood's *Cat's Eye*," *Nora* 2.6 (1998), pp. 104–05.
27. Margaret Atwood, "Spotty-Handed Villainesses: Problems of Female Bad Behavior in the Creation of Literature," January 1994. http://owtoad.com/villainesses.html
28. Margaret Atwood, *Cat's Eye* (Toronto: McClelland and Stewart, 1988), p. 229.
29. Hermione Lee, "Writers in Conversation: Margaret Atwood," Interview, VHS video film, Roland Collection No. 43, 52 minutes, color, Northbrook, Illinois.
30. Margaret Atwood Papers, Thomas Fisher Rare Book Library, University of Toronto. 2001 Accession. Box 8: Folder 19.
31. Margaret Atwood, *The Blind Assassin* (Toronto: McClelland and Stewart, 2000) p. 497; Atwood Papers, 2001 Accession. *The Angel of Bad Judgment*, Box 1.
32. See Bouson, *Brutal Choreographies*, p. 25.
33. The novel's descriptions of the tricky Button Factory photographs, sometimes seeming to be the same but existing in several variants, don't seem consistent, possibly deliberately so. Atwood seems to be warning us not to confuse the different levels of fiction and "reality." In the cut black and white photograph of Iris and Alex, if Iris was on the left and the hand of the "other sister," who sets things down, is Iris's, either the photograph in the Epilogue cannot be of Iris and Alex, Laura is the writer of the book, or the speaker of this chapter is Laura: unlikely possibilities.

34. Eve Kosofsky Sedgwick, "Gender Asymmetry and Erotic Triangles," *Feminisms: An Anthology of Literary Theory and Criticism*, eds. Robyn R.Warhol and Diane Price Herndl (New Brunswick, NJ: Rutgers University Press, 1991), pp. 524–31.
35. Sharon R. Wilson, "Frankenstein's Gaze and Atwood's Sexual Politics in *Oryx and Crake*," Paper, "Margaret Atwood: The Open Eye" symposium, University of Ottawa, April 2004.
36. Margaret Atwood, *Oryx and Crake* (New York: Doubleday, 2003), pp. 313, 322.

FURTHER READING

Books of general interest for Atwood

De Cordova, Richard. *Picture Personalities: The Emergence of the Star System in America*. Urbana: University of Illinois Press, 1990.

Dyer, Richard. *Stars*. London: British Film Institute, 1992. 2nd edition.

Frye, Northrop. *The Bush Garden: Essays on the Canadian Imagination*. Toronto: Anansi, 1971.

Gadpaille, Michelle. *The Canadian Short Story*. Don Mills, Ontario: Oxford University Press, 1988.

Gibson, Graeme. *Eleven Canadian Novelists*. Toronto: Anansi, 1973.

Gledhill, Christine, ed. *Stardom: Industry of Desire*. London: Routledge, 1991.

Gorjup, Branko, ed. *Mythologizing Canada: Essays on the Canadian Literary Imagination*. Ottawa: Legas, 1997.

Haraway, Donna. *The Haraway Reader*. New York: Routledge, 2004.

Howells, Coral Ann. *Contemporary Canadian Women's Fiction: Refiguring Identities*. New York and Basingstoke: Palgrave, 2003.

Huggan, Graham. *The Post-colonial Exotic: Marketing the Margins*. London and New York: Routledge, 2001.

Hutcheon, Linda. *The Canadian Postmodern: A Study of Contemporary English–Canadian Fiction*. Toronto: Oxford University Press, 1988.

Splitting Images: Contemporary Canadian Ironies. Toronto: Oxford University Press, 1991.

James, Edward and Farah Mendlesohn, eds. *The Cambridge Companion to Science Fiction*. Cambridge: Cambridge University Press, 2003.

Ketterer, David. *Canadian Science Fiction and Fantasy*. Bloomington and Indianapolis: Indiana University Press, 1992.

Kröller, Eva-Marie, ed. *The Cambridge Companion to Canadian Literature*. Cambridge: Cambridge University Press, 2003.

Kudchedkar, Shirin, ed. *Postmodernism and Feminism: Canadian Contexts*. New Delhi: Pencraft International, 1995.

McKibben, Bill. *Enough: Genetic Engineering and the End of Human Nature*. London: Blooomsbury, 2004.

Marangoly, Rosemary George. *The Politics of Home: Postcolonial Relocations and Twentieth-Century Fiction*. Cambridge: Cambridge University Press, 1996.

Marshall, P. David. *Celebrity and Power: Fame in Contemporary Culture*. Minneapolis: University of Minnesota Press, 1997.

Moodie, Susanna. *Roughing It in the Bush; or, Life in Canada (1852)*. Boston: Beacon Press, 1987.

Moylan, Tom. *Scraps of the Untainted Sky: Science Fiction, Utopia, Dystopia*. Boulder, CO: Westview Press, 2000.

New, W. H. *Land Sliding: Imagining Space, Presence and Power in Canadian Writing*. Toronto: University of Toronto Press, 1997.

Orbach, Susie. *Hunger Strike: The Anorectic's Struggle as a Metaphor for Our Age*. London: Penguin, 1986.

Rao, Eleonora. *Heart of a Stranger: Contemporary Women Writers and the Metaphor of Exile*. Naples: Liguori Editore, 2002.

Scheier, Libby, Sarah Sheard, and Eleanor Wachtel, eds. *Language in Her Eye: Views on Writing and Gender by Canadian Women Writing in English*. Toronto: Coach House, 1990.

Staines, David, ed. *The Canadian Imagination: Dimensions of a Literary Culture*. Cambridge, MA: Harvard University Press, 1977.

Wilson, Edward O. *The Future of Life*. New York: Knopf, 2002.

Books on Atwood

Bouson, J. Brooks. *Brutal Choreographies: Oppositional Strategies and Narrative Design in the Novels of Margaret Atwood*. Amherst: University of Massachusetts Press, 1993.

Cooke, Nathalie. *Margaret Atwood: A Biography*. Toronto: ECW Press, 1998.

Cuder, Pilar. *Margaret Atwood: A Beginner's Guide*. London: Hodder and Stoughton, 2003.

Davey, Frank. *Margaret Atwood: A Feminist Poetics*. Vancouver: Talonbooks, 1984.

Davidson, Arnold E. *Seeing in the Dark: Margaret Atwood's "Cat's Eye."* Toronto: ECW Press, 1997.

Fee, Margery. *The Fat Lady Dances: Margaret Atwood's "Lady Oracle."* Toronto: ECW Press, 1993.

Grace, Sherrill. *Violent Duality: A Study of Margaret Atwood*. Montreal: Véhicule Press, 1980.

Hengen, Shannon. *Margaret Atwood's Power: Mirrors, Reflections and Images in Select Fiction and Poetry*. Toronto: Second Story Press, 1993.

Howells, Coral Ann. *Margaret Atwood*. Basingstoke: Macmillan, 1996. 2nd edition, 2005.

Ingersoll, Earl G., ed. *Margaret Atwood: Conversations*. London: Virago, 1992. 2nd edition.

Keith, W. J. *Introducing Margaret Atwood's "The Edible Woman": A Reader's Guide*. Toronto: ECW Press, 1989.

Mycak, Sonya. *In Search of the Split Subject: Psychoanalysis, Phenomenology, and the Novels of Margaret Atwood*. Toronto: ECW Press, 1996.

Rao, Eleonora. *Strategies for Identity: The Fiction of Margaret Atwood*. New York: Peter Lang, 1993.

Reynolds, Margaret and Jonathan Noakes. *Margaret Atwood: The Essential Guide*. London: Vintage, 2002.

Staels, Hilda. *Margaret Atwood's Novels: A Study of Narrative Discourse*. Tubingen and Basel: Francke Verlag, 1995.

Stein, Karen F. *Margaret Atwood Revisited*. New York: Twayne, 1999.

Sullivan, Rosemary. *The Red Shoes: Margaret Atwood Starting Out*. Toronto: HarperFlamingoCanada, 1998.

Thompson, Lee Briscoe. *Scarlet Letters: The Handmaid's Tale*. Toronto: ECW Press, 1997.

Wilson, Sharon Rose. *Margaret Atwood's Fairy-Tale Sexual Politics*. Jackson, MS and Toronto: University Press of Mississippi and ECW Press, 1993.

Woodcock, George. *Introducing Margaret Atwood's Surfacing: A Reader's Guide*. Toronto: ECW Press, 1990.

Collections of critical essays on Atwood

Davidson, Arnold E., and Cathy N. Davidson, eds. *The Art of Margaret Atwood: Essays in Criticism*. Toronto: Anansi, 1981.

Dvorak, Marta, ed. *The Handmaid's Tale: Margaret Atwood*. Paris: Ellipses, 1998.

Lire Margaret Atwood: "The Handmaid's Tale." Rennes: Presses Universitaires de Rennes, 1999.

Grace, Sherrill E., and Lorraine Weir, eds. *Margaret Atwood: Language, Text and System*. Vancouver: University of British Columbia Press, 1983.

Lacroix, Jean-Michel, and Jacques Leclaire, eds. *Margaret Atwood: "The Handmaid's Tale"/"Le Conte de la servante": The Power Game*. Paris: Presses de la Sorbonne Nouvelle, 1998.

McCombs, Judith, ed. *Critical Essays on Margaret Atwood*. Boston: G. K. Hall, 1988.

Mendez-Egle, Beatrice, ed. *Margaret Atwood: Reflection and Reality*. Edinburg, TX: Pan American University Press, 1987.

Nicholson, Colin, ed. *Margaret Atwood: Writing and Subjectivity: New Critical Essays*. Basingstoke and New York: Macmillan and St. Martin's Press, 1994.

Nischik, Reingard M., ed. *Margaret Atwood: Works and Impact*. Rochester, NY: Camden House, 2000.

Sandler, Linda, ed. *Margaret Atwood: A Symposium. The Malahat Review* 41 (January 1977).

Scheckels, Theodore F., and Paul Martin, eds. *Recent Work on Recent Atwood*. Edmonton: Spotted Cow Press. Forthcoming.

Turcotte, Gerry, ed. *Margaret Atwood: Entering the Labyrinth: "The Blind Assassin."* Wollongong, NSW: University of Wollongong Press, 2003.

Van Spanckeren, Kathryn, and Jan Garden Castro, eds. *Margaret Atwood: Vision and Forms*. Carbondale and Edwardsville: Southern Illinois University Press, 1988.

Vevaina, Coomi S., and Coral Ann Howells, eds. *Margaret Atwood: The Shape-Shifter*. New Delhi: Creative Books, 1998.

Wilson, Sharon Rose, ed. *Margaret Atwood's Textual Assassinations: Recent Poetry and Fiction*. Columbus: Ohio State University Press, 2003.

Wilson, Sharon Rose, Thomas B. Friedman, and Shannon Hengen, eds. *Teaching Atwood's "The Handmaid's Tale" and Other Works*. New York: Modern Language Association of America, 1996.

York, Lorraine, ed. *Various Atwoods: Essays on the Later Poems, Short Fiction, and Novels*. Toronto: Anansi, 1995.

Critical and theoretical essays

Atwood, Margaret. "Survival, Then and Now." *Maclean's*, 1 July 1999: 54–58.
Barzilai, Shuli. "Who Is He? The Missing Person Behind the Pronoun in Atwood's *Surfacing*." *Canadian Literature* 164 (Spring 2000): 57–79.
Beer, Janet. "Doing It with Mirrors: History and Cultural Identity in *The Robber Bride*." *British Journal of Canadian Studies* 13.2 (1998): 306–16.
Beran, Carol. "Images of Women's Power in Contemporary Canadian Fiction by Women." *Studies in Canadian Literature* 15.2 (1990): 54–76.
Bouson, J. Brooks. "'It's Game Over Forever': Atwood's Satiric Vision of a Bioengineered Posthuman Future." *Journal of Commonwealth Literature* 39.3 (2004): 139–56.
Campbell, Josie. "The Woman as Hero in Margaret Atwood's *Surfacing*." *Mosaic* 2.3 (1978): 17–28.
Cixous, Hélène. "The Laugh of the Medusa" (1975). *Feminisms: An Anthology of Literary Theory and Criticism*. Eds. Robyn R. Warhol, and Diane Price Herndl. New Brunswick, NJ: Rutgers University Press, 1991: pp. 334–49.
Davey, Frank. "Alternate Stories: The Short Fiction of Audrey Thomas and Margaret Atwood." *Canadian Literature* 109 (1986): 5–14.
Duncan, Isla. "Margaret Atwood's Reworking of the Wendigo Myth in *The Robber Bride*." *British Journal of Canadian Studies* 14.1 (1999): 73–84.
Dvorak, Marta. "Writing Beyond the Beginning: or, Margaret Atwood's Art of Storytelling." *Commonwealth Essays and Studies* 22.1 (Autumn 1999): 29–36.
"Margaret Atwood's Cat's Eye: or, The Trembling Canvas." *Etudes anglaises* 54.3 (2001): 299–309.
"The Right Hand Writing and the Left Hand Erasing in Margaret Atwood's *The Blind Assassin*." *Commonwealth* 25.1 (Autumn 2002): 59–68.
Garretts-Petts, W. F. "Reading, Writing, and the Postmodern Condition. Interpreting Margaret Atwood's *The Handmaid's Tale*." *Open Letter*. Seventh series 1 (Spring 1988): 74–92.
Haag, Stefan. "Ecological Orality and Silence in Margaret Atwood." *Canadian Poetry* 47 (Fall–Winter 2000): 14–39.
Heller, Arno. "Margaret Atwood's Ecological Vision." *Nationalism v. Internationalism: (Inter)National Dimensions of Literatures in English*. Eds. Wolfgang Zach, and Ken. L. Goodwin. Tubingen: Stauffenberg, 1996: pp. 313–18.
Howells, Coral Ann. "Margaret Atwood's Discourse of Nation and National Identity in the 1990s." *The Rhetoric of Canadian Writing*. Ed. Conny Steenman-Marcusse. Amsterdam and New York: Rodopi, 2002: pp. 199–216.
Hunt, Richard. "How to Love This World: The Transpersonal Wild in Margaret Atwood's Ecological Poetry." *Ecopoetry: A Critical Introduction*. Eds. J. Scott Bryson, and John Elder. Salt Lake City: University of Utah Press (2002): pp. 232–44.
Ingersoll, Earl G. "Engendering Metafiction: Textuality and Closure in Margaret Atwood's *Alias Grace*." *American Review of Canadian Studies* (Autumn 2001): 385–401.

Kellner, Hans. "Narrativity in History: Poststructuralism and Since." *History and Theory* 26.4 (1987): 1–29.
Mackey, Eva. "Death by Landscape: Race, Nature, and Gender in Canadian Nationalist Mythology." *Canadian Woman Studies* 20.2 (Summer 2000): 125–30.
Morton, Stephen. "Postcolonial Gothic and the New World Disorder: Crossing Boundaries of Space/Time in Margaret Atwood's *The Robber Bride*." *British Journal of Canadian Studies* 14.1 (1999): 99–114.
Murray, Heather. "Women in the Wilderness." *(A)Mazing Space: Writing Canadian Women Writing*. Eds. Shirley Neuman, and Smaro Kamboureli. Edmonton: Longspoon/NeWest, 1986: pp. 74–83.
Nischik, Reingard M. "Speech Act Theory, Speech Acts, and the Analysis of Fiction." *Modern Language Review* 88.2 (1993): 297–306.
"Teaching the American Short Story: New Approaches to an Old Favourite." *Der Fremdsprachliche Unterricht* 3 (1999): 28–33.
Relke, Diana. "Myths of Nature and the Poetry of Canadian Women: an Alternative Reading of Literary History." *New Literature Review* 23 (1992): 31–49.
Rogerson, Margaret. "Reading the Patchworks in *Alias Grace*." *Journal of Commonwealth Literature* 33.1 (1998): 5–22.
Staels, Hilda. "Atwood's Specular Narrative: *The Blind Assassin*." *English Studies* 85.2 (April 2002): 147–60.
Wilson, Sharon Rose. "Deconstructing Text and Self: Mirroring in Atwood's *Surfacing* and Beckett's *Molloy*." *Journal of Popular Literature* 3 (Spring/Summer 1987): 53–69.
A checklist of new Atwood criticism appears annually in the Newsletter of the Margaret Atwood Society. http://www.mscd.edu/~atwoodso/

INDEX

Alias Grace 36, 88–89, 92–93, 183, 185
  historical novel 23
  identity 93, 185
  notoriety 36, 88
  trickster narrator 88, 92
Anderson, Benedict 103
Animals in That Country, The 132–33, 135–36
  "Backdrop Addresses Cowboy" 135
  "I Was Reading a Scientific Article" 136
  "Progressive Insanities of a Pioneer" 16, 132
Ankersmith, F.R. 88
Art of Margaret Atwood, The 7
Atwood, Margaret
  artistic development 15–19
  biographies 38–40
  early years 12–15
  interpreting Canada 20, 24–25, 152
  literary celebrity 1–2, 9–10, 25, 34–35, 37
  writing, on 22–23, 30, 97, 141, 173
  works, see specific titles
Ayre, John 39

Bakhtin, Mikhail 119
Baudelaire, Charles 153–54
Becker, Susanne 32, 35
Beckett, Samuel 178
Blind Assassin, The 24, 61–62, 67–68, 95, 100, 185–86
  narrative techniques 64, 96–97, 119–20, 127–28, 186
  title 185
Bluebeard's Egg 148–50
  "Resplendent Quetzal, The" 149
  "Salt Garden, The" 177
  "Scarlet Ibis" 149–50
  "Significant Moments in the Life of My Mother" 116, 118–19, 121
  "Uglypuss" 116
Bodily Harm 20–21, 50–52
Bonheim, Helmut 145
Bottle 84
  "Faster" 84
  "King Log in Exile" 84
  "Post-Colonial" 108
Buñuel, Luis 46

Callaghan, Morley 13
Canada
  literary context 6, 13
  national identity 3, 25–26, 100–01, 107, 112, 140, 148
  victim complex 18
Cat's Eye 36, 63, 66–67, 101–02, 103, 182–84
celebrity, discourse of 3, 28–35, 40
  website 33
Circe 140
Circle Game, The 15, 133–35
  "Circle Game, The" 133
  "City Planners, The" 134
  "Explorers" 135
  "Place: Fragments, A" 134
  "Pre-Amphibian" 134
  "Settlers" 16, 24–25, 135
  "This Is a Photograph of Me" 131, 134
Cixous, Hélène 58, 59, 63, 65, 90, 165
Cluett, Robert 7–8
Cooke, Nathalie 34, 39, 40
Cordova, Richard de 40
Critical Essays on Margaret Atwood 8

Dancing Girls 148
"Polarities" 148
"Travel Piece, A" 177
"When It Happens" 177
Davidson, Arnold 7, 9
Davidson, Cathy N. 7
Davies, Robertson 124
Day of the Triffids, The (Wyndham) 163
Double Persephone 14, 24, 132, 133
Dyer, Richard 29–30
dystopias 5, 125–27, 161–73
HT/O&C comparisons 162–64, 170
traditions of 163–64

Edible Woman, The 17–18, 60–61, 93, 182
Ellmann, Maud 65
environmentalism 4, 48, 72–84, 122, 161, 183

Faulkner, William 118
feminism 17, 162–64
see also women
Foucault, Michel 44–45, 52, 54, 86
Franklin, Sir John 74
Frye, Northrop 14, 19, 124, 132

Gallant, Mavis 124
Garden Castro, Jan 8
George Marangoly, Rosemary 106
Givner, Joan 39
Gledhill, Christine 28, 40
Good Bones
"Female Body, The" 62
"Gertrude Talks Back" 155, 156–58
"Little Red Hen, The" 155–56
"Men at Sea" 153–55
Gothic 49, 66, 139
Grace, Sherrill 7, 130, 176
Gulliver's Travels (Swift) 164, 169, 170

Haliburton, Thomas Chandler 115, 126
Hamlet (Shakespeare) 156
Handmaid's Tale, The 21, 52–54, 87–88, 165–69, 182
context 161
environmentalism 161
female bodies 167–68
Gilead 52–54
human rights 163
memory, traumatic 167
narrative strategies 91, 164, 166, 168, 169
resistance, escape 54, 167
Haraway, Donna 73–74
Harvard University 14–15
Hassan, Ihab 94
history 4, 9, 16, 86–97, 137
Hite, Molly 66
home, concept of 4, 100, 101, 105–06, 108–09, 112
Howells, Coral Ann 66, 68, 93, 176
Huggan, Graham 28–29
humor 4, 33–34, 114–28, 156
burlesque 115, 126
Canadian 114, 116
carnivalesque 115, 119, 127
irony 65, 114, 120–21, 127, 134
oral tradition 115
orality 118, 119
polyphony 119–20
tall tales 115, 117, 126
voice 119–20
Hutcheon, Linda 89
hybridity 107, 119

immigrants 100, 104–05, 108
"In Search of *Alias Grace*" 92, 96
Interlunar 77, 141–42
"After Heraclitus" 142
"Burned House, The" 77
"Lesson on Snakes" 142
"Psalm to Snake" 141
"Quattrocento" 142
intertextuality 7, 47, 96, 97, 125, 153, 179
parody 68, 124–25, 126, 156–57
Island of Dr Moreau, The (Wells) 164

Jones, Dorothy 61
Journals of Susanna Moodie, The 16–17, 91–92, 136–37
"Afterword" 91, 136
"The Double Voice" 137
Joyce, James 117

Kesterton Lecture 72, 75–76
King, Barry 31
King, Thomas 124, 126
Kroetsch, Robert 126

Lady Oracle 20, 35–36, 65–66, 125, 182
Laing, Ronald D. 146
landscape 135, 137

language
écriture féminine 59–60, 69, 167
poetics of inversion 153
poetics of metamorphosis 5, 130–31, 135, 143
word play 90–91, 123–24
words, Snowman and 110–11, 172
writing the body 58–60, 61, 64–65
see also humor
Laurence, Margaret 16
Leacock, Stephen 126
Life Before Man 80–81, 186–87
Lifton, Robert Jay 130
liminality 109

McClelland, Jack 17
McClintock, Anne 135
McCombs, Judith 8
McKibben, Bill 163
McLuhan, Marshall 17–18, 21
Macpherson, Jay 14
Malahat Review, The 6–7
Margaret Atwood: Language, Text, and System 7–8
Margaret Atwood Society Newsletter 2
Margaret Atwood's Textual Assassinations 10
Margaret Atwood: Vision and Forms 8
Margaret Atwood: Works and Impact 9–10
Margaret Atwood: Writing and Subjectivity 8–9
Merrick, Helen 164
Metamorphoses (Ovid) 132
Miller, Perry 21
Montefiore, Jan 47
Moodie, Susanna
Life in the Clearings 16, 92
Roughing It in the Bush 16, 136
Morning in the Burned House 142–43
"Fire Place, A" 143
"Half-Hanged Mary" 90
"Morning in the Burned House" 143
"Shapechangers in Winter" 143
"Waiting" 132–33
"You Come Back" 142
Moving Targets 24
Munro, Alice 28
Murder in the Dark 158
"Instructions for the Third Eye" 158, 178
myths and fairy tales 132, 138, 140, 155, 156–58, 179

Negotiating with the Dead 16, 24–25, 37–38
Nicholson, Colin 8
Nineteen Eighty-Four (Orwell) 161
Nischik, Reingard 9, 176
"Notes on *Power Politics*" 43, 45, 48, 54, 55

Onley, Gloria 45
Orbach, Susie 61
Oryx and Crake 24, 46, 55, 82–83, 108–12, 117–18, 169–73, 186–87
consumerism 82, 161
context 161, 172
genetic engineering 82, 108, 163, 170
"human" 82, 83, 170
science versus art 83, 108, 163, 170
survival narrative 163–70, 177
title 162
Osborne, Carol 102
Ostriker, Alicia 48
outsiders 100, 101, 102–04, 109–10

Paradise Lost (Milton) 173
Piercy, Marge 181
photographs 33, 95, 134, 136, 185–86, 189
poetry 4–5, 76–77, 130–43
politics, sexual
Alias Grace 62
Blind Assassin, The 61–62
Bodily Harm 50
Cat's Eye 151
Dancing Girls 146
"Female Body, The" 62
Handmaid's Tale, The 62
Power Politics 45, 49–50, 138
Surfacing 49–50
Wilderness Tips 152
You Are Happy 138
see also power politics
postcolonialism 9, 101–02, 179
postmodernism 6, 86–87, 91, 118, 153, 168, 179
power politics 3–4, 8, 43–48, 55
definition of 44–45, 51
national 43
war 54–55, 186
see also politics, sexual
Power Politics 43, 45–49, 54–55, 138–39
"accident has occurred, The" 49
"At first I was given centuries" 54
"Imperialist, keep off" 43–55

"My beautiful wooden leader" 47, 139
"Small tactics" 49
"Their attitudes differ" 47
"They are hostile nations" 48
"They eat out" 46
"They travel by air" 49
"Yes at first" 139
"You did it" 47
"You fit into me" 46
Procedures for Underground 76–77, 137–38
"Archaeologists, For" 77
"Blazed Trail, A" 77
"Chrysanthemums" 77
"Cyclops" 137
"Fishing for Eel Totems" 77
"Procedures for Underground" 138
"Projected Slide of the Unknown Soldier" 138
"Return Trips West" 77
"Soul, Geologically, A" 77
Proteus 130
Purdy, Al 138

Renzetti, Elizabeth 39
research 7, 8, 171, 184
Richler, Mordecai 124
Robber Bride, The 87, 93–94, 102–07
Zenia 87, 93–94, 103, 105, 107
Rosenthal, Caroline 37
Rouse, Roger 106
Rubbo, Michael 34, 40
Rushdie, Salman 89, 91

Sandler, Linda 6
satire 6, 30–31, 46, 122–24, 169
Horatian 115
Juvenalian/Swiftian 115, 117
Menippean 121, 124
see also humor
"schizoid" 146
science fiction 97, 162, 170
Second Words 22
"Amnesty International address" 20, 44, 51, 52
Sedgwick, Eve Kosofsky 186
Shelley, Mary 126, 164
short fiction 5, 9, 145–59
space 130–31
Spivak, Gayatri 60
storytelling 63–64, 78, 95–96
Handmaid's Tale, The 88, 165–66, 169
Oryx and Crake 162, 171, 187
Strange Things 74–75
Introduction 14, 24
"Eyes of Blood" 74
Sullivan, Rosemary 38, 133, 135–36
Surfacing 18, 49, 78–80, 91, 178–82
survival 74–75, 81, 165, 176–78, 183–84, 187
Survival 18, 44, 45

Thomas Fisher Rare Book Library 7, 11, 171
Tiffin, Helen 51
To the Lighthouse (Woolf) 170
Traill, Catherine Parr 16
True Stories 21, 52, 141
"Notes Towards a Poem that Can Never Be Written" 52, 141
"True Stories" 88
Twain, Mark 114, 118, 119, 126
Two-Headed Poems 21, 140–41
"Two-Headed Poems" 22, 140

Van Spanckeren, Kathryn 8
Various Atwoods 9
villainesses 183
vision 5, 178
art, visual 8, 22, 34
blindness 185, 187
cover designs 46, 93, 95, 139
vision imagery
Alias Grace 185
Blind Assassin, The 64, 185–86
Cat's Eye 182–83
Circle Game, The 134
Journals of Susanna Moodie, The 137
Oryx and Crake 46, 55, 186–87
Surfacing 180–81

Webster, Mary 89, 98
Weir, Lorraine 7
wilderness 79–80, 132–33, 137
Wilderness Tips 150–52
"Age of Lead, The" 120, 121–22
"Death by Landscape" 151
"Hairball" 150–51
"Uncles" 116–17
"Weight" 121, 151
"Wilderness Tips" 122

Wilson, Edward 72–73
Wilson, Sharon R. 10
Wolf, Naomi 63, 65
women
- female bodies 3, 58–70, 167–68
- gender revisionism 156–57, 158
- victims, as 139, 151, 158
- writers, as 60, 62–63, 65–66, 68–69, 165

"Writing *Oryx and Crake*" 72

York, Lorraine 9
You Are Happy 140
- "Circe/Mud Poems" 140

CAMBRIDGE COMPANIONS TO LITERATURE

The Cambridge Companion to Greek Tragedy
edited by P. E. Easterling

The Cambridge Companion to Roman Satire
edited by Kirk Freudenburg

The Cambridge Companion to Old English Literature
edited by Malcolm Godden and Michael Lapidge

The Cambridge Companion to Medieval Women's Writing
edited by Carolyn Dinshaw and David Wallace

The Cambridge Companion to Medieval Romance
edited by Roberta L. Krueger

The Cambridge Companion to Medieval English Theatre
edited by Richard Beadle

The Cambridge Companion to English Renaissance Drama, second edition
edited by A. R. Braunmuller and Michael Hattaway

The Cambridge Companion to Renaissance Humanism
edited by Jill Kraye

The Cambridge Companion to English Poetry, Donne to Marvell
edited by Thomas N. Corns

The Cambridge Companion to English Literature, 1500–1600
edited by Arthur F. Kinney

The Cambridge Companion to English Literature, 1650–1740
edited by Steven N. Zwicker

The Cambridge Companion to English Literature, 1740–1830
edited by Thomas Keymer and Jon Mee

The Cambridge Companion to Writing of the English Revolution
edited by N. H. Keeble

The Cambridge Companion to English Restoration Theatre
edited by Deborah C. Payne Fisk

The Cambridge Companion to British Romanticism
edited by Stuart Curran

The Cambridge Companion to Eighteenth-Century Poetry
edited by John Sitter

The Cambridge Companion to the Eighteenth-Century Novel
edited by John Richetti

The Cambridge Companion to Gothic Fiction
edited by Jerrold E. Hogle

The Cambridge Companion to Victorian Poetry
edited by Joseph Bristow

The Cambridge Companion to the Victorian Novel
edited by Deirdre David

The Cambridge Companion to Crime Fiction
edited by Martin Priestman

The Cambridge Companion to Science Fiction
edited by Edward James and Farah Mendlesohn

The Cambridge Companion to Travel Writing
edited by Peter Hulme and Tim Youngs

The Cambridge Companion to American Realism and Naturalism
edited by Donald Pizer

The Cambridge Companion to Nineteenth-Century American Women's Writing
edited by Dale M. Bauer and Philip Gould

The Cambridge Companion to Victorian and Edwardian Theatre
edited by Kerry Powell

The Cambridge Companion to the Literature of the First World War
edited by Vincent Sherry

The Cambridge Companion to the Classic Russian Novel
edited by Malcolm V. Jones and Robin Feuer Miller

The Cambridge Companion to the French Novel: from 1800 to the Present
edited by Timothy Unwin

The Cambridge Companion to the Spanish Novel: from 1600 to the Present
edited by Harriet Turner and Adelaida López de Martínez

The Cambridge Companion to the Italian Novel
edited by Peter Bondanella and Andrea Ciccarelli

The Cambridge Companion to the Modern German Novel
edited by Graham Bartram

The Cambridge Companion to the Latin American Novel
edited by Efraín Kristal

The Cambridge Companion to Jewish American Literature
edited by Hana Wirth-Nesher and Michael P. Kramer

The Cambridge Companion to Native American Literature
edited by Joy Porter and Kenneth M. Roemer

The Cambridge Companion to the African American Novel
edited by Maryemma Graham

The Cambridge Companion to Canadian Literature
edited by Eva-Marie Kröller

The Cambridge Companion to Contemporary Irish Poetry
edited by Matthew Campbell

The Cambridge Companion to Modernism
edited by Michael Levenson

The Cambridge Companion to American Modernism
edited by Walter Kalaidjian

The Cambridge Companion to Postmodernism
edited by Steven Connor

The Cambridge Companion to Postcolonial Literary Studies
edited by Neil Lazarus

The Cambridge Companion to Australian Literature
edited by Elizabeth Webby

The Cambridge Companion to American Women Playwrights
edited by Brenda Murphy

The Cambridge Companion to Modern British Women Playwrights
edited by Elaine Aston and Janelle Reinelt

The Cambridge Companion to Twentieth-Century Irish Drama
edited by Shaun Richards

The Cambridge Companion to Homer
edited by Robert Fowler

The Cambridge Companion to Virgil
edited by Charles Martindale

The Cambridge Companion to Ovid
edited by Philip Hardie

The Cambridge Companion to Dante
edited by Rachel Jacoff

The Cambridge Companion to Cervantes
edited by Anthony J. Cascardi

The Cambridge Companion to Goethe
edited by Lesley Sharpe

The Cambridge Companion to Dostoevskii
edited by W. J. Leatherbarrow

The Cambridge Companion to Tolstoy
edited by Donna Tussing Orwin

The Cambridge Companion to Chekhov
edited by Vera Gottlieb and Paul Allain

The Cambridge Companion to Ibsen
edited by James McFarlane

The Cambridge Companion to Flaubert
edited by Timothy Unwin

The Cambridge Companion to Proust
edited by Richard Bales

The Cambridge Companion to Thomas Mann
edited by Ritchie Robertson

The Cambridge Companion to Kafka
edited by Julian Preece

The Cambridge Companion to Brecht
edited by Peter Thomson and Glendyr Sacks

The Cambridge Companion to Walter Benjamin
edited by David S. Ferris

The Cambridge Companion to Lacan
edited by Jean-Michel Rabaté

The Cambridge Companion to Nabokov
edited by Julian W. Connolly

The Cambridge Companion to Chaucer, second edition
edited by Piero Boitani and Jill Mann

The Cambridge Companion to Shakespeare
edited by Margareta de Grazia and Stanley Wells

The Cambridge Companion to Shakespeare on Film
edited by Russell Jackson

The Cambridge Companion to Shakespearean Comedy
edited by Alexander Leggatt

The Cambridge Companion to Shakespeare on Stage
edited by Stanley Wells and Sarah Stanton

The Cambridge Companion to Shakespeare's History Plays
edited by Michael Hattaway

The Cambridge Companion to Shakespearean Tragedy
edited by Claire McEachern

The Cambridge Companion to Christoher Marlowe
edited by Patrick Cheney

The Cambridge Companion to Ben Jonson
edited by Richard Harp and Stanley Stewart

The Cambridge Companion to John Donne
edited by Achsah Guibbory

The Cambridge Companion to Spenser
edited by Andrew Hadfield

The Cambridge Companion to Milton, second edition
edited by Dennis Danielson

The Cambridge Companion to John Dryden
edited by Steven N. Zwicker

The Cambridge Companion to Aphra Behn
edited by Derek Hughes and Janet Todd

The Cambridge Companion to Samuel Johnson
edited by Greg Clingham

The Cambridge Companion to Jonathan Swift
edited by Christopher Fox

The Cambridge Companion to Mary Wollstonecraft
edited by Claudia L. Johnson

The Cambridge Companion to William Blake
edited by Morris Eaves

The Cambridge Companion to Wordsworth
edited by Stephen Gill

The Cambridge Companion to Coleridge
edited by Lucy Newlyn

The Cambridge Companion to Byron
edited by Drummond Bone

The Cambridge Companion to Keats
edited by Susan J. Wolfson

The Cambridge Companion to Mary Shelley
edited by Esther Schor

The Cambridge Companion to Jane Austen
edited by Edward Copeland and Juliet McMaster

The Cambridge Companion to the Brontës
edited by Heather Glen

The Cambridge Companion to Charles Dickens
edited by John O. Jordan

The Cambridge Companion to George Eliot
edited by George Levine

The Cambridge Companion to Thomas Hardy
edited by Dale Kramer

The Cambridge Companion to Oscar Wilde
edited by Peter Raby

The Cambridge Companion to George Bernard Shaw
edited by Christopher Innes

The Cambridge Companion to W. B. Yeats
edited by Marjorie Howes and John Kelly

The Cambridge Companion to Joseph Conrad
edited by J. H. Stape

The Cambridge Companion to D. H. Lawrence
edited by Anne Fernihough

The Cambridge Companion to Virginia Woolf
edited by Sue Roe and Susan Sellers

The Cambridge Companion to James Joyce, second edition
edited by Derek Attridge

The Cambridge Companion to T. S. Eliot
edited by A. David Moody

The Cambridge Companion to Ezra Pound
edited by Ira B. Nadel

The Cambridge Companion to W. H. Auden
edited by Stan Smith

The Cambridge Companion to Beckett
edited by John Pilling

The Cambridge Companion to Harold Pinter
edited by Peter Raby

The Cambridge Companion to Tom Stoppard
edited by Katherine E. Kelly

The Cambridge Companion to Herman Melville
edited by Robert S. Levine

The Cambridge Companion to Nathaniel Hawthorne
edited by Richard Millington

The Cambridge Companion to Harriet Beecher Stowe
edited by Cindy Weinstein

The Cambridge Companion to Theodore Dreiser
edited by Leonard Cassuto and Claire Virginia Eby

The Cambridge Companion to Willa Cather
edited by Marilee Lindermann

The Cambridge Companion to Edith Wharton
edited by Millicent Bell

The Cambridge Companion to Henry James
edited by Jonathan Freedman

The Cambridge Companion to Walt Whitman
edited by Ezra Greenspan

The Cambridge Companion to Ralph Waldo Emerson
edited by Joel Porte and Saundra Morris

The Cambridge Companion to Henry David Thoreau
edited by Joel Myerson

The Cambridge Companion to Mark Twain
edited by Forrest G. Robinson

The Cambridge Companion to Edgar Allan Poe
edited by Kevin J. Hayes

The Cambridge Companion to Emily Dickinson
edited by Wendy Martin

The Cambridge Companion to William Faulkner
edited by Philip M. Weinstein

The Cambridge Companion to Ernest Hemingway
edited by Scott Donaldson

The Cambridge Companion to F. Scott Fitzgerald
edited by Ruth Prigozy

The Cambridge Companion to Robert Frost
edited by Robert Faggen

The Cambridge Companion to Ralph Ellison
edited by Ross Posnock

The Cambridge Companion to Eugene O'Neill
edited by Michael Manheim

The Cambridge Companion to Tennessee Williams
edited by Matthew C. Roudané

The Cambridge Companion to Arthur Miller
edited by Christopher Bigsby

The Cambridge Companion to David Mamet
edited by Christopher Bigsby

The Cambridge Companion to Sam Shepard
edited by Matthew C. Roudané

The Cambridge Companion to Edward Albee
edited by Stephen J. Bottoms

CAMBRIDGE COMPANIONS TO CULTURE

The Cambridge Companion to Modern German Culture
edited by Eva Kolinsky and Wilfried van der Will

The Cambridge Companion to Modern Russian Culture
edited by Nicholas Rzhevsky

The Cambridge Companion to Modern Spanish Culture
edited by David T. Gies

The Cambridge Companion to Modern Italian Culture
edited by Zygmunt G. Baranski and Rebecca J. West

The Cambridge Companion to Modern French Culture
edited by Nicholas Hewitt

The Cambridge Companion to Modern Latin American Literature
edited by John King

The Cambridge Companion to Modern Irish Culture
edited by Joe Cleary and Claire Connolly